"COLVILL SMILED."

The Legend of the 1st Minnesota
Volunteer Regiment at Gettysburg.

July 2, 1863. May the Legend Never Die.

First paperback edition: 2025.

Book design by Kip Johnson.

ISBN 979-8-9926669-2-2 (paperback edition).

Library of Congress Control Number: 2025903922

Printed at The Print Shop, Otter Tail Power, Fergus Falls, MN.

Published by Hoffbeck of Minnesota, Barnesville, Minnesota.

Contact: Steven R. Hoffbeck
406 9th St. SE
Barnesville, MN 56514
Email: stevehoffbeck@yahoo.com

Printed in the United States of America.

This book is for

my grandchildren,

Andrew and Samuel;

Maia, Noah, Shai, and Aria.

(and for those who arrive later).

Colonel William Colvill.

Colonel William Colvill as a civilian after he had come home to Minnesota, having recovered from his grievous wounds, but needing a cane to help him walk.
Photo from 1865 or 1866, when he was 35 years old.
Credit: Minnesota Historical Society.

"COLVILL SMILED."

The Legend of the 1st Minnesota Volunteer Regiment at Gettysburg.

July 2, 1863. May the Legend Never Die.

"Love is as Strong as Death.
Its Passion is as Relentless as the Grave."
Song of Songs 8:6.

"A flood cannot put out love.
Rivers cannot drown love."
Song of Songs 8:7.

PROLOGUE

For those men who fought in the Civil War, which raged from 1861 to 1865, the twin themes of "Love" and "Death" predominated.

The "Death" theme was plain to perceive for every soldier. The fear of death could be masked, yet it was unavoidable.

Most Civil War soldiers learned to look away from death's door; they did not think about it.

The "Love" theme might seem to be out of place in wartime.

Yet the love of a soldier for his family; his wife or his sweetheart; his home, his state; his flag, or his country, was in his heart, no doubt.

This book tells the stories of two Minnesotans from Red Wing, William Colvill and Martin Maginnis, who loved their country and who volunteered to defend the honor and the flag of the Union.

They joined the First Minnesota Volunteer Regiment and traveled east to fight on battlefields in Virginia, in Maryland, and in Pennsylvania. They were a long ways from Minnesota.

By the end of the war, they had experienced all the emotions, privations, and fears of army life and combat.

This volume contains what may be found regarding the writings and speeches of William Colvill and of Martin Maginnis, so the reader will become better-acquainted with these two Civil War officers from Minnesota, and become better-acquainted with the legends surrounding the "old Minnesota First" regiment, especially, the 'famous charge at Gettysburg.'

A quote from Oliver Wendell Holmes, Jr. (1841-1935), a Civil War soldier who later became a Supreme Court Justice, gives a deep perspective of that time period in American history:

"The generation that carried on the war has been set apart by its experience. Through our good fortune, *in our youth our hearts were touched with fire.*"

"It was given to us to learn at the outset that life is a profound and passionate thing."

("Memorial Day: An Address ... May 30, 1884," *Speeches By Oliver Wendell Holmes, Junior* (Boston: Little, Brown, and Company, 1891), p. 11).

Colvill and Maginnis returned home to Red Wing after the war was over, and each forged his own path in life. Each man got married, had a career, cared for their families and friends, and grew old and grey. They carried scars in their bodies from wounds suffered in combat and they had war-memories in their minds and hearts from their times on the Civil War battlefields where their names became legendary to future generations of Minnesotans.

May the legend of the "immortal Minnesota First" Regiment never die.

L to R: Ane Marie, Larry, Jeffrey, Alvina, Steven, Brenda, Raymond, Dana, Janice Hoffbeck at our family farm 5 miles northwest of Morgan, Minnesota. 1963. Author's photo.

INTRODUCTION

I was born in 1953, which means I am pretty old.

If we zoom back in time to 1963, I was 10 years old, which meant that I was pretty young, and that year was significant because it marked the 100th anniversary of the Battle of Gettysburg in the Civil War (1861-1865).

There was a well-known magazine called *Life* back then, and *Life* published a series of articles featuring the big Civil War battles that had happened a century before, year by year, from 1961 through 1965.

My mom and dad subscribed to *Life* magazine, and, being a boy who loved to read, I read the articles and looked at the illustrations, ingraining those images into my thinking----visions of the Blue and the Gray, U.S.A and C.S.A. (Confederate States of America); Union soldiers, Rebel soldiers, the 'Johnny Rebs'; Springfield rifles and Enfield rifles; cannonballs and Minie balls; Abraham Lincoln and Jefferson Davis; generals Robert E. Lee and U.S. Grant.

In 4th grade, all of my classmates and I had to memorize the Gettysburg Address speech of Abraham Lincoln; and I still remember most of it today---"Four score and seven years ago our fathers brought forth on this continent a new nation, conceived in Liberty and dedicated to the proposition that all men are created equal. Now we are engaged in a great civil war, testing whether that nation, or any nation so conceived and so dedicated, can long endure."

Lincoln's words were in my brain, and I had *night-time* **dreams that I was a Union soldier** in *imaginary Civil War battles* that took place in the open fields around our dairy-farm located near the town of Morgan in southwest Minnesota. I would run to charge against the gray-clad forces of the Johnny Rebs, carrying my heavy, nine-pounds in weight, Springfield rifled-musket.

Yet in my recurring dreams, sometimes the rifle would not fire and I did not know why it had no gunpowder or bullet in it. At times in my dreams when my gun wouldn't work, I would lie down and "play dead," lying motionless and pretending to be unconsciously-deceased, hoping the Confederate soldiers would pass me by and then I could survive the dreamland battle.

Sometimes my brothers----Larry, Jeffrey, and Dana----and I would be Civil War re-enactors, for we acted out battles on the lawn and in our grove of trees and along the dusty gravel roadway that went along the edge of our Hoffbeck farm. We had toy cap-guns, one was a Fanner 45 with Shootin' Shell two-piece play bullets with plastic noses, using Greenie stickum caps; mine was a Colt Navy revolver with a blue barrel, modeled after the 1861 version.

In evening battles, after dark, each brother got 3 paper caps in his toy cap-gun and found a place behind a tree or bush for an ambush. There would be a flash of light as the cap exploded, and a puff of smoke, and a shout of "Got you!" So when you got 'hit,' you had to fall to the ground, playing 'dead' for the count of ten, and then you were alive again, so you could get up to resume the battle until all your meager ammunition of caps was gone.

In 6th grade, in Minnesota History class, our teacher covered the basics of the story of our North Star State, including a mention of the legend of the First Minnesota Volunteer Regiment and its famous charge at the Battle of Gettysburg.

In my Morgan High School U.S. History class, 10th grade, our teacher, Mr. Paul Grogan (a wiry former U.S. Marine, the coolest teacher) memorably taught about slavery, rebellion, Civil War battles, and victory at Appomattox, and helped give me a lifetime love of history and how Minnesota's history mirrors the larger U.S. history, and vice-versa. As renowned-author Sinclair Lewis, a native Minnesotan, once said: "To understand America, it is merely necessary to understand Minnesota."[1]

Mr. Grogan also introduced me to unforgettable stanzas of "The Charge of the Light Brigade," the war poem of Alfred, Lord Tennyson, that helped me understand a question about fighting real-life battles in Minnesota.

The goal of this book is to fit the Civil War experiences of Minnesotans into the big picture of American history. For those who are willing to read this book, the author wants to explain what happened to the First Minnesota Regiment on the second day of the Battle of Gettysburg, July 2, 1863, so that the story of their famous charge against enemy lines will be quite clearly understandable. In order to do this, there will be three retellings of the "Charge of the 1st Minnesota." I will attempt to tell this story in three different ways.

The first one will be very short in length.

The second will be a little bit longer, with more details.

And the last retelling will be told mainly through the words of two of the officers in the First Minnesota Volunteer Regiment, Colonel William Colvill, and First Lieutenant Martin Maginnis. These two men had worked together as newspapermen in Red Wing, and had gone hunting and fishing, in the years just prior to the outbreak of the Civil War. They were friends, fishing buddies, co-workers, and fellow leaders of the regiment.

The problem in writing the story of the First Minnesota Regiment at Gettysburg is that it was too hard for each soldier to know all the details of this big battle, because *each man could not see very far*, due to thick gunsmoke and the deep confusion of hand-to-hand combat and close-in fighting. Therefore, anyone attempting to capture the very truth and essence of combat will only partially succeed.

However, let's start this tale, anyway.

In the briefest form, the story goes like this.

"First Minnesota," replied Col. Colvill!

General Winfield Hancock asked: "What regiment is this?"
Colvill said: "First Minnesota." Gettysburg, July 2, 1863. Advertisement artwork,
poster, 1961. Credit: Colvill file, Goodhue County Historical Society, Red Wing, MN.

CHAPTER ONE
Long Story Made Very Short

At the battle of Gettysburg, on the second day of fighting, July 2, 1863, the Confederate soldiers were pushing back the Union lines near Cemetery Ridge and the situation was desperate.[1]

U.S. reserve troops could not reach the critical point for another five or ten minutes.

Eight companies of the First Minnesota regiment, numbering only 262 men, were close by, awaiting orders.

General Winfield S. Hancock yelled out: "What regiment is this?"

"First Minnesota," replied Colonel William Colvill.

"Charge those lines," commanded Hancock.

The Minnesotans immediately charged, as ordered, being thrown in to hold the gap for five minutes until reinforcements arrived. And the men of the 1st Minnesota did it; they saved the day at Gettysburg. Union reserves got there in less than ten minutes.[2]

In fact, the First Minnesota held its position for fifteen minutes, not just for five, yet at a tragic price, for, in that time, 37 died and 121 were wounded. Colonel Colvill was gravely wounded, but survived.

The next day, the remainder of the First Minnesota Volunteer Regiment helped stop "Pickett's Charge," and the U.S. Army of the Potomac won the Battle of Gettysburg.

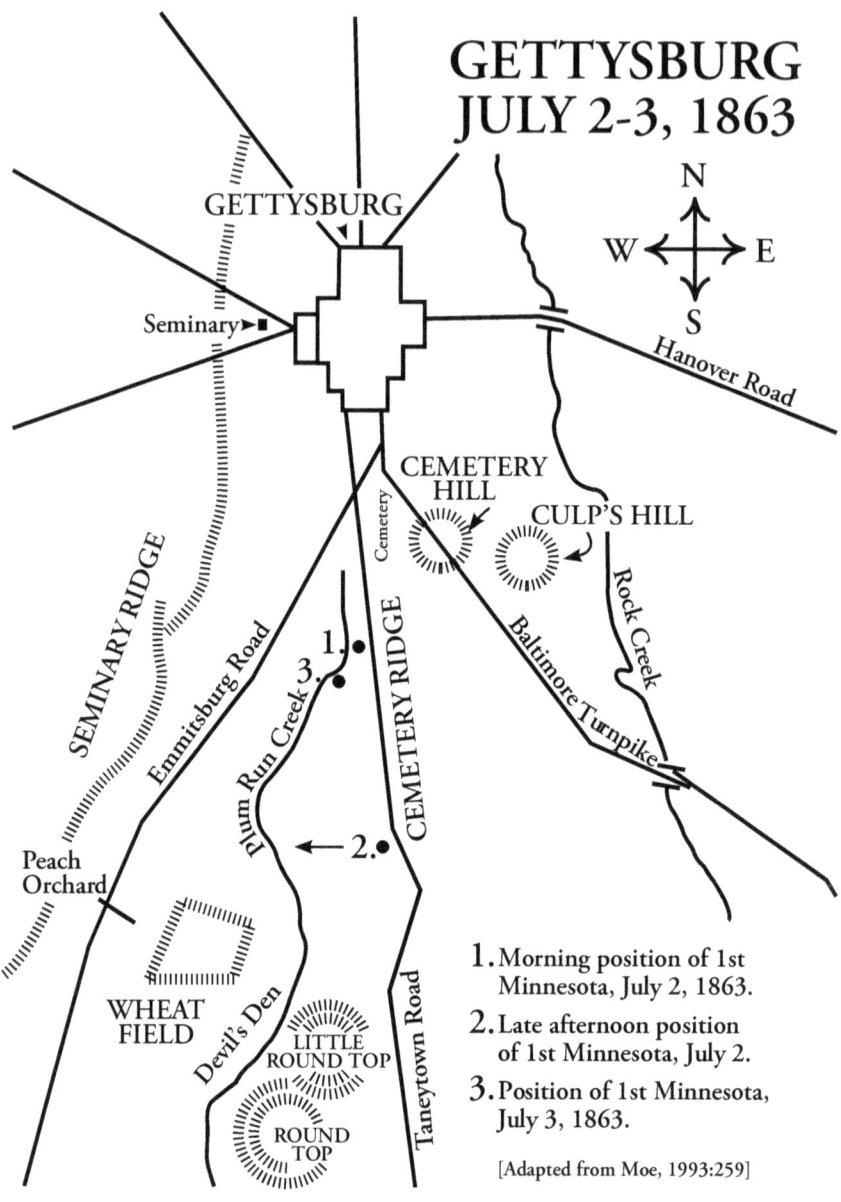

GETTYSBURG
JULY 2-3, 1863

1. Morning position of 1st Minnesota, July 2, 1863.
2. Late afternoon position of 1st Minnesota, July 2.
3. Position of 1st Minnesota, July 3, 1863.

[Adapted from Moe, 1993:259]

Illustration. Map of Gettysburg battlefield. Gettysburg, Pennsylvania, July 2-3, 1863. Adapted from Moe, 1993: 259, by Steve Hoffbeck.

CHAPTER TWO
Long Story Made A Little Bit Longer

"History was made," from July 1 to July 3, 1863, at Gettysburg, Pennsylvania. And the First Minnesota "helped write red pages of history."[1]

In mid-June, 1863, Confederate General Robert E. Lee "chose a bold maneuver," moving north from Virginia. Lee, with his Army of Northern Virginia, about 75,000 strong, marched through Maryland and then crossed into Pennsylvania, in order to again bring the war to northern soil and take supplies for the use of his soldiers.[2] President Abraham Lincoln, upon learning that Lee's forces were marching forth, ordered the U.S. Army of the Potomac, about 90,000 in number, to follow and counteract the Confederates.

The two armies collided at a little town called Gettysburg, where the greatest battle of the Civil War took place. The shooting began when a C.S.A. brigade, seeking food and supplies in the town, encountered Union cavalry outside Gettysburg on July 1. They attacked----and fighting escalated during that day as more and more Union and Confederate troops joined the battle. At the end of the day, the C.S.A. held the upper hand, forcing Union troops to retreat through Gettysburg's streets and then Union soldiers occupied the high ground at Cemetery Hill. The main body of the U.S. troops, commanded by General George G. Meade, arrived during the night and established strong defensive positions on Culp's Hill and Cemetery Hill, and on Cemetery Ridge, south of town.

Lee's army occupied Seminary Ridge, just a mile west of the Union lines.

The First Minnesota Regiment arrived at Cemetery Ridge before dawn on July 2 and by afternoon the regiment's eleven companies were spread along the ridge on the south side of the Union lines, with nine of the companies (A, B, D, E, F, G, H, I, K), totaling 262 men, being positioned on Cemetery Ridge to protect an artillery battery.

General Lee, confident that his Confederate soldiers could defeat any Union army, ordered attacks on both ends of the U.S. positions on July 2, the second day of the Gettysburg battle. Lee sent General R.S. Ewell's troops against the Union's north side, but Ewell's attack failed to dislodge the entrenched Union forces.

On the south end of the Union's position, Confederate General James Longstreet's soldiers had more success, for they almost took over the hill called Little Round Top. When U.S. General D.E. Sickles advanced too far westward, he was "dangerously exposed" to the Confederate attack, and the Southerners broke through Sickles' lines. There was severe fighting at the adjacent "Wheatfield," bringing heavy losses for both sides. It was at this point, in the late afternoon, that the First Minnesota Regiment had to face its fate.[3]

The eight companies were protecting a group of cannons, but had little to do at first. The officers of the First Minnesota ordered them to "lie down" in the space in front of the cannons, so as to be not easily seen and to be not so easily struck by stray bullets or by bouncing cannonballs. Through the smoke produced by black gunpowder, the Minnesotans could see the disaster unfold as the Confederates shot and killed and pushed through Sickles' Union soldiers. When their fellow U.S. soldiers ran from the fight, the situation became dire and close to disastrous. The Rebel troops were smashing into Union troops, pushing them back and moving towards Plum Run Creek and ready to advance upwards to Cemetery Ridge, threatening to capture the high ground and split the entire U.S. defensive position with deadly potential to win the whole battle.

As C.S.A. soldiers advanced, Company F was sent towards Little Round Top (to the immediate south) as skirmishers, separating from the other eight companies of the 1st Minnesota.[4]

The commander in charge of this portion of the battlefield, General Winfield S. Hancock, looked at the situation and immediately realized he had to get reinforcements or the C.S.A. troops would seize the advantage and the battle might be lost.

General Hancock ordered reinforcements to hurry over to save the position. However, those troops were a half mile away and would arrive too late to turn back the Southerners.

Seeing that Colonel William Colvill with his First Minnesota Regiment was the nearest supporting regiment, Hancock gave an order: "Charge those lines," pointing to the Confederate brigade, less than 400 yards away. He needed five minutes of time to allow reinforcing troops to advance ½ mile.[5]

Immediately, Colonel Colvill lined up his men and this "thin blue line a hundred yards long, charged."[6]

The men of the First Minnesota advanced down the slope at double-quick time towards the 1,600 Confederate troops nearing Plum Run, a dry creek bed at the foot of Cemetery Ridge. The 262 Minnesotans were outnumbered five to one, yet still they charged, speeding up to a full run, with bayonets pointed at their enemies.

Bullets directed at the First Minnesota tore into their bodies. Confederate cannons fired cannonballs and canister shot and case shot into the Minnesota men, wounding many of them and killing others.

The Minnesotans kept charging, and fired a volley of bullets into the Rebel soldiers. The First Minnesota found cover among the boulders and bushes in the Plum Run creek bed and reloaded and shot furiously into the Confederate lines. The Rebels, stunned and disorganized by the unlikely attack, broke and fell back.

Firing continued for at least fifteen minutes, and relief came when the 82nd New York Regiment arrived along the northern side of the Minnesotans, and a Union brigade came on their southern side to rescue them.

The Minnesota regiment "had plugged the hole in the ranks and held the field" as Union cannons opened fire on the Confederates and the First Minnesota's survivors were able to retreat to the top of Cemetery Ridge.

The skillful movement of reinforcements by the Union generals and the advantage of the higher ground on Cemetery Ridge allowed the U.S.A. to beat back the C.S.A.'s attacks at a critical time on the second day of battle, July 2.

That day was the "grandest, and most glorious day in the history of the regiment," wrote Sergeant James A. Wright, yet it was also the "saddest" and "bloodiest" day for the First Minnesota.[7]

There were only 47 men who were standing after the "Charge of the First Minnesota" and the combat at Plum Run creek bed was over. In those fifteen minutes of agony, 215 of the 262 Minnesotans were either wounded so they could not stand up, or were killed in action. The loss was terrible.

The price in blood and life that the Minnesotans had paid was extremely high, for the initial reports stated that "more than two-thirds" of them were either wounded or killed on July 2nd.[8]

William Colvill, age 31, Red Wing, Minnesota 1861 (or 1862).
Credit: U.S. Army Military History Institute.

Yet the battle of Gettysburg was not over.

Day Three, July 3rd would be the decisive day.

Union General George Meade judged that C.S.A. General Robert E. Lee, having weakened the U.S. lines with his attacks on the northern end at Culp's Hill and at the southern end near Little Round Top would try to overwhelm the very center of U.S. defenses at Cemetery Ridge.

General Lee concluded that the Union defenses were strong at Culp's Hill and near Little Round Top, and that meant that the Union center might be relatively weak. Believing that his Southerners could defeat the Northerners in any pitched battle, he thought that his men could pierce through the very middle of Cemetery Ridge, flow all around behind the Union rear, destroying their supply-lines and communications and win the victory. It was a gamble to charge headfirst across open fields directly into the U.S. defenses, but he did it anyway.

The morning was spent arranging cannons to the best advantage for both sides. Union soldiers fortified their defenses on Cemetery Ridge by digging rifle-pits and stacking logs and rocks to strengthen a stone wall that ran along the front of the ridge. U.S. troops used every little hill, ravine and ridge as natural protection from bullets and cannon-fire.

That afternoon, at 1 p.m., 140 Confederate cannons loosed a cannonade upon Cemetery Ridge. In response, 60 union artillery pieces bombarded the Rebels' cannons, which had targeted the U.S. cannons. For nearly two hours, the big guns fired.[9]

Then the U.S. cannons ceased fire in order to mislead the Confederates into "thinking that they had silenced them," when it was, in reality, a wise move to cool the guns and conserve ammunition.[10]

At 3 p.m., 13,000 Confederate soldiers, with three brigades from General George Pickett's division leading the way, began a mile-long march across the open fields towards Cemetery Ridge.

U.S. cannon fire from the front and sides put the advancing C.S.A. ranks into a deadly crossfire. As the Rebels neared the Union defenses, they broke into an all-out run, and they were cut down by a shattering Yankee rifle-fire. Only 5,000 Southerners made it to the top and some small groups of C.S.A. soldiers penetrated the Union lines. However, the U.S. reinforcements engulfed them, killing or capturing the Rebels who made it that far, forcing them to retreat from the ridge. "Pickett's Charge" had failed, for the Confederates had lost over 5,000 soldiers, overall, in one hour.

The men of the 1st Minnesota, positioned just 300 yards from the last gasp of Pickett's Charge, had joined in the fearsome struggle of repulsing the C.S.A.'s final assault, capturing 500 Confederate soldiers. It was a glorious, yet grim, day, as 70 more Minnesotans were killed or wounded.

Thankfully, the battle of Gettysburg was over on that third day, on July 3, 1863.

General Lee's army, crippled by its heavy casualties, began a withdrawal to Virginia on July 4th.

The Union army also marched away, in order to block any intended actions of the Rebels against Washington, D.C.

Both sides left behind 51,000 soldiers, either wounded, dead, captured, or missing. (23,000 for the U.S.; 28,000 for the Confederates, in the three days).

Gettysburg was a major turning point in the Civil War----never again would Lee's armies invade the northern states. Pickett's Charge became known as the "high-water mark of the Confederacy," for the C.S.A.'s fortunes went downhill after going disastrously uphill into the U.S. guns at Cemetery Ridge.

The outlines of this 1st Minnesota Regiment story are generally known but not often thought about.

The question may be asked "Why did these Minnesotans, on July 2, charge directly into the onrushing Confederates, "into the valley of death that day," outnumbered as they were?[11]

In a word: Duty.

The soldiers of the 1st Minnesota Volunteer Regiment did what good soldiers were supposed to do, what they were ordered to do.

CHAPTER THREE
A Long Story Made Understandable

How do modern-day people understand these men of the Civil War times of the 1860s?

The best way is to look at two of these dutiful men.

Here are the storylines of William Colvill, and Martin Maginnis, of Company F, First Minnesota Volunteer Infantry, both from Red Wing.

Both of them were well-educated, both were newspapermen, both showed great endurance in wartime marching, both were courageous in battle.

Both men lived through their Civil War service, though both had been wounded in battle.

Colvill was Irish and Scottish, mainly Scottish. Maginnis was Irish-American.

In Christian faith, Colvill was Episcopal. Maginnis was a strong Catholic.

William Colvill was eleven years older than Martin Maginnis and was a mentor and friend of Maginnis.

Both men had been born in upstate New York.

William Colvill was born in 1830 in the town of Forestville, Chautauqua County, N.Y., located about six miles from Lake Erie's shores. His grandfather, William Colvill, and his father, William Colvill II (called William Colvill, Junior), had immigrated to the U.S. in 1820 from Kirkaldy, Scotland. His mother, Mary C. Love, was of Irish extraction and the Love family had arrived in America

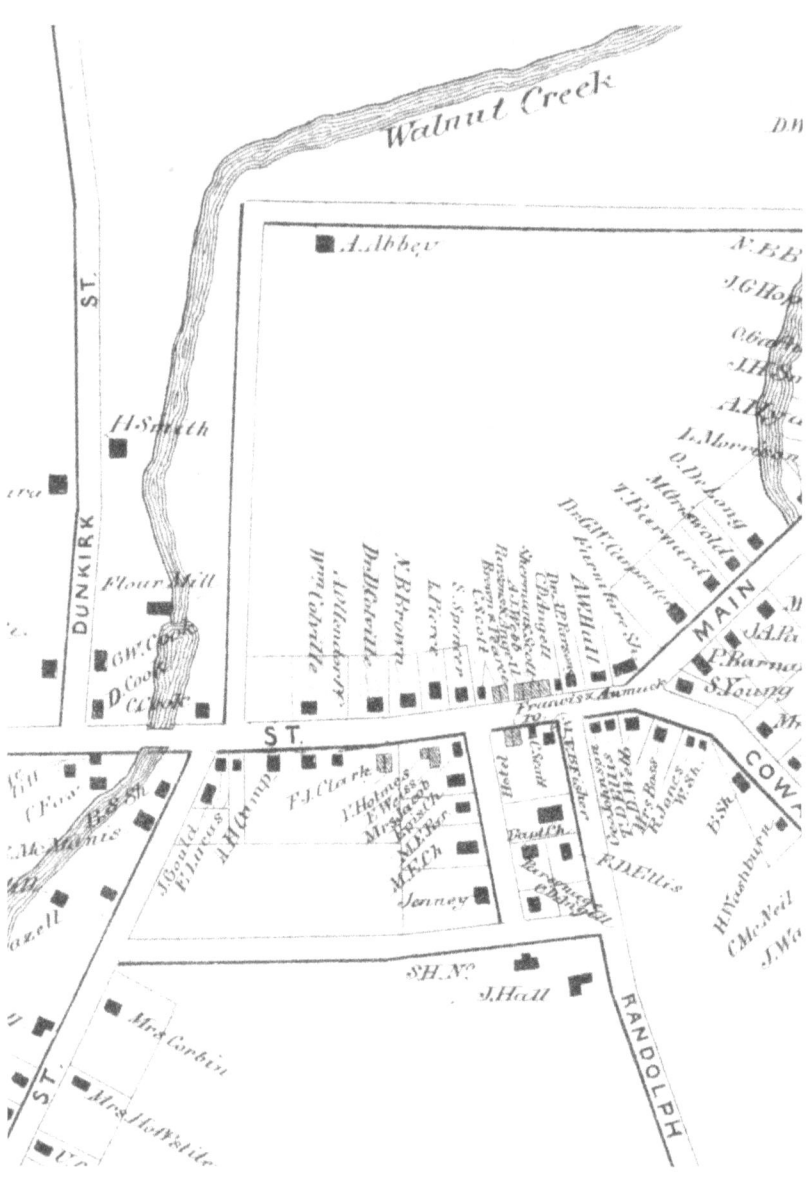

Forestville, NY, Chautauqua County, 1867. Colvill family residences near Walnut Creek. William Colvill home (father of Colvill of Minnesota), who had a 151-acre farm; and Dr. David G. Colvill home (uncle of Minnesota's Colvill).
Credit: The New York Public Library Digital Collections.

prior to the Revolutionary War. Her grandfather, Robert Love, had been an American soldier in that war.[1]

According to a history of Forestville, grandfather Colvill established a farm there and bought the local gristmill. William Colvill, Jr., the son, operated a store in Forestville, the firm of "Camp & Colvill, and also took over the farm;" and had 5 children: Jane, Elizabeth, Mary, William of this story, who actually was "William Colvill III," and George.[2]

William Colvill III (hereafter referred to simply as 'William Colvill,' because that is what he went by; or, sometimes, by the name of "William Colvill, Jr.") got his education at Fredonia Academy, located eight miles from Forestville, N.Y., and then was a schoolteacher for one winter. He moved to Buffalo, where he read law in the office of future-president Millard Fillmore, and was admitted to the N.Y. bar in April 1851.[3]

William Colvill worked as a lawyer in Forestville for three years and then journeyed to the western frontier, to Red Wing, Minnesota, in 1854, when he was 24 years old. He worked in real-estate sales immediately, and then opened a law office in 1855. At this same time, Colvill established his own newspaper, calling it the *Red Wing Sentinel*. He was a man with talent and ambition and skills well-suited for Minnesota Territory, and he became among the "leading citizens" of Red Wing.[4]

Colvill had a commanding presence for those days. He was considered to be a *giant of a man* because he stood six-feet-five-inches tall, when the average height of a man was about five-foot-eight.

Martin Maginnis was another young man blessed with real talent. Born in 1841, in Wayne County, N.Y., (a county located just east of Rochester, on the south shore of Lake Ontario), Martin was the first-born son of Patrick and Winnifred Maginnis. Both Patrick and Winnifred were born in Ireland; and they immigrated to America prior to Martin's birth. The family moved to Minnesota Territory in 1854, when Martin was only 13 years old. Patrick Maginnis soon staked out a farm in Belle Creek township, just 17 miles from Red Wing.[5]

Martin got his early years of schooling at Macedon Academy, N.Y., and later he attended Hamline University in Red Wing, where

Martin Maginnis of Red Wing, likely 1862, about 21 years old.
First Minnesota Volunteer Regiment. Credit: NDSU Archives, Fargo, ND.

he "gained a well-rounded and useful education with emphasis upon Christian, classical, and scientific training." Hamline was the "first institution of higher learning established in Minnesota Territory." The list of faculty included Reverend Peter Akers, who taught Biblical literature and was "known for his anti-slavery convictions and writings."[6]

Maginnis always had a distinctive personality and Irish-American voice, partly because of his Irish accent----acquired directly from his father Patrick and his mother Winnifred, as both of them were born and raised in Ireland. Everyone in his childhood home spoke English with an Irish lilt, so Martin Maginnis naturally spoke with a "rich brogue." In that time period in American history, it was easy to know if someone was Irish, for anyone could tell as soon as he opened his mouth to speak. Some appreciated the accent, some discriminated against it.[7]

The association of Martin Maginnis with William Colvill began in 1855 when the 25-year-old Colvill, along with Dan S. Merritt and James C. Hutchins, started the *Red Wing Sentinel* newspaper. Martin Maginnis was 14 years old when he learned the printer's trade from Colvill and the others at the *Sentinel*, running errands, sweeping floors, building fires in the wood-stove, delivering newspapers, putting type back in type-cases; eventually moving upward to setting type and reporting and writing. By 1859, when he was age 18, Martin Maginnis became the "printer and chief editor," all the while taking classes at Hamline University, and he bought half of the business.[8]

In contrast to Colvill's gigantic stature, Maginnis was five-foot-eight-and-a-half-inches in height. One was tall, the other was average.

Colvill and Maginnis became like brothers in those years before the Civil War, for Colvill's own younger brother, George (about the same age as Martin Maginnis), was faraway, in New York state. As Maginnis later wrote about William Colvill: "In my boyhood's days he first taught me how to use a gun in the game-filled bottoms of the Mississippi River," that flowed alongside Red Wing. All seasons of the year yielded wild game in the nearby woods and fields: white-tailed deer abounded in the winter; April and October were alive with ducks and geese; summer provided grouse, woodcock, and prairie chickens; and wild passenger pigeons were abundant during spring nesting and in fall, when they feasted on acorns.[9]

Martin also wrote that Colvill "taught me how . . . to cast a fly in the crystal trout streams that emptied into [the] mighty current" of the Mississippi. They caught brook trout in the crystal-clear, "gently rippling" streams flowing from springs bubbling from the wooded bluffs above Red Wing; from brooks named 'Spring Creek,' 'Hay Creek,' and 'Bullard's Creek,' Maginnis and Colvill landed plenteous "speckled trout."[10]

"We ourselves," wrote Colvill in 1859, "have often had the startling pleasure of landing trout of two pounds and upwards from the streams of Minnesota and Wisconsin, and know where the places are now."[11]

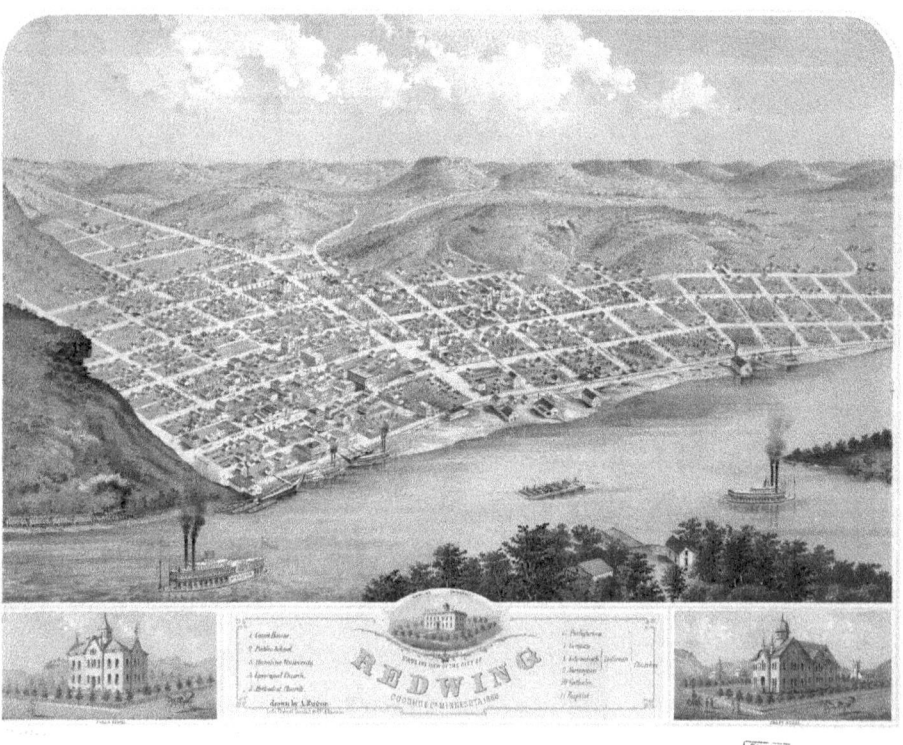

Bird's eye view of Red Wing, 1868, alongside the Mississippi River.
Credit: Library of Congress. Public domain.

Colvill also looked after the intellectual development of the younger Martin Maginnis, as Colvill published the Red Wing newspaper, with Maginnis learning every part of the business. In order to develop Maginnis's writing skills, Colvill shared his own collection of books he had brought with him from New York. As Maginnis noted: "In his well-stocked library----one of the best that was brought so early into the territory of Minnesota---I read with him poetry, romance, history and philosophy, and sometimes law."[12]

They both sought a wiser, wider perspective because the issues of slavery and the rights of states within the U.S. republic in the later 1850s were so divisive. Colvill and Maginnis were Democrats, with an emphasis on the idea of true democracy----namely, that the people in a state or territory must decide for themselves if they wanted to have slavery within their own boundaries. In the election year of 1860, with these explosive issues in the forefront of the news, Colvill sold his share of the *Red Wing Sentinel*, on February 4, 1860, to William W. Phelps of Red Wing (who had just finished a two-year term as one of Minnesota's two Congressmen in Washington, D.C.) seeing a "storm coming" within the Democratic Party. He wisely did not want to inflame his own neighbors against him. Maginnis, however, continued to publish the newspaper, with fainting hopes that moderate viewpoints could fix the deep divides between North and South.[13]

As the time of the 1860 presidential election neared, the issues that Colvill and Maginnis wrote about in the *Red Wing Sentinel* became difficult to process to their readership. Colvill and Maginnis, were both supporters of the Democratic Party, but when Southern Democrats agitated for a radical pro-slavery platform, the party split up into two separate branches---Northern and Southern. Being Democrats, Colvill and Maginnis were dismayed when the candidate they supported, Illinois Senator Stephen Douglas, lost the election after Southern Democrats nominated and voted for their own extreme pro-slavery man, John Breckinridge. The vote in Red Wing went overwhelmingly for Abraham Lincoln's election---the Goodhue County vote-count was 1,352 for Lincoln; with 429 for Douglas; and 17 for Breckinridge.[14]

After Abraham Lincoln won the presidency in November, 1860, some Southerners wanted to secede (to leave) the Union. South

Carolina seceded from the U.S. in December, 1860, and within six weeks, six more states left the Union. On February 4, 1861, these states formed a separate nation, the Confederate States of America (C.S.A.).

When the C.S.A. attacked Fort Sumter, S.C., in April, and it surrendered on April 14, 1861, President Lincoln responded powerfully. The very next day, Lincoln issued a proclamation calling for 75,000 troops as a show of force to quell this rebellion against the U.S.[15]

Martin Maginnis published a call "To Arms!, To Arms!," in his Wednesday, April 17th, *Sentinel,* underneath a warlike eagle whose beak carried a banner screaming: "The Union---It Must Be Preserved." The eagle called the men of Red Wing to a Friday, April 19th, mass meeting in the Goodhue County courthouse to organize a company of volunteers in answer to Lincoln's call to raise an army.[16]

The city of Red Wing was in a "blaze of enthusiasm," and the people turned out in such numbers that the courthouse was "crowd-

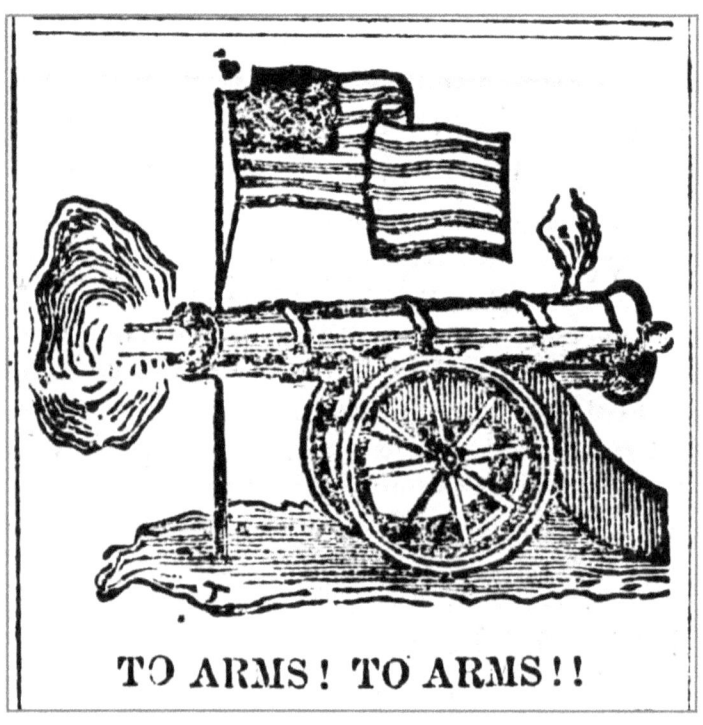

Martin Maginnis's Red Wing Sentinel, April 17, 1861. The call: "To Arms! To Arms!"
Red Wing rapidly formed a company of 100 men for the First Minnesota
Volunteer Infantry regiment.

ed to suffocation." There was a "spirit of adventure that always accompanies the commencement of a war."[17]

In that patriotically-charged place, Reverend Matthew Sorin spoke to the people, and his "words were flaming swords" that "set fire to all hearts" of the citizens in this "war meeting." Others, including William Colvill, gave "stirring speeches," and enthusiasm rose to a crescendo with a call for volunteers to sign their names in the Secretary's enrollment-book on an oaken desk up front.[18]

As soon as the Secretary opened his book, two vigorous men, William Colvill and A. Edwards Welch, immediately jumped up and "raced for the Secretary's desk," hurdling over the backs of the chairs in order to "get through the crowd."[19]

Welch was quicker, but slipped and fell at the desk, "just as his hand touched the pen."[20]

Colvill suddenly seized the elusive pen, saying, "Excuse me, Ed, but you will be next," and thus Colvill "wrote his name for the Union army," becoming the first man to enlist in Goodhue County.[21]

Ed Welch next signed his name, and a host of others followed, including Martin Maginnis.

Colvill, standing 6-foot-5-inches tall, was looked up to as a leader, and he organized this company of volunteers. His men elected him as their Captain, unanimously, followed by "three hearty cheers" for Colvill, who then gave a "few remarks amid tumultuous cheers." Then came more voting, whereby the men selected Ed Welch as 1st Lieutenant, and Martin Maginnis as 1st Sergeant.[22]

"It was no wonder," wrote Maginnis about Colvill, "that I should go out as first sergeant in the company that he raised at the first call to arms," because Colvill had proven to be "an older friend and companion-----a kind and voluntary tutor, my mentor in politics and leader in everything." Colvill was like a big brother to Maginnis.[23]

It was perfectly natural for William Colvill to volunteer to serve in the war, for his great-grandfather on his mother's side of the family, had been a soldier in the Revolutionary War. Great-grandfather Robert Love (1757-1846) was a private in a Massachusetts regiment, serving "in the siege of Boston, Battle of White Plains, Capture of Burgoyne and Oriskany." When William Colvill was a youngster, he had "heard him relate many incidents of his early life of his service in the Revolutionary War," and he had sat at the feet of his great-grandfather and "heard the story of their sufferings and victory."[24]

Love of his country was deeply-instilled in William Colvill. Indeed, it was just two years previously, in 1859, that Colvill had given a Fourth of July speech at Bay City, just across the Mississippi River from Red Wing, and he praised the "glorious soldiers of the Revolution, who, at the call of their country, left the dear enjoyments and ties of home and family to brave the horrors of war." Colvill loved the "temple of Independence" that had been built "upon the slaughtered bodies of many brave men," and he declared that the union of the states should always be defended in order to "perpetuate their memories." These American soldiers, motivated by "patriotism and brotherly love," had bought freedom on the battlefields of the Revolutionary War, which were "crimson with their blood."[25]

"To honor the flag of freedom," Colvill said, "let us swear that we will not be unworthy of our glorious heritage, and that the liberty for which our fathers fought, the independence which they gained, and the union which they formed and cemented with their blood, shall be perpetuated forever!"[26]

There were fifty men who enrolled on that first day, and more were needed. So, the next day, Colvill "took a light wagon and went out into the country" around Red Wing, "stopping at the pioneer farm houses and asking the young men to join him." Years later, Colvill said that "he returned with four wagon loads of men" to help fill the ranks.[27]

And so, a total of 100 men made up the company called the Goodhue Volunteers. They traveled by steamboat to Fort Snelling to join the other nine companies of the First Minnesota regiment during the month of May 1861. The men said goodbyes to their wives, sweethearts, and families at the levee along the Mississippi River at Red Wing. Each volunteer knew that he might not come home again, ever.

At Fort Snelling, their commander was Colonel Willis A. Gorman, who had been an officer in the Mexican War, so he had knowledge of military training. Battlefield movements and marching and target practice filled the days. These civilians immediately began training to become "well disciplined" soldiers. The men had to "drill, drill, drill, until their muskets, and all military movements" became "as familiar as the tools and movements of the peaceful occupations," whether as a farmer or a lumberjack or a newspaperman.[28]

The *1,000 men* of the First Minnesota Volunteers had within them the "young energy" of the frontier, who were among the first to spring to the defense of the Union and the American flag. As Maginnis later wrote, these were "men who could shoot and march and ride and do anything demanded" in that time of war. "They were men who could write books or practice law or conduct colleges," alongside some who knew how to "build a locomotive or a steamboat."[29]

Colvill understood that the soldiers of the First Minnesota Regiment had qualities that would make them a "powerful factor" in the Union army. They were muscular men, farmers and lumberjacks, and the Minnesota climate helped make them strong and forceful. He said: "Many of them were lumbermen, just out of the woods, hardy physically," and able to handle exposure to any kind of weather, not easily fatigued, and "at home" in difficult conditions. These Minnesotans had "shooting ability" because they were outdoorsmen, but their frontiersmen skills were even more essential in the U.S. military, because "there were roads to be made, bridges to be built or destroyed, railroads . . . to be operated, in order to get to the enemy before fighting him." Colvill recalled that "We were rough men," and perhaps it appeared that "we were awkward, but we were handy men on several occasions" during the war.[30]

Among the soldiers in the First Minnesota there were some who knew how to handle an axe, or a cant hook for moving heavy logs or breaking log-jams on a river; or to plow and plant and harvest a wheat field; while others, like Colvill and Maginnis, were newspapermen who could speak words to inspire and motivate their brothers in arms. The regiment was made up of "clerks, farmers, mechanics, students, doctors, lawyers, teachers, college professors," and "lumbermen," who left their callings in life to preserve their nation. Most had been born in another state, but there were many of German and Irish origins, and there was also a sprinkling of Swedes and Norwegians among them. Almost all were younger than 30 years old (Colvill was age 31); with a majority being under age 20 (Maginnis was 19 years old at that time).[31]

Each volunteer had a feeling of patriotic fervor in his throbbing soldier's-heart, in varying temperatures from warm to hot, even if he did not know the full extent to which he would end up sacrificing some portion of his life, or if he would be fated to bleeding-out all of his life-blood for the Union.

For Captain William Colvill, who had never been in the military, it was a vital necessity for him to learn how to be an officer.

So Colvill got the best book on weapons and combat maneuvers available at that time----entitled *Rifle and Light Infantry Tactics*. This was the standard U.S Army manual for training soldiers to get them ready for battle. Colvill read it and put its methods into practice. Colvill "made a complete study of the profession of arms," wrote Maginnis, because "from the first he loved all the literature and science and traditions of war." By his serious studying and through experience, Colvill became a "complete master" of the details of military service and "demands of discipline."[32]

These men from Red Wing were strong, willing to serve the Union, and ready to learn how to be good soldiers, yet within each man there was the "question of life or death": 'Would he return to Minnesota alive?'[33]

In the last week of June, Colvill and Maginnis and the 1st Minnesota went to the warfront, all the way to Washington, D.C., to guard the capital. These 900-plus Minnesotans had military drill every day during June, and they even had a visit one day from President Abraham Lincoln.[34]

It was not long before the First Minnesota would participate in its first battle.

It was in July of 1861, when the regiment "crossed over into Virginia and took a leading part in the Battle of Bull Run." The Union army had to win the war by invading and conquering the South, whereas the Southerners did not need to conquer the North, they only had to defend their own territory. The logical way for the U.S. to win the war quickly would be to capture Richmond, the C.S.A. capital. Because Washington, D.C., and Richmond were only 100 miles apart (as a bird flies), it seemed possible to quickly 'capture the capital' and end the war. However, the geography made it hard to get from one city to the other, with ten rivers to cross, *each river making*

38

a line of defense; and ridges and swamps to navigate, and so Union forces had to follow a few good roads and the main railway line to Richmond. The most direct path went through Manassas village, located near a creek called Bull Run that flowed from the Bull Run Mountains nearby. The land was "wooded, rough and difficult," with plenty of ambush places for the Confederates to make earthworks for concealing artillery and troops around the town called Manassas.[35]

The battle of Bull Run, July 21, 1861, was the first time in combat for the First Minnesota regiment. All of the men were afraid of dying that day for they were to be placed in the battle in the very "forefront of duty and danger." They had to overcome their fears.[36]

Before the battle, Martin Maginnis was "certain of victory," but Captain Colvill was unsure of how it would go.[37]

Union General Irvin McDowell had a good plan for his 35,000 troops, but it was too complicated, it was too elaborate, for the newly-trained soldiers and inexperienced officers.[38]

The Minnesota regiment, led by Colonel Gorman, started marching toward the field of battle at 2 o'clock in the morning, and they marched for six miles through the woods in order to get around to the far side of the Confederate positions.

The First Minnesota did well in its first battle, engaging in several attacks against Confederate positions, pushing the Rebels back "about a half mile" and capturing three batteries of cannons.[39]

Then, the Confederates held strong on their "second line of defenses," with cannons hidden along wooded hills.[40]

That afternoon, the Minnesotans were in "the advance of the army," wrote Maginnis, in the "post of honor----and as it proved of danger and death---the right flank regiment of the battle."[41]

At that time, Maginnis and Colvill and their fellow soldiers "took their position facing . . . a heavy piece of woods" where, even though "no enemy could be seen," it was filled with Rebel soldiers, concealed in woods and brush, ready to counterattack.

"Colonel Gorman gave the word in clear tones," recalled Maginnis. Gorman said "Steady! Steady Minnesota! *Aim low!* Fire!"

"And we poured a thousand rifle bullets into the woods."

"That volley seemed the signal to unchain Pandemonium" as "a masked battery on our left, within a hundred yards, opened a terrific fire; and all along the line of the woods, not over thirty feet from us . . . rolled out upon us a sheet of flame and a storm of bullets from the Alabama and Mississippi infantry. Terrific and sudden was that shower of grape and canister, balls, and bombs; bullets and bursting shells, which tore through our ranks and raged along our line, beyond all I had ever read of or imagined, and mowed down our gallant lads like grass before the scythe."

"Our troops held manfully before it, and answered their fire."[42]

It was in the early part of the Battle of Bull Run that Maginnis was wounded. "I received a piece of lead in the cheek," Maginnis recalled years later, "that might have made a bad wound had it struck a little squarer." Captain H.R. Putnam evaluated Maginnis's condition and found that the "wound was not very serious," and they advanced on the battlefield together.[43]

"The enemy made a desperate charge," wrote Maginnis, yet "Company F never lost an inch of ground" at that point in the battle.[44]

And then, the Southern cavalry, the famous "Black Horse Guards," all of them riding all-black steeds, charged down the hill, "shaking the ground and filling the air with dust . . . . and they moved down upon us. We closed up our ranks and poured a steady, murderous fire into them. Horses and men fell together in masses, and not one-third of the dashing horsemen went back to tell the tale of their repulse. The ground was covered with their dead, [and] their horses."

Another regiment of Southerners attacked and after 15 minutes of fighting, Maginnis and his company "drove them back," following Captain Colvill. "We drove them up into the woods," as noted by Maginnis; and Colvill "took a Mississippi Colonel and three men prisoners with his own hand."

In those next minutes, "friend and foe were intermingled, and a thousand desperate hand to hand conflicts were going on with muskets, pistols, bayonets, and even knives," and "we drove them back behind their batteries, back to their rifle pits, back on the solid columns of thousands that they still had in reserve."

"And those fresh thousands" of strong reinforcements attacked, forcing the First Minnesota and the other Union troops to fight their way out of the woods as best as they could, "dragging with us the prisoners we had taken," wrote Maginnis.

"Col. Gorman was again rallying the remains of the regiment," but the "day, the battle, all----was lost."

"In obedience to orders," recalled Maginnis, "sullenly and gloomily, we took our backward march," in retreat, "carrying off our wounded."

"Gorman had succeeded in getting the regiment into something like order," so that they "fell back . . . in pretty good shape," towards Washington, D.C., providing a somewhat-organized rearguard cover for the unorganized Union retreat.

Winslow Homer, "Bayonet Charge," illustration from 1862, not of the 1st Minnesota Regiment, yet showing the desperation on the faces of soldiers from both sides. Credit: Smithsonian American Art Museum. [Free to use]. Source: Winslow Homer, "The War for the Union 1862—A Bayonet Charge," from Harper's Weekly, July 12, 1862.

In the middle of the "last fight of the day," Captain Colvill had a close call with death. His first battle could have been his last.[45]

Colvill and men were moving away from a difficult zone, under their commander's "order to retire," and Colvill was among the last to leave. He tried to help a wounded soldier along the way, but was interrupted by the rapid approach of "a platoon of the enemy."[46]

Colvill heard a flood of footsteps close-by, and, immediately, Confederate soldiers sprang "out of the woods" in a "left wheel" movement directly "into the road."

The C.S.A. infantrymen instantly saw a huge, six-foot-five-inches-tall man just several yards in front of them, and the sudden motion of the enemy troops "startled" Colvill as swiftly as a partridge whirring up from the bushes while hunting had surprised him in the past----with a **WHRRRRRRRR** sound. The Confederates were just "as much" startled by the sight of Colvill.

"Instinctively" Colvill took off running, pell-mell, as fast as he could towards a ravine that was about 25 yards away, and close to the woods. He sprinted for his life over that short distance faster than a "race horse" could have covered it, even though Colvill's energy was just about totally spent from the exertions and stress of that long day.

As Captain Colvill reached the edge of the ravine, he heard the distinctive sound of the rifle barrels slapping down into the hands of the Confederate soldiers (from the regular position on their right-hand shoulders), ready to aim and fire.

So Colvill *jumped forward*, with a "mighty leap," with his "feet thrown out" in front of him, and he was flying through the air. He landed in the ravine, flat on his back, skidding, with his "head crouched downward," at the very "same instant" that the enemy soldiers pulled their triggers.

"*A hundred bullets*," or even more, "*buzzed like a nest of hornets past my head*," recalled Colvill some years later.

Without losing his head, Colvill immediately sprang right back up and he "rushed down" the ravine to safety, out of the direct line of fire, behind the banks of the nearby creek. "Glancing back," Captain Colvill saw a look of total astonishment on a whole "row of blank faces" in the line of the Confederates, who simply could not believe that their deathly volley had missed such a big target.

Colvill, what with his adrenaline-fueled leap, allied with the 'Hand of the Almighty,' lived through a volley of lead balls whizzing an inch or two above his head---a mere one-half-second from his own obliteration.

At Bull Run, Captain Colvill and the First Minnesota Regiment had fought well, but then the wider Union effort turned this battle into a demoralizing defeat; and it ended with a disorganized retreat for the bulk of the U.S. army. Colvill avowed that the First Minnesota men, at the end of the day, were "bringing up the rear in good order." This was the "regiment that didn't run at Bull Run."[47]

As another soldier from Red Wing summed up this first battle: "Fighting was natural" for the 1st Minnesota, however, "we hadn't learned *how to retreat*."[48]

American war eagle. Defend the honor and the flag of the U.S.
Author's photo, 2013. Old Sturbridge Village, Massachusetts.

CHAPTER FOUR
What the First Minnesota Regiment Learned at Bull Run

It was a bitter first taste of battle at Bull Run, for the 1st Minnesota regiment had suffered repeated attacks due to its position at the farthest right side of the U.S. forces. Because they were in the "thickest of the fight" in the thickets, the Minnesotans had more men killed or wounded than any other Northern regiment, losing 42 killed; 108 wounded; and 30 missing (captured) of their total numbers of about 900 (a 20 percent casualty rate).[1]

This first battle would prove to be the *worst single day of the war* for the 1st Minnesota----because 42 men died on that day.

The lesson of Bull Run was this: each man slowly came to understand that if he did his duty and did not act in a foolhardy way, he would be more likely to live through each battle than to die on the battlefield. He would be more likely to be wounded than to be killed. At Bull Run, about 12 percent of the Minnesota regiment had been wounded, and about 5 percent were killed. According to Frank Haskell, a Civil War officer from Wisconsin who examined the numbers, the "proportion of the killed to the wounded" in the war's battles was "*one* to *five*, rarely less than five."[2]

This idea, that many more soldiers would *be wounded rather than be killed* in battle, was directly connected to the *"Aim Low"* order of Colonel Willis Gorman, who had learned it by his experience in the Mexican War of 1846-1848. The main reason for commanding the troops to *"Aim Low"* was to encourage each man to shoot his gun. Even though it seems strange to urge a soldier to shoot his gun, it was necessary in war because an average man would not want to kill another man; he would be reluctant to take the life of another man. It has been deduced that 80 percent of Civil War soldiers did not shoot their weapons at their enemies on the battlefield. Some, if they did shoot, would deliberately aim high so that they would not harm anyone. Some soldiers who did not want to shoot their own rifles, would just load their rifles and keep passing the loaded-rifles to the soldier who was willing to shoot. The best shooters would keep up a constant fire from these rifles passed to them, reloaded again and again.[3]

As a Civil War veteran noted: "Out of every regiment," of a thousand men total, "not more than 100 men were fighters" who "shot to kill." The others would be "nervously throwing away ammunition" by shooting high, thinking that the very sound of his rifle-shots could force the Confederates to retreat.[4]

Another factor was involved in a soldier's response to the order to "Aim Low." The soldier understood that if he shot an enemy in the feet or in the legs, the enemy-soldier would be less likely to die, but would be taken out of action. A wounded soldier would have to be carried away from the battlefield by a fellow soldier. The mathematics of this were unmistakable, because if each wounded soldier was immediately helped by his buddy and taken to a field hospital for medical help, then there would be fewer enemy soldiers available to fight. Soldiers also came to understand if both sides would aim low, at the enemy's feet, then more men would be wounded rather than killed by their bullets. It might seem obvious that anyone would rather be wounded than to be killed, however, upon reflection, it eventually dawned upon Civil War combatants that a wounded soldier might be hobbled for the rest of his life.[5]

Before the battle of Bull Run, Martin Maginnis had wondered "what may a day bring forth?" Afterwards, he was thankful for surviving his first battle, yet he could not help but wonder how he and his fellow Minnesotans *made it at all* through the Battle of Bull Run.[6]

"In the din of battle," wrote Martin Maginnis, "we were all kneeling----not for fear, but for accuracy in taking aim. Our boys were cool" even at one time when the enemy soldiers were between Company F and the rest of the regiment. Just then Lieutenant Ed Welch shouted: "Stand fast, for God's sake, Company F!"

Maginnis stated: "And we 'stood fast,'----"for 'God's sake."

Ultimately, Maginnis marveled as to "why the enemy did not surround us and sweep us from the field, God in his mercy alone knows."[7]

After Bull Run, President Abraham Lincoln reorganized the Union army's leadership.
Author's collection.

CHAPTER FIVE
The Army of the Potomac

After Bull Run, President Lincoln appointed a new commander, General George McClellan, and McClellan created the
"Army of the Potomac" to organize the disorganized Union forces
guarding the nation's capital. McClellan made sure that his regiments
learned how to march and maneuver by being instructed, drilled, and
disciplined during the winter of 1861-62. The almost-unending drills
taught the men about "company, battalion and line maneuvers," before being sent forth again into battle.[1]

General McClellan, as Maginnis said later, had the magnificent "organizing hand," that gave the U.S. army the "discipline that was
needed to fit it for its task" of defeating the Rebel forces. "That discipline was superb," asserted Maginnis, "if it in the wider sense means
that obedience to duty which keeps men in line when they fight, and in
column when they march, to fight again tomorrow, and to march the
night after, until energy is exhausted and obedience mechanical." What
McClellan provided from 1861 to 1862 made his men into a true army,
that Maginnis called the "best disciplined army on this planet."[2]

Command of the 1st Minnesota changed, too. It was now led
by Colonel Napoleon J.T. Dana, West Point-educated and, in the
view of Martin Maginnis, "the great master of skill and discipline,"
who ensured that the "training of the regiment was of the best." Maginnis, himself, got a promotion from sergeant to Second Lieutenant.[3]

Union General George McClellan decided to attack the
Confederate capital of Richmond, Virginia, from a southern direction, rather than through Bull Run again. So the 1st Minnesota, again

with new leadership----under Colonel Alfred Sully---was a part of the 100,000-man army that McClellan led to the Virginia Peninsula in March of 1862, advancing along the York River to within six miles of Richmond by late May. This was called the 'Peninsular Campaign.'

At the Battle of Fair Oaks, May 31-June 1, the Confederates attacked, and the Minnesota regiment was in action, on the extreme right side of the U.S. forces, therefore, the Union troops got no closer than six miles of entering Richmond. General Robert E. Lee then assumed command of Confederate forces; and Lee's Rebel army pushed the Union army away, back down the peninsula in the Seven Days' Battles (June 25-July 1, 1862).

In a skirmish at Nelson's Farm, near White Oak Swamp, Monday, June 30th, Captain William Colvill was hit by a bullet in his shoulder, two inches below his left collar-bone. Colvill got medical attention from Dr. Daniel Hand, who found a "quiet fence corner for him," where Dr. Hand removed Colvill's shirt and found a "dangerous wound." The doctor removed the musket-ball from Colvill's chest, and insisted that Colvill "must keep quiet," and rest.[4]

Soon thereafter, Dr. Hand went back to where Colvill was lying and "told him we were retreating, and he must be left behind."[5]

"I did not think he could make the march," recalled Dr. Hand, but Colvill "just pulled his tall form from under the fence and said: 'No,'" that he would go with the army, that he "would not be left" behind.

There was no wagon or cart to carry Colvill, but Major George N. Morgan, also of the First Minnesota, came by, and Major Morgan offered to let Captain Colvill ride his horse.

Colvill would not accept riding Morgan's horse, instead Colvill "took a firm grip of the horse's tail, and off they started," with Colvill, being steadied by the horse's strength, walking haltingly to safe haven at Harrison's Landing. He needed two months to recover from this serious wound, going to his old hometown of Forestville in New York state, where he could stay with his family. His mother and father lived there, and his uncle, David G. Colvill, was a physician there. His sister, Mary and her husband Daniel Sherman also had their home in Forestville. As he was recuperating, he received a promotion from captain to major.[6]

THE ARMY OF THE POTOMAC—OUR OUTLYING PICKET IN THE WOODS.—Sketched by Mr. W. Homer.

"In the Woods," by Winslow Homer. The Minnesotans had used the sheltering trees of the North Woods at Antietam to their great advantage. "The Army of the Potomac-- Our Outlying Picket in the Woods," Harper's Weekly, June 7, 1862. #1996.63.48. Credit: Smithsonian American Art Museum. [Free to use.]

Martin Maginnis was "slightly wounded," shot in his left shoulder at Savage's Station, June 29th, yet was "never off duty."[7]

The last of the Seven Days' battles came at Malvern Hill, July 1st, where Union troops held the high ground, a great defensive advantage. The Confederate army suffered severe losses charging uphill across open fields into cannon-fire. Despite the victory at Malvern Hill, Union forces had utterly failed in its mission to capture Richmond.[8]

The soldiers of the First Minnesota regiment endured summer's heat, mud, illness, marching, and battle during the Peninsular Campaign and its Seven Days' fights, before being ordered back to guard the fortifications around Washington, D.C.

The next major battle for the Minnesotans came in September, 1862, when the South took the offensive. Robert E. Lee's Confederate army invaded Maryland, hoping to win a great victory on Northern soil, in hopes that Great Britain or France would officially recognize the Confederate States of America as a separate nation. Lee's plan threatened Pennsylvania and threatened Washington, D.C. The Confederates wanted to "carry the horrors of war into the heart of the North," rather than have battles in war-worn Virginia. If Lee's armies did well, the North might agree to a ceasefire and end the war with Southern independence a reality.[9]

Things did not go the way General Lee wanted them to go. Fate intervened when a Union soldier found a document entitled "Special Order 191," which was a copy of Lee's invasion-plans wrapped around three cigars, which had been lost by a careless Southern officer. After getting this information, the U.S. army marched forth in order to intercept the Confederate forces. The armies of the North and South clashed at the Battle of Antietam, in Maryland, on September 17, and that one day became the bloodiest single day in the Civil War. 23,000 soldiers were killed, wounded in action, or missing after twelve hours of brutal combat (these were the totals for *both* sides). The Battle of Antietam ended the Confederate Army's first invasion into the North and led Abraham Lincoln to issue the preliminary Emancipation Proclamation, his plan to release slaves into freedom, which would eventually lead to the end of slavery in the U.S.

William Colvill, now a major, had recovered enough from his June wounds to return to the 1st Minnesota Regiment on August 31, in time to help Colonel Alfred Sully lead them at Antietam.[10]

Again, the Minnesota men were in another of the most desperate battles in the war, at Antietam. Obeying orders as always, the regiment was sent into battle near the town of Sharpsburg, moving from the East Woods across an open area and then facing a deathly Confederate ambush in the West Woods. Advancing under heavy artillery fire, the Minnesotans fought for a time "behind a rail fence" where the loss became heavy and they managed to retreat in a fairly-good line of battle. They made a stand near a farm house, then moved back to form a "strong position" behind a stone fence before going into the shelter of the North Woods, where Union cannons saved them from deeper losses. As it was, 118 of the enlisted men were casualties, with 15 killed, 79 wounded, and with 24 missing in action.[11]

As a reward for his leadership on the Antietam battlefield, Colvill was promoted again, from major to lieutenant colonel.[12]

Among the wounded at Antietam was Martin Maginnis. He was shot through his leg, a flesh wound, and was in a field hospital for one week before rejoining his company.[13]

Later in 1862, Maginnis and Colvill and the 1st Minnesota Regiment were in the battle of Fredericksburg, December 13, a disaster for the North. The key point here was that the Confederate army held the high ground. The Southerners fortified the heights above the town, and Union troops vainly charged again and again, uphill, into deadly musket-fire and cannon-fire, losing 12,000 soldiers killed or wounded in a day. The Minnesota men were fortunately assigned to guard cannons located near the city on that day and were spared from the foolish headlong frontal charges into heavily-dug-in defenders.[14]

The regiment was not in the worst of the combat in early 1863, when Chancellorsville was the scene of another clash of armies.

Indeed, the first months of 1863 were a time of winter camp along the Rappahannock River.

Lincoln's Emancipation Proclamation was a major step in abolishing
the curse of slavery. Author's collection.

CHAPTER SIX
What the Men of the First Minnesota Learned Along the Way

The soldiers of the First Minnesota Infantry had become veterans of war. They knew what it meant to be a 'good soldier,' for they had learned many lessons along their pathway since leaving their beloved North Star State back in 1861.

They had learned that there were times to form a battle line and there were times to take cover behind a fence or in the edge of the woods.

There were times to lay down flat on the ground to avoid cannon fire.

They came to understood that "great battles are won with artillery," as Napoleon had written decades earlier. They learned the benefits of Union artillery and the hazards of facing enemy cannons that used four types of ammunition aimed at them----solid shot cannonballs; explosive shells; case shot which held shrapnel or round shot; and canister, a tin-can containing *27 iron balls, each over one inch in diameter.*[1]

Expert artillery crews could hit buildings, bridges, or small groups of men at maximum range of one mile with a round iron cannonball, 12 pounds in weight. It has been said that a smooth-bore cannon could hit a barn a mile away, and the rifled-cannon Parrot guns could accurately hit a window on a barn a mile away. Cannoneers would aim a solid-shot cannonball to bounce and tumble and roll along the ground like a bowling-ball, and a soldier had to keep his eyes open to try to dodge it towards the end of its flight.

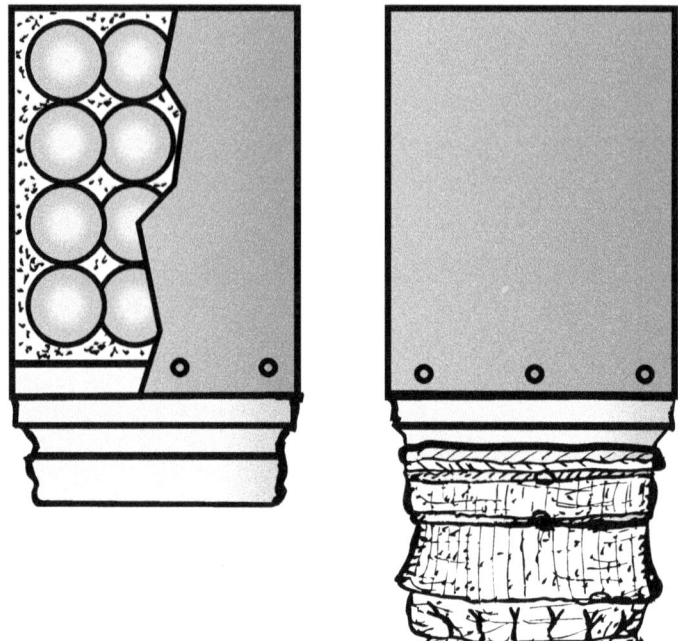

Cut-away view of canister (on left), showing the iron shot, packed in sawdust, inside a large tin can that just fit inside the cannon's barrel, used at close range. When fired, its effect was like a giant shotgun. A gunpowder bag was attached to the wooden base of the tin canister before firing, to power the iron balls (on right). Steve Hoffbeck drawing, adapted from N.P.S., "Weapons, Accouterments and the Soldier," nps.gov/history/history/paal/thunder-cannon/chap4.htm; and Jack Coggins, Arms and Equipment of the Civil War (Mineola, NY: Dover Publications, 1962); and Standard U.S. Field Artillery Smoothbore Ammunition, 1849-1865.

Cannons could also fire case shot, a hollow iron ball filled with gunpowder and about 75 iron balls, timed to explode about 15 feet overhead, fired from about 400 yards away.

The deadliest of all was canister, in the shape of a large tin-can, filled to the brim with 27 iron balls (over one inch in diameter), because it was used at close-range. When fired, the tin-can ruptured when it left the muzzle of the cannon, turning the cannon into a giant shotgun. It was used against the First Regiment when the Minnesota soldiers got within 300 yards and closer. Canister was greatly feared because these murderous cans, when fired at point-black range, would kill or maim anyone that it hit that got caught in its hail of shot.

1864 A Shell Is Coming. Two soldiers take shelter behind a tree. Object # 47.91.25(182). Title: Life in Camp, Part 1: A Shell is Coming. Artist: After Winslow Homer. Louis Prang & Co. Date: 1864. Credit: Metropolitan Museum of Art. Public Domain.

Because the artillery crews had to see what they were shooting in order to aim the cannons, the soldiers being shot at could also see the cannons, so it was wise to have a position at the edge of the woods. It was better to have the trees be hit by cannon balls, rather than have a soldier being hammered by one. Taking whatever cover was available was of great value to preserve one's life and limbs.

The soldiers of the 1st Minnesota came to know that diseases could be as bad as bullets. They were taught by Colonel N.J.T. Dana early on to be careful in their "sanitary arrangements," regarding cleanliness in latrines, for Colonel Dana had learned all about best practices in his Mexican War service long before. The Minnesota regiment had fewer losses to disease than other sloppier regiments, losing 27 enlisted men and 2 officers who died of various diseases over the course of their three years of service in the war.[2]

Oddly enough, Colvill and Maginnis and their fellow soldiers gained a measure of protection against disease germs because they drank so much coffee. The caffeine helped them have energy to march long distances per day even though exhausted; kept their minds thinking fast in the day of battle; and a hot cup of coffee gave them warmth on cold winter days. Even more importantly, because the Minnesota men boiled the coffee over a fire or over hot coals, the boiling killed whatever germs were lurking in the water (although they did not necessarily know much about germ-theory).[3]

CAMPAIGN SKETCHES.

THE COFFEE CALL.

Boiled coffee fueled Colvill and Maginnis and the men of the First Minnesota as they endured wartime encampments. Winslow Homer, Campaign Sketches, "The Coffee Call." Credit: Library of Congress.

The Minnesotans in the Army of the Potomac learned the best ways to live in a winter camp in Virginia and how to endure tenting life when marching on a campaign. Each soldier had a tent-mate; and, while on the march, each pair of tent-mates cooked their own food.

The Minnesota soldiers lived for months at a time on basic foods----coffee and sugar, hard-tack crackers, and salt pork. The tent-mates between the two of them carried one coffee pot, a small frying-pan, and a hatchet for cutting wood for a fire to prepare their simple fare.[4]

When the regiment was in winter camp, they built a small hut as a bakery to make bread for all the men. They also got beans, and used a 'bean hole' to bake pork and beans. First thing in the evening, they filled several huge iron kettles with beans and salt-pork and soaked the beans. Then they dug a trench and made a huge fire in it. After the wood turned to hot coals, they shoveled out the hot coals, placed the massive kettles in the trench, scooped the coals back into the trench and around the kettles, and then covered it all with soil--with a small airhole for ventilation. Leaving it to bake overnight, they had a big breakfast of pork-and-beans the next morning.[5]

Regarding tents while on the march, every Minnesotan carried a half tent, "each about five and a half-feet square," so, after a day's march, two soldiers would put their two halves together, buttoned at the top. Maginnis and Colvill shared a shelter-tent in the first year of the war, as Maginnis later wrote. These shelter tents were said to work "pretty well for a short man," like Maginnis, but would "hardly cover a long one, like our Captain" Colvill.[6]

The men of the First Minnesota had to learn how to get along with each other and how to cope with all the different personalities that made up the regiment. Some were easy-going, some were crochety, some were argumentative, some were pious, some were accepting, some were judgmental. They were of all types of men who had to find a way to work together in order to have the best chance to make it out of a battle alive.

They were like brothers and could disagree and still march together and they might offend each other, yet still fight a battle beside their fellow Minnesotans. These soldiers ate together, drank coffee together, and groused about the way the war was going, together.

In the first year of the war, Martin Maginnis and William Colvill of Company F, who had gone hunting and fishing and camping-out in the woods surrounding Red Wing before the war, continued this comradeship. Each knew the ways of the other really well.

Like a younger brother to an older brother, Martin Maginnis modelled himself after Colvill. Colvill had an imperturbable manner when faced with danger, and a stoic way of dealing with physical pain and discomfort.

As Sergeant James A. Wright, who also was in Company F from Red Wing, observed after seeing Colvill in battle at Bull Run in 1861 and in the Seven Days of 1862, he wrote that Colvill was "a man of iron nerve and will," who "certainly could face danger with the *greatest show of indifference* of any man I ever knew."[7]

Colvill, concluded Wright, was always "there in an emergency and ready to meet it without fuss or flourish."

Still, Colvill was admired by the men of his regiment because "he was not a man without feelings and sensibility." Wright "thought sometimes that the thermometer or his real feelings might not have registered greatly different from the rest of us if the record had been made public."

The bravery shown by Colvill was something that Maginnis aspired to match, even if done incompletely

Maybe Maginnis tried too hard to emulate his mentor.

As observed by 2nd Lieutenant Mark Hoyt, who also was in Company F and was from Red Wing, in the first year of the war, these two, Colvill and Maginnis were quite a pair, the captain and the sergeant.

Hoyt (1838-1864) wrote in his diary on April 29, 1862, that "Colvill is as incomprehensible a mixture of sense and nonsense---
goodness and evil----
precaution and carelessness---
dirt and cleanliness---
life and laziness---
as human eyes ever contemplated."[8]

Hoyt commented that "Maginnis is a kind of pocket edition," in other words, a smaller version, "of the [same] inexplicable character."

"The one is the infallible oracle of the other." So that "what Colvill don't know Maginnis will tell you has yet to be revealed to man."

Colvill, in the view of Maginnis, "holds the keys to the temple of universal wisdom," and Maginnis "borrows them now and then, makes an entry and an investigation and returns glorifying the inevitable Colvill."

The two men were "not divided" in their worldviews and in their agreed-upon ways of soldiering and surviving the hardships of marching and fighting in battles.

By 1863, Colvill and Maginnis and their Minnesota Volunteer Regiment had persevered. Colvill was promoted to colonel, and Maginnis had become a lieutenant, both rising through the ranks. They were in Virginia, a long way from home. As an observer wrote, these Minnesotans had a "gunpowdery grimness" about them, "not seen in unfought men." Maginnis wrote later that the story of his service in the Army of the Potomac was too often a "sad but glorious story of bootless efforts, useless sacrifices." He and his fellow soldiers were oftentimes "worn out in marches without objects; wasted in battle that had no results; tainted with inactivity; baffled by interference and delay;" as they "struggled, fought and bled" in hope of a decisive defeat of the rebel Confederacy. To him, "there never had been an army that owed less to brilliancy of leadership, or the inspiration of genius; what it *lost* was often from the lack of its direction; what it *won* was dearly paid for in its own patriotic blood."[9]

Confederate cannons at Seminary Ridge.
Author's photo, 2017, at Gettysburg.

CHAPTER SEVEN
The Legend of Colvill and the 1ˢᵗ Minnesota at Gettysburg

The second invasion of the North by the Confederates under the command of Robert E. Lee took place in June of 1863. This time the Rebel cavalry and army entered Maryland and then marched right into the southern part of Pennsylvania.

General Lee decided to carry the fight into the North rather than fight another major battle in Virginia. His plan was to draw the Union army away from Richmond. If his Confederate army could gain a victory, it would bring "intense excitement at home" to inspire more new recruits for its depleted ranks, and it might help "give the Southern government the European recognition it was longing for."[1]

Robert E. Lee knew his army "would be attacked in force sooner or later," and because Lee thought his army was invincible, his Southerners would win if "he could choose his own battle ground."

If Lee's army would lose a major battle during this invasion, "he could fall back, and be no worse off than losing a battle in Virginia."

This penetration into Maryland and thence into Pennsylvania was risky, but it was a calculated risk for the Confederate forces.[2]

The Union Army of the Potomac, now commanded by General George G. Meade, followed the Confederate army northward to intercept it because of the danger the invasion posed to Baltimore and Washington, D.C., and to Pennsylvania. Meade's goal was to cut lines of communication between Lee's army and the C.S.A. capital at Richmond and then to fall upon Lee "with all force."[3]

The two armies approached each other near Gettysburg, a crossroads town, located alongside "one of Pennsylvania's loveliest valleys" with wooded ridges on both sides and a "stretch of fields and meadows," alive and green, between. The clash began when advance-C.S.A. forces ran into Union cavalrymen on July 1. For the next three days, the Northern army numbering 90,000 fought the Southern army of 75,000 men in the most legendary battle of the Civil War.[4]

The 1st Minnesota Regiment was among the Union armies marching to Gettysburg. These Minnesotans made up only a small portion of the massive Federal army. Although the Minnesota regiment had started out in 1861 with over 1,000 soldiers, they had endured two years of battles, hardships, and illnesses, so there were only 300 men remaining. Yet, these few, the 300, ended up playing a major role on the second day of Gettysburg, on July 2nd. Leadership by this time this time had been passed to William Colvill, who had been promoted to the rank of colonel in May of 1863, and he was fully in command of the regiment.[5]

On the first day, July 1, Union cavalry and troops fought the Confederates and got pushed back from the west side of the town of Gettysburg, moved back through the town and established a position on Cemetery Ridge on the high ground there. The Union position was selected, "almost by accident," due to the timing of the end of the first day of battle.[6]

Union General Meade sent General Winfield S. Hancock forward to inspect the U.S. position and Hancock pronounced it to be strong. Meade gave orders to "mass the army there" upon Cemetery Ridge; and Union regiments, including the First Minnesota, marched miles and miles with little rest to get there in time for the clash of armies.

The key point for General Meade at Gettysburg was simple: the Union had the advantage of holding the ***higher ground*** at Cemetery Ridge.

Union troops and artillery therefore had the **stronger** position.

General Lee and his Confederate Army took its positions in the town itself and on the north side of Gettysburg, and also occupied Seminary Ridge, which ran south of the Gettysburg Lutheran

Seminary. Seminary Ridge was west of Cemetery Ridge. The C.S.A. had lost the choice of positions and Lee had to take the "poorer one and make the best of it." The Rebel commanders "could not know that Meade would be able to bring [basically] his whole army up before the Confederate attack."[7]

The First Minnesota regiment marched to Gettysburg, arriving at Cemetery Ridge at about 5:40 a.m., about an hour after sunrise, on July 2.[8]

"The morning was foggy, sultry and murky," wrote Martin Maginnis of that somber day upon which the legend of the First Minnesota came to be.[9]

The first assignment for eight companies of the Minnesota regiment was near the center of Cemetery Ridge, in a reserve role, to be ready to move to reinforce the regiments on the front-lines, as needed. The other three companies got assigned elsewhere that day: Company F to the skirmish line, Company C to provost guard at division headquarters, and Company L (Sharpshooters) to guard an artillery battery.[10]

It is important to note that the 1st Minnesota regiment actually numbered 489 men at Gettysburg, however, there were ***101 soldiers who were "reported as 'absent sick,"*** and who were unable to fight in the battle, thereby reducing the total number from 489 to 388 men. In order to get to Gettysburg, the regiment had marched punishing distances for days and days, winnowing out the weakest and leaving only the strongest soldiers for this ultimate battle-test. These were the fittest of the fit, even if near exhaustion.[11]

Throughout the morning, the *262* Minnesotans in those *eight* companies heard cannons firing and some rifle-fire from skirmishers from both armies.

In the afternoon, heavy fighting took place to the left of the position of the 1st Minnesota.

Union troops had been in a solid line, connected from regiment to regiment, until General Daniel Sickles took his regiments a half-mile forward to an "intermediate ridge . . . forming along the Emmetsburg road to the orchard . . . to the foot of Round Top," seeing that this ground was a bit higher than where his men had been. Sickles' goal was to block the Confederate path to Round Top; the goal of C.S.A. General Longstreet was to fight his way through Sickles' troops in order to gain the heights of Round Top. "Every man in Longstreet's corps knew that to gain that hill was to gain a victory over Meade's whole army," and, likewise, every man in Sickles' lines "realized the importance of the position," and fought resolutely to hold on, rather than "yield the ground." Below Round Top was the place to "gain all or lose all." The problem for Sickles was that his troops had lost connection with the other Union regiments on both sides of his soldiers. The Confederate forces, seeing the gap opening, attacked heavily with infantry and artillery fire, placing their "heaviest blow" there. The Union commander in the nearby zone, General Winfield S. Hancock, observing the assault upon Sickles and the vulnerable area, immediately sent Union reinforcements to fill the gap and to send other Union troops to help General Sickles so that Sickles would not be overwhelmed.[12]

The 1st Minnesota Regiment at Gettysburg was a unit of the Second Corps at Gettysburg, under the command of General Winfield S. Hancock, known as "Hancock the Superb." Artist: Alfred Waud. "Hancock at Gettysburg." Credit: Library of Congress. Public Domain.

The First Minnesota regiment had been in a fairly-safe reserve position, but General Hancock ordered it to move. The First Regiment "hurried with a battery along the ridge," as Colvill later wrote, to provide protection for the cannons of Battery C, 4th U.S. Artillery.[13]

Colvill noted that his men were placed on the side of a "shallow, gently sloping ravine," about "30 rods" downhill from the cannons. 30 rods was a distance of 165 yards, a distance which may be better understood in modern-times as just over one-and-one-half football fields. From this position, the Minnesotans could protect the Union cannons.[14]

Having plenty of experience of exposure to enemy cannons, the men of the First regiment were lying down, prone upon the ground, to reduce the chance of being hit by Confederate cannon-fire. Even though they were lying down, they were on high ground, providing each soldier with a "full view" of the battle unfolding below them.[15]

As recalled by Martin Maginnis, the clash between the Union soldiers of Gen. Sickles and the other regiments sent into the fray against the Confederate forces of General James Longstreet was a vortex of battle: "Although obliged to keep low and not expose ourselves to the cannon balls, shells, and bullets, which . . . went whistling and bursting above and around us, we beheld a grand sight."[16]

"Below and before us on the plain," wrote Maginnis, "The battle was fiercely raging. Every movement of the opposing troops was discernible, and we watched them with the anxiety of spectators so deeply were we interested in the result; though but little of this could be seen in the faces of the men, who, long accustomed to conceal their emotions beneath the mask of reckless indifference, were with apparent unconcern, criticizing impartially the fighting of friend and foe."[17]

The battle below them intensified as the Southerners attacked the Union regiments of Sickles "from both sides with extreme fury." Union General Sickles had made a mistake by disconnecting his troops from the other Union divisions, but he had an even bigger problem because his division was also outnumbered by Rebel divisions. It was clear to Martin Maginnis that General Robert E. Lee had sent his "heaviest forces to break through" the Union lines on this part of Cemetery Ridge in order to cut off Little Round Top, and from the heights of Little Round Top, Confederate artillery would make Cemetery Ridge useless as a defensive position and Lee's C.S.A. army would win the battle of Gettysburg. The whole battlefield was at stake on this afternoon on July 2nd.[18]

At first, Maginnis saw clearly the Blue and Gray soldiers in a green landscape of fields and woods, but that changed after a short time. Because the black-gunpowder used in cannons and rifles was not modern *smokeless* gunpowder, every time soldiers fired their weapons, every gun spewed forth accumulating vapors of thick white smoke. "Soon the view became more obscured," explained Maginnis, "for though the sun shone brightly, the air was damp and the smoke hung heavily over the fight, sometimes in rolling, cloudy masses, and again, like a well-defined wall, conforming to the lines of battle, rising high in the air."[19]

Through this heavy smoke, Maginnis and the men of Minnesota could see the "charging battalions, the darkened forms of the combatants, and the banners wildly tossing to and fro above the surging masses, looming gigantically in the maze between us and the declining sun." At times, "the sulfurous pall would hide everything from view, save when the flashes gleaming redly through the darkness revealed the position of the batteries, and we would intently listen, endeavoring to tell from the yelling and cheering which came up from the chaotic turmoil to which side the advantage leaned, while the rattle of small arms and deep bass of artillery made the music of the battle . . . . Then the breeze would roll up the smoky curtain and none could repress a shout of joy to see that our men were still crowding the fight, and every heart felt the meaning of those expressive words of our national anthem, 'our flag is still there.'"[20]

Colonel Colvill also commented on the black-powder smoke that spread over the field of battle. "The effect of the low-lying smoke," wrote Colvill later, "was to magnify objects; men looked very tall."[21]

On that afternoon, General Lee's "entire line advanced to engage" the Union troops "everywhere" in an all-out effort to prevent Union troops from sending sufficient reinforcements to save Sickles' position.[22]

At a key point, Union General Sickles was wounded, and his lines gave way "under a severe cross fire," and began to retreat. As Maginnis remembered it, he wrote that "the contest was sharp and heavy," and "success trembled in the balance" until "fresh battalions of the foe came down and our gallant boys gave way;" retreating while carrying back their fellow Union soldiers who had been "slightly wounded." Squads of men would rally as they went backwards, "now and then to empty their guns once more at their pursuers; but all organized, concerted and effective action" by Sickles' "broken ranks" was "at an end," as Confederate cannons poured canister shot into the retreating groups. The Union men were "reeling and staggering back," as the Rebels "showered rapid volleys" of lead bullets into their backs.[23]

Sickles' retreating soldiers had been overwhelmed and were running through and past the position of the 1st Minnesota regiment. "We met Sickles's men coming up and across the ravine," William Colvill recalled later, "Gen. Hancock was with us" at that moment. Hancock was riding his horse in order to survey the battlefield and the general "immediately dismounted and with all his energy sought to rally them," and Colvill and Maginnis and the other Minnesota officers tried to help Hancock in stopping Sickles' troops. "It was useless," wrote Colvill, "they were perfectly demoralized." Those soldiers did not stop until they got nearly to Rock Creek, about a mile away.[24]

"Then the Rebel skirmish line," wrote Colvill, "came in sight . . . looming through the smoke, and pushed down the slope into the bottom . . . . and this skirmish line opened a scattering fire upon us."[25]

The Confederate soldiers were following on the heels of the retreating Union men, and the forward momentum of the Southern army put them near the dry creek bed named Plum Run, located at the bottom of the slope down from Cemetery Ridge, where there were plenty of rocks, thickets of small trees, and bushes for cover. Colvill judged the distance from his position to the bottom of the slope at Plum Run to be "about fifteen rods," in other words, about 82 yards (for modern people to understand it, you would think of being on the 18-yard-line of a football field and you are going to the goal line that is 82 yards away).[26]

The critical time of decision had arrived. "The Rebels' first line" of massed troops, according to Colvill, began advancing and "moved rapidly down into the hollow" just below the position of the First Minnesota.[27]

The cannons that the Minnesotans were guarding opened fire with canister shot, "at short range" on the Confederate infantry and the enemy began "advancing through the smoke" towards the Union artillery position.[28]

"Just then," Maginnis recalled, General Winfield S. Hancock rode up again, and the general saw the Southerners approaching. Hancock looked to his right, where he had ordered reinforcements from General Alpheus Williams' division, but those troops were not yet there, they were "still five minutes distant." Before the reinforcements could get there, the Confederates would have captured the artillery battery and would have gained the "very heart of the position" on Cemetery Ridge. Hancock, "with the eye of a true commander," saw that the only Union soldiers between the Rebels and the cannon emplacement were "252 officers and men" of the First Minnesota---- *he had expected to see the troops of Alpheus Williams who were supposed to have followed the Minnesota regiment.* "If Hancock could only stop that charging mass for five minutes," he could block the Rebels from taking the cannons and from destroying the Union supply wagons, located just one hundred yards from that spot. According to Maginnis, Hancock was "unable to conceal his agitation," and the general "asked in almost anguished tones: 'Great God! Is this all the men we have here?'"[29]

At that time, General Hancock, riding his favorite bay horse, approached Colvill, not knowing his name, but Hancock clearly perceived that Colvill was the leader of the regiment. Hancock pointed to the Confederate regiment advancing from the west, waving their Rebel flags, and Hancock said to Colvill: "Do you see those colors?"[30]

"Yes sir," replied Colvill.

"Well," commanded Hancock, "capture them."

Colvill smiled. And then Colvill said, "*I will, General.*"[31]

General Hancock "rushed to the right near the battery . . . and gave the order: "Minnesota Forward!"" Commanding the men "with all his force and action."[32]

"The Critical Moment at The Battle of Gettysburg, Seven O'clock P.M., July 2nd, 1863."
Col. William Colvill, receiving the order from General [Winfield S.] Hancock to
"Charge Those Lines." Drawing by Josias King. Gen. Hancock is shown, on his horse,
giving the order to "Charge those lines," to Col. William Colvill. The aide to Gen.
Hancock is on the other horse. Colvill and the other officers of the 1st Minnesota Regiment were all on foot. Colvill was behind the men as they charged so that he
could adjust their position with his orders, as necessary. Drawing by Josias King.
Credit: Minnesota Historical Society.

"The men of the regiment," wrote Colvill later, all heard Hancock's order and "saw him as he delivered it, and turned their heads to me . . . ready for my order, which was immediately given."

"Forward!" shouted Colonel Colvill, and the regiment arose, at once, as if they were one man "and, as if on review, stepped down the slope towards the enemy," now only about 100 yards away.[33]

The order was repeated: "FORWARD DOUBLE QUICK," and immediately the First Minnesota obeyed. As Martin Maginnis looked back at that day, he wrote: "It is an easy thing to charge when the enemy is retreating and the battle is going well, but it requires steady troops to even hold a position when the line is breaking away on every side." He believed that "it was a strange order to give a handful to charge that advancing mass that had just carried two of our best divisions off their feet." Yet, it was an order the Minnesotans would "unquestionably obey."[34]

"The regiment charged," wrote Gen. Hancock, "in column of fours" that formed into a line, "shoulder to shoulder," with every gap "closed up," as they had been so well-trained to do.[35]

71

All of the officers of the First Minnesota were dismounted, with the horses being "grouped at a little distance" to the rear, "just up the Ridge." A couple of men were most likely assigned to hold those horses, reducing the number of soldiers available to charge at the enemy troops.[36]

The 1st Minnesota started "double quick" down the slope "*in a beautiful line*," almost 100 yards from end to end, side by side. Colvill wrote that "as the regiment started," he believed that "the swinging of the *gleaming muskets* as the right shoulder shift was made in one time and two motions corresponding to the steps of the advance . . . seemed to emphasize the unity" of the men. "The *gleam of the muskets* . . . . It was grand. The regiment moved as one man, taking up its swinging gait down the slope."[37]

The Minnesotans were charging forward, with fixed bayonets, towards Confederate troops that outnumbered them by a 20-to-1 ratio, and was made up of several "regiments of the Alabama brigade," and portions of a Mississippi brigade, "all of whom had lost their order and alignment," and who became "mingled in one advancing mass" of troops. "Behind them in alignment came . . . a Florida brigade" that was supporting the Rebel advance.

Maginnis later wrote: "As soon as our movement was noticed, the advancing mass" of Alabama and Mississippi troops "stopped and opened a murderous fire upon us."

The First Minnesota's soldiers had covered about 30 yards before the enemy's "cannon opened on us, and shell and solid shot tore through the ranks, and the more deadly Enfield rifles of their infantry were centered on us alone. At every step fell our men, yet no one wavers . . . without word or cheer, but with silent, desperate determination." In that first round of deadly enemy fire, wrote Maginnis, "one-quarter of our men had already fallen." The Minnesotans had held their fire-----waiting, waiting to fire their rifles at the opportune time.[38]

Just after the Confederates fired that deathly first volley into the "beautiful line" of the 1st Minnesota, the Minnesota's officers gave the order: "CHARGE, men!"[39]

No more silence. "With a *wild cheer*," recalled Maginnis, "we *ran* at them." The final fifty yards of ground was at a dead run.

There was no turning back.

They set their teeth on edge as they ran the 50-yard-dash of their lives. They all ran as fast as they could go, realizing they would all get shot to pieces if they did not move fast. "In an instant," wrote Colvill, "we were upon their line, which was standing among the rocks and gullies" in the creek bottom.[40]

The idea was to run to Plum Run creek to "fire a low-aimed volley," and "then rush in with the bayonet."[41]

And so the Minnesota men gave the Rebels what Colvill called "the First Minnesota volley," namely, at close range, "every gun discharged *full in their faces*" at the close range of only 16-and-a-half feet away.[42]

Maginnis wrote that they ran right up close to the enemy soldiers in order to "empty our guns with the muzzles at their very hearts." And that fearsome volley cut through a "perfect swath" of "Southerners," who sank "upon the ground." Those other Confederates "gave way," springing out of the gully to avoid Minnesota's piercing bayonets---running "back upon their second and third lines."[43]

The men of Minnesota put into deadly practice what they had previously learned, to "aim low."

As one veteran of the First Minnesota later narrated the events: "As we crossed the little stream the order came: "Halt. Ready! At their legs aim! Fire!" And "as the volley sounded, came the order, "With bayonet! Charge!, and at them we went."[44]

"Our volley," he said, "had done fearful execution in wounds, though but few were killed. We had damaged more legs than I like to think of now, and before the enemy had recovered from the surprise of our unexpected attack, we were among them, striking and stabbing right and left."[45]

The rocks and brush and thickets along Plum Run creek gave some protective cover for the Minnesota soldiers who marched and ran the 82 yards to get there. Plum Run creek was a "dry gully some 4 to 5 feet wide and 2 feet deep," and was of benefit to the First Minnesota. "Every man straining every nerve," was "loading and firing from amidst the rocks," shooting into the second Confederate line that was coming down towards the creek bed.[46]

The "supporting lines" of Florida soldiers were so "confused" by the Charge of the First Minnesota, that they began to "wildly commence firing through the mass in front, slaughtering their own men by hundreds," thereby "throwing the whole column into confusion, while the Rebel artillery from the rear fired on friend and foe alike." The Confederate officers tried to "stop the firing and restore order" to enable their soldiers to try to overwhelm the Minnesotans.[47]

Lieutenant Martin Maginnis, who was in charge of Company H (not his original Company F), made it all the way down to "brush and trees" along the banks of Plum Rum creek, but Colonel William Colvill was severely wounded just upon reaching the dry creek bed. As Colvill told his story of that day, he wrote that he had been running down the slope, through "blinding smoke," situated "immediately behind the colors," and when he reached the bushes along Plum Run creek, there "came a shock like a sledge hammer on my backbone between the shoulders."[48]

Colvill had been hit by a "Minie ball which penetrated at the top of the right arm, passed under the shoulder blade, struck the

First Minnesota Regiment charging at the Confederates, pushing them back, July 2, 1863. Colonel Charles P. Adams; Major Mark Downie; and Colonel William Colvill with upraised swords (Colvill at far right); with 3 captains who died in the battle, Louis Muller; Wilson B. Farrell; and Nathan Messick, all fallen. Bronze sculpture (shallow-relief) by Jacob Fjelde, on the Minnesota monument at Gettysburg (dedicated 1897). Credit: "Veggies," Wikimedia Commons. [Free to use].

backbone and lodged in the flesh about the middle of the shoulder blade." That bullet, Colvill wrote, "turned me partly round, and made me 'see stars.'"[49]

Situated right next to Colonel Colvill was Captain Henry C. Coates, of Company A, and Coates said to Colvill: "Colonel, you are badly hurt."[50]

Colvill replied: "I don't know; take care of the men."[51]

As Colvill later wrote about his perilous position by the creek, "just then I was putting my foot on the ground; there was a sharp pang through it." He had been shot in his foot by a bullet that came from the right side, "striking the right foot at the ankle joint, crushing that and smashing up the joint," so that his leg "gave way." He fell heavily forward onto the ground. "I saw just beside me a gully," he recalled, "not more than two feet wide and less in depth. As I struck the ground," he wrote, "I rolled over into it." I "listened . . . to the bullets zipping along the ground and thought how fortunate for me was the fact of the gully."[52]

Unfortunately for the First Minnesota regiment, the Confederates recovered enough from their setback to advance and began to overlap the ends of the Minnesota lines in the rocks, because the Confederates had a much longer line of troops. If help did not arrive, all of the Minnesotans would be hit by Rebel gunfire. As Colvill put it: "The uppermost thought of all was: *can we hold the enemy till relief comes*?"[53]

Fortuitously, the first five minutes of the heroic charge of the 1st Minnesota had accomplished their objective, namely, to slow down the Confederate advance before the Rebels could sweep up Cemetery Ridge. The expected Union reinforcements came in the nick of time, within five minutes.

As Maginnis wrote, the five minutes "time had been gained, and at that instant," a battery of Union cannons "on our left opened" and poured a "few rapid volleys into the confused mass" of the Confederate forces and "swept it from the field."[54]

On the right side of the First Minnesota's perilous position, according to Colvill, came the "crack, crack" of a thunderous volley from the cannons of the "eighty-second New York" regiment, pouring fire into the Rebel troops. Union soldiers, a "whole brigade," the expected reinforcements, came directly into the rocky creek bed to help in the hand-to-hand combat against the Rebels.[55]

The thin ranks of the Minnesota First "were filled from the rear" by a whole legion of "stabbing, striking and swearing" blue-coated Union soldiers. "The reinforcements had come," and they helped push the Rebels back from Plum Run creek.[56]

"The enemy in front had disappeared," wrote Colvill, "and we turned to those on our right . . . who were cut off from escape. They ceased firing and shouted to us not to fire; they surrendered," and, amazingly, the 1st Minnesota took 400 Confederates as prisoners.[57]

The First Minnesota was supposed to hold the line for five minutes, and they extended that time and held the line for fifteen minutes, but in that short time, they had *saved the day*.

Still, they paid a big price. This July 2 battle at Gettysburg was the worst day of the war for the Minnesota First, not because of totals killed in action, but because of the large number of men who were seriously wounded in action.

They started out on the charge with 262 men in a line moving ahead. By the end of the day, at nightfall, there were 47 who were able to stand and walk, according to most tabulations. Those who have written about the famous "Charge of the First Minnesota" regiment, calculate that 215 of the men were casualties--- either killed or wounded. The official report, however, listed 157 men who had been either killed or wounded on July 2, allowing that 104 were able to stand and walk.[58]

In the official report written by Captain Henry C. Coates, the list of those killed in action on July 2 numbered 35, and he numbered the wounded on that battlefield slope, on that day, as 123 or 124 men. Of those 123 (or 124) wounded men, some were mortally wounded and died from their wounds in the days and weeks after the battle.[59]

If an observer focuses on the number of Minnesota men who died on the Gettysburg battlefield on that day, according to the earliest count by Captain Coates, a total of 35, and compares that number (from July 2) to the regiment's very first battle, at Bull Run, it must be noted that more died at Bull Run, a total of 42. The situation was much different, however, because the regiment sent about 900 soldiers and officers into the Bull Run battleground (5% died), whereas there were only 262 who were still available for duty on the second day of the Gettysburg battle (13%). To provide perspective, at the Battle of Antietam, in September of 1862, 15 of the men of the First Minnesota died.[60]

It must also be noted that the First Minnesota was shot to pieces at Gettysburg in such a short time, in a mere hundred yards of forward motion, in *fifteen minutes* of fury, so that 35 lay dead and so many were incapacitated by wounds. At Bull Run, the time in actual combat, shooting and being shot at, was three hours, not in fifteen minutes, and those 42 Minnesotans who died at Bull Run that day were not in one small area of the battlefield.[61]

The number of wounded men was extremely high, much higher than the other major battles in which the regiment had served, due to the nature of the "Charge of the First Minnesota," which was a frontal assault moving directly into a vastly greater number of Confederates. The worst time came when the enemy troops partially-surrounded the Minnesota men, resulting in bullets hitting the soldiers from several different directions. Quite a few of the Minnesotans were hit by more than one bullet, disabling them from walking and forcing them to wait for someone to carry them back to a field hospital. So many of the officers and men would never be able-bodied enough to return to the regiment after Gettysburg.[62]

As the sun set in the west on the battlefield, Colonel Colvill needed help, being severely wounded in his shoulder and ankle. He was fully conscious, as he wrote later, "I saw it grow dark; then it became quiet. I saw the stars shining out overhead."[63]

"Presently I hear the voices of our men," continued Colvill. "The boys were then looking up the dead and wounded, in one case where their search had found a comrade and they were taking his last words for his home and family."[64]

The Minnesota soldiers, who were able, helped the wounded. They found Colonel Colvill and carried him to a field hospital; as they did for all their wounded comrades. They gathered their dead and moved them back up the ridge, as best they could, yet unburied.

That night was not much for sleeping, for all knew the battle would continue the next day, July 3. Martin Maginnis was in the Union line, awaiting whatever would happen between the Blue and the Gray. His old friend and fishing companion, William Colvill, not with the regiment, being wounded, was in pain, awaiting surgery.

"Red and fiery through the morning mists," wrote Maginnis, "arose the sun on the third of July." He was among the 47 able-bodied soldiers of the First Minnesota, who were ordered to take a place in the front line, right in the middle of the Union front-lines on Cemetery Ridge, looking across the "red field of Gettysburg" at the Confederate positions on Seminary Ridge, just a mile away, knowing full well that the armies would resume the "bloody work which darkness had suspended." In the ensuing day, the regiment's numbers grew to be about 100 men total as the soldiers and officers from Company F and Company C came back from their other duties.[65]

The strong 100 of the Minnesota First "were lying close upon the ridge," and they were very wise. "The men with their bayonets scratch up the hard earth and gravel, fill their knapsacks with it, and pile them in line with such stones and rocks as they can gather" for protection from bullets and cannon shot, and they lay down behind the improvised wall.[66]

On July 3, the Minnesotans were near the center of the Union lines at Cemetery Ridge. U.S. commanders made sure that "every exposed situation had been fortified, hundreds of rifle-pits excavated, and every ravine would be packed with Federal infantry." There were some natural protections for these Union defenders, consisting of "stone walls, hills and ridges," and the U.S. artillery "could pour its fire over the heads" of the Union soldiers, and could also hit the charging Confederates with a crossfire of canister shot when the Rebels came into close range.[67]

Morning passed without combat, indeed, a "silence fell upon the battlefield" as the Rebels aligned their artillery in preparation for their infantry attack upon the Union army.[68]

"Suddenly the stillness was broken," recalled Maginnis, "by two signal guns from the Confederate lines," at 1:00 o'clock in the afternoon, and then "all their batteries opened, and a hundred-and-fifteen cannon poured a cataract of iron" into the Union lines.[69]

It was the "great cannonade," and each side bombarded the other side. As Maginnis later wrote, he experienced a "deafening roar that shook the solid hills." Over his head, as he lay safely on the ground behind his sandbag-like knapsack-backpack, there flew "solid shot, shell, short bars of railway iron, spikes from improvised canister----all things that could be rammed into and shot out of a cannon were tearing and plowing up the ground." The shelling smashed Union cannons and artillery-crews, leaving "heaps of mangled horses and men."[70]

The artillery-crews on both sides were firing a total of "230 pieces of artillery... all firing as fast as men could serve them." The rumble was "consolidated into one terrible roar, which alarmed cattle in the fields fifteen miles away, and was plainly heard by human ears forty miles away." Every soldier "sought cover" to avoid being hit. "Showers of dirt, flung high in air by the shells, descended upon men lying in the ravines." The men of the First Minnesota hugged the ground beneath them. The shells flew overhead, "seemingly in and from all directions," wrote Sergeant James A. Wright, "howling, shrieking, striking, exploding, tearing, smashing, and destroying," but the Confederate fire was aimed at the U.S. cannons, so the enemy shells "struck in front of us and bounded over us." Wright wrote that he "commended my soul to God, shut my teeth *hard*, and lay flat on the ground----expecting every minute to be blown to atoms." But Maginnis and Wright and the others were not hurt by this awful cannonade.[71]

After an hour-and-a-half of artillery fire, at 2:30 p.m., 13,000 Confederate soldiers emerged from the woods of Seminary Ridge, led by three brigades from General George Pickett's division, and began a three-fourths-mile-long advance across the open fields towards Cemetery Ridge.[72]

Martin Maginnis and the men of the First Minnesota regiment watched "Pickett's Charge" as it unfolded. All the Union soldiers reportedly kept a "deep silence as a hundred thousand pairs of eyes" stared at the advance of "Pickett's division of Virginians in double-line of battle, flags rippling and bayonets gleaming."[73]

"Line after line" of Confederates, recalled Maginnis, came forth and closed up into a heavy order of battle, massed and directed upon our center," heading right into the "heart of the Union" front-lines.[74]

The Rebels marched forth, "elbow to elbow in unbroken line," a line that was about one-and-one-half miles from end-to-end, until Yankee cannons ripped into the gray-clad troops, with a crossfire. The ground became a "field of blood."[75]

General Winfield Hancock riding along Union lines during C.S.A. bombardment prior to Pickett's Charge, Gettysburg, July 3, 1863. Credit: Library of Congress. "Battle of Gettysburg," ca. 1887. https://www.loc.gov/item/2003663828/.

When the time was right, "suddenly from the ground" rose the Union line, and as the command: "Fire!" rang out, a "crashing volley" was "poured into the advancing columns." Maginnis and his fellow Minnesotans were told to hold their fire until the Confederates were within optimal firing range, and were, once again, ordered to "fire at their feet," which counteracted, somewhat, the "tendency to overshoot" through aiming too high. So they aimed low, partly because that was all that they could see of the Rebels---their enemies were covered with smoke from the knees up, due to their own rifle-fire. In this "withering fire," Confederate soldiers fell in "swaths as if death had swept them with his scythe."[76]

Still the Confederate infantry moved forward, with a "wild yell," the Rebel yell, and their "charging lines" ran forward towards the "angle," which would be the "high-water mark" of the Confederacy. Only 5,000 Southerners got to that spot, and then small groups of Rebel soldiers penetrated the Union frontlines in a final assault.[77]

The Confederates captured a battery of U.S. cannons, planting Virginia's Rebel flag on the battery. Seizing the moment, the men of the First Minnesota and other regiments counter-charged, rushing pell-mell to the "angle." The fearsome struggle assumed the "shape of a melee," recalled Maginnis, as the Confederates tried to hold what they had won. In this "vortex" of combat, through the gun smoke, the First Minnesota helped reclaim that ground at the top of Cemetery Ridge. After a "deadly exchange of fire," the "flag of Virginia" was ripped down, replaced with the U.S. "stars and stripes."[78]

Pickett's Charge was a disastrous defeat for the Confederates, leaving 5,000 of their original 13,000 soldiers dead in one hour of battle. The battlefield was heaped with dead and wounded. As one Virginia soldier wrote about the third day of the Battle of Gettysburg: "Hell could never be so bad."[79] The Rebels who had not been killed or captured retreated toward Seminary Ridge. General Robert E. Lee "had played his last card, and lost."[80]

In the fighting on July 3rd, the losses of the 1st Minnesota totaled 12 dead and 32 men wounded, far less than on the previous day, yet serious numbers due to the fact that there were only about 100 of them on the battleground that day.

Nonetheless, the Minnesotans, almost decimated, had helped repel 'Pickett's Charge,' on the third day of battle at Gettysburg; and Union soldiers captured "nearly the entire rebel force who remained alive." Maginnis and his First Minnesota regiment, themselves, "took about 500 prisoners" and captured the flag of the 28th Virginia regiment. The Union's "cheers of victory" echoed from the Gettysburg battlefield.[81]

When General George Meade was told that "the enemy's attack is repulsed," Meade said: '**Thank God.**"[82]

The Blue and the Grey. Author's collection.

CHAPTER EIGHT
The Aftermath

On July 4th, General Robert E. Lee withdrew his Confederate army, going back towards Virginia. His 'invincible' army was crippled by its heavy losses. All those who were able to move left Pennsylvania.

The men of the First Minnesota spent the night of July 3 on the crest of Cemetery Ridge, resting as best they could, not knowing if there would be another day of fighting on July 4.

When the Union commanders realized that Lee's army had gone away, the Minnesota men were still positioned on Cemetery Ridge, overlooking the "valley of death beneath." They were exhausted and it was difficult to focus on anything other than the present moment, because everything was "sprinkled with blood," on bodies, cannons, uniforms, horses, rocks, the soil, anything they touched. They spent some time then to "hastily bury our dead."[1]

On the morning of July 5th, the Minnesotans, numbering only about one-hundred able-bodied soldiers, moved southward, and "marched in pursuit of the enemy," through Maryland and back into Virginia.[2]

About a month after the Gettysburg battle, Captain Henry C. Coates sent an official report numbering the dead and wounded of the First Minnesota regiment.[3]

Day by day, the list showed the severity of the losses.

On the day of the Charge of the First Minnesota, July 2, there were 2 officers who died on that day, along with 33 enlisted men who had been killed in action, for a total of 35 in that single day.

On July 3, in action in helping defeat "Pickett's Charge," 2 officers were killed in action that day, with 10 enlisted men dying, for a single-day total of 12.

These totals from each day in the first reports did **not** include those who died from their wounds in the days following the battle. The list gave the names of 3 officers who died from their injuries later, and the list provided the names of 14 enlisted men who died after the battle was over, for a total of 17 who died later.

And so, the total number of deaths for the regiment (for the two days at Gettysburg) had been published as being 64 in an early report. [4]

Similarly, a newspaper report from 1864 listed the total deaths for the 1st Minnesota for the two days at Gettysburg as 69 "men killed or who have died." That newspaper story placed the two-day total of wounded soldiers at 149. Different sources of information provide different totals of those 'killed in action' and 'wounded in action,' however, it is clear that the two-days of battle of Gettysburg was deadlier than previous battles, with the proportion of dying to being wounded being far worse than on other battlefields. [5]

At the end of the battle, 272 men remained on duty for the 1st Minnesota, including the 101 men who had been listed before the battle as "absent sick." [6]

The Minnesotans had been such a "splendid regiment" in the early years of the Civil War, never wavering. Yet they were so few by the time of the last day at Gettysburg, that they had become "the ***shattered old thunderbolt.***" The First Minnesota had been so vital to the Union, but so weakened by losses at Gettysburg so as to be hardly existing. [7]

Martin Maginnis survived Gettysburg. Due to the loss of so many officers in the regiment, he was promoted from lieutenant to captain. [8]

Colonel William Colvill was in bad shape, with one Minie bullet lodged in his back near his shoulder-blade and another still stuck in his shattered ankle. Those who saw him did not think he could live very long.

Colvill was placed in a tent in the field hospital, with the other wounded men from the First Minnesota located a "short distance away." Quite a number from the Minnesota regiment had been wounded in their legs, as was Colvill, and there were "thirty amputa-

A surgeon and his assistants at work, trying to help wounded Union soldiers.
Winslow Homer drawing, "Surgeon At Work," for Harper's Weekly.
Credit: Metropolitan Museum of Art. Public domain.

tions among them in all." Colvill refused an amputation of his own leg, and he said he was the "only one of them that recovered."[9]

At that point, Colonel Colvill "was given up for dead, but his great vitality pulled him through" a miasma of poor medical treatment, infection, and agonizingly-slow recovery. His condition was dire, his prospects dim.[10]

Even so, the day after the Battle of Gettysburg was July 4th, Independence Day, and Colvill said he had a "very interesting experience in the field hospital" on the Fourth of July. He said that "some Rebel officers passed through my tent" on the way to where the "rebel wounded were lying in great numbers on a hillside some thirty rods (165 yards) away, in the pouring rain." The groaning of the wounded Confederates "had been horrible all night," and the Rebel officers hoped to ease their pain by visiting them. As Colvill observed, one of the officers, "in a clear, sweet voice struck up a camp meeting hymn," and "instantly the groans and cries ceased" as "all joined with him in the hymn . . . a familiar one to them," but "new to me." The chorus of men singing became a "grand refrain from thousands of wounded men."

"The singer then made a prayer," remembered Colvill, and "after that---no groans or complaints."

Colvill never forgot the singing or the prayer and God's answer to the prayer.

Colonel Colvill would also always remember the kindnesses of a family in the town of Gettysburg who opened up their home and gave him a room and a bed to help him in his wounded agony.

It was the family of James Pierce, a prosperous Gettysburg butcher, who provided shelter for him.

As Tillie Pierce, the fifteen-year-old daughter of James Pierce, wrote the story, there were "several soldiers" who came to the Pierce house a "few days after the battle" and asked Mrs. Pierce if "she would allow them to bring their wounded Colonel" to the Pierce home because "they would like to have him kept at a private house." The soldiers said "they would send two nurses along to help wait on him."[11]

Mrs. Pierce gave her consent, according to the written account of Tillie Pierce, "as we had a very suitable room."

"The officer," wrote Tillie, "was carried to the house on a litter, and was suffering greatly." After the soldiers "got him upstairs, and were about placing him on the bed, it was found to be too short, so that foot-board had to be taken off and an extension added," for "the Colonel was a very tall man and of fine proportions."

"He had been severely wounded in the right ankle and shoulder," remembered Tillie, and the shoulder wound extended to his spine.

Mrs. Pierce "waited on him constantly," as did the two nurses from the First Minnesota Regiment-----Milton Bevans of Red Wing's Company F, and private Walter S. Reed, from Company G, who "could not have been more devoted" to his care.

The Pierce family could see that Colonel Colvill was "highly esteemed by all his men," for many of them "visited him at the house, and even wept over him in his suffering and helplessness . . . . they always spoke of him as one of the bravest men in the army."

Medical help for Colvill was delayed, due to the sheer numbers of wounded who required treatment. There were many men shot in the legs and arms and the surgeons in the field hospitals had been continually "probing and picking bullets from the flesh," or "sawing and cutting off" those ruined limbs, so that there were heaps of limbs stacked near the field hospitals. It took 10 days before the Army surgeons were able to help Colvill at the Pierce house, and their first step was to remove the bullet from Colvill's back, *a week-and-a-half* after he had been shot. The ankle wound was more difficult to treat.[12]

"The surgeons," wrote Tillie, "at first wanted to amputate his foot, saying it was necessary in order to save his life." But Colvill objected to this and "said that if his foot must go he would go too."

The surgeons relented, finally extracting the Minie-ball bullet from Colvill's ankle-----*two weeks* after the battle had ended.[13]

The recuperation from the wounds, and from the surgeries, took a long time.

"Before long," wrote Tillie Pierce, "his sister came, who with tender care and cheering words no doubt hastened his recovery." This sister was Mary (Colvill) Sherman, who traveled to Gettysburg from the Colvill's original hometown of Forestville, New York.[14]

"Several months elapsed" before Colvill was able to leave the Pierce home, being able to move around, somewhat, "on a pair of crutches."

"As he was leaving the house," wrote Tillie Pierce, "he could hardly express fully his thanks and appreciation of our kindness; and on parting kissed us all, as though he were bidding farewell to his own kith and kin." The tenderhearted Pennsylvanians had come to love this wounded Minnesota officer, and "felt as though one of our own family were leaving."

The tall Colonel, recalled Tillie, "promised that whenever he was able he would come back to see us."

The two nurse-attendants from the First Minnesota, Bevans and Reed, assisted Colvill out of the house. As they were leaving, Private Reed gave young Tillie Pierce a "gun and bayonet," and said to her: "I bought it with my own money, and I give it to you; and if anyone comes after it, and wants to take it from you, just tell them that the gun was bought and paid for by the soldier who gave it to you."[15]

A few weeks after that, a U.S. Provost Marshal came to Gettysburg in order to collect all weapons and materials belonging to the federal government, and someone informed him that there was a gun at the Pierce house.

Before long, two soldiers came to the door of the Pierce's and asked Tillie if there was a "musket about the house."

Tillie said: "Yes, sir; but it is mine."

They informed her that the "Provost Marshall had sent them after it, and that they would have to take it."

Tillie told the men what Private Reed had said about the gun, that this gift had been "bought and paid for by the soldier who gave it" to her. "Whereupon they expressed their sorrow, but added, they would have to obey."

In her indignation, Tillie said: "If they are mean enough to take the gun they can have it; but it is *my* gun."

"They seemed sorry as they rode away" with Tillie's "highly-prized treasure," but it was gone.

However, about two hours later, Tillie "saw the same two soldiers returning on horseback, one of them having a gun on his shoulder."

The soldiers wanted to see Tillie and the two men looked "quite pleased" as they said to Tillie: "The Provost Marshal heard you were such a good Union girl," that he has "sent back your gun, and we are very happy to return it to you." Tillie was so pleased that she was able to keep this gift from the Minnesotans.

When Colvill left the Pierce's house, he wanted to go back home to Minnesota, however, his physical condition would not allow such a long trip. Instead, in September, 1863, the wounded colonel had "treatment at the Cotton Factory Hospital," in Harrisburg, Pennsylvania, which had been established as a U.S. military hospital. By late October, he traveled the shorter distance to his father's house, in his original hometown in Forestville in New York state, where his father and mother still lived, and the town where his sister Mary Sherman and her family lived. There David G. Colvill, M.D. (his 63-year-old uncle), and Amos R. Avery, M.D., treated Colonel Colvill's lingering wounds---his ankle and foot wound was "inflamed" with infection, and they recommended the "utmost quiet and rest for his recovery."[16]

Colvill also was cared for by a nurse named Jane E. Morgan, who had grown up in Oneida, N.Y. Together, his sister, Mary Colvill Sherman, and nurse Jane Morgan helped care for him until he regained enough strength to travel home to Minnesota in February of 1864. This formerly-powerful giant of a man had been greatly diminished by terrible suffering, being brought low by the wounds of war inflicted upon him.[17]

CHAPTER NINE
The First Minnesota Regiment Goes Home

Because the First Minnesota regiment had experienced such heavy losses at Gettysburg, President Lincoln's administration sent Captain Martin Maginnis and the rest of the men to New York City, along with three other regiments, to put down the violent 'Draft Riots.' It turned out to be "an easy job." Rioting was "mostly over," because the first U.S. troops to arrive fired upon the rioters with their "big Springfield muskets . . . and the mob fled."

"On reaching New York," Maginnis later recalled, "we were hurried to the Treasury building and we found the riot had been largely quelled, except in a few corners, which we soon settled." For a while, the regiment set up camp in Central Park, and cooked some "beans in holes in the ground" as they had done in other camp-grounds. In gratitude for their service, the "good people of New York and Brooklyn" provided dinners and picnics and warm hospitality for the Minnesota regiment.[1]

The First Minnesota had a "joyful time," remembered Maginnis, "until we were ordered back to the front to eat hard-tack and dodge Minie balls." At the small battle of Bristoe Station in October, Maginnis led his company of the 1st Minnesota, and he continued his captaincy through the last field service of the regiment in the Mine Run campaign of November to December, 1863.[2]

After all the marching and all the patrols and skirmish duties and all the many battles, the year of 1864 brought an end to the three-year enlistments for Maginnis and all the men of the regiment.

In early February, friends and politicians in Washington, D.C., honored the men of the regiment before they traveled home to Minnesota. There, they were feted with a banquet at the National Hotel, decorated with evergreens on the walls and flowery bouquets on the tables. Colonel Colvill, still being "unable to move" on his own power, had to be carried into the banquet hall by two of his soldiers from the regiment.[3]

The regiment traveled back home to Minnesota in February, 1864, transported by railway to Wisconsin and then by horse-drawn sleighs. William Colvill, "though yet very weak from his wounds received at Gettysburg and illness following, accompanied the regiment on its return home."[4]

Their fellow Minnesotans gave them a hearty welcome, first at Reed's Landing; then at Wabasha; again at Red Wing, once more at Hastings; and, finally, in St. Paul, where they were greeted with a half-mile-long parade, and treated to a welcome-home reception. Colonel Colvill wanted to take part in the big reception get-together, "but found himself so much exhausted by the journey and the excitement" of all the well-wishes of the townspeople along the way, that "it was deemed best for him" to remain in his hotel room. Colvill still could not walk on his own power, and needed help from Captain Thomas Sinclair, who carried the big, six-foot-five-inches-tall colonel from place to place, moving Colvill "to and from his room or carriage." Captain Sinclair was so strong that he lifted the "wounded hero as easily and lightly" as any mother would carry a child, and so devoted to his commanding officer that he cared for him as a son would for a father.[5]

After the coming-home celebration was over, as families reunited and gave thanks for the return of these veteran soldiers, there was both happiness and sorrow. Joy that the men had returned, yet sorrow for those who had been lost on the battlefields of Virginia, Maryland, and Pennsylvania over the course of the three-year enlistment. It was bittersweet, with scars, for "scarcely a man of them [had] escaped either death or wounds."[6]

For William Colvill and for Martin Maginnis, it was a time of recovery and reckoning.

HOME FROM THE WAR.

Home From War. The men of the First Minnesota Regiment returned home in February of 1864, and their families gave them a hearty welcome. Credit: Metropolitan Museum of Art. Public Domain. Artist: Winslow Homer. "Home From the War," 1863. Public Domain.

Colonel Colvill was partially disabled by the wounds inflicted upon him, and it took quite some time for him to get back upon his feet. This he did eventually, using a cane to help him walk, yet he would never again be fully able-bodied because his ankle and foot had been so shattered by a lead slug at Gettysburg in the glorious charge against the Johnny Rebs.[7]

Despite the handicap, William Colvill went back to work in Red Wing as editor of the *Goodhue County Republican* newspaper, taking over the job from an old friend. Being a lifelong Democrat, it appeared to be an odd juxtaposition of political loyalties to be in charge of a Republican newspaper, however, Colvill had proven his loyalty to the Union and the principles of the American Republic through his devotion to flag and country and Minnesota that he had shown to all through his military service. He had "sealed his love for the Union with his blood."[8]

Colvill also reopened his law office in Red Wing, and he ran for public office in the fall season of 1864. Local voters honored this genuine war hero by electing him to the Minnesota state House of Representatives. One of his finest efforts in his term of office was to be a proponent of a law that called for a state-wide vote to amend the state Constitution to provide voting rights for all of Minnesota's black men. Colvill spoke to his fellow legislators, laying out a "lengthy argument" in favor of the bill. "He said he wished to carry out the principles of the Declaration of Independence, that 'all men are created free and equal.'" Colvill believed that the right to vote would provide "a chance to rise above the present oppressed and unfortunate conditions" for black Minnesotans. Although the amendment failed in the latter part of the year 1865, voters approved these voting rights in 1868.[9]

Immediately after the legislature adjourned, in February, 1865, Colvill gained appointment as colonel of the First Minnesota Heavy Artillery, but he was not physically well enough to get to the assignment in Chattanooga, Tennessee, until May.[10]

Bigger events intervened.

The Civil War ended, as a Minnesota newspaper headline of April 14, 1865, read: "Surrender of Gen. Lee!"[11]

Edwin Stanton, U.S. Secretary of War, sent a message to Union General U.S. Grant: "**Thanks be to Almighty God** for the great victory with which he had this day crowned you and the gallant army under your command." [Emphasis mine].[12]

A mere five days later, this height of happiness fell away into gloom. It was a "National Calamity----President Lincoln No More." Word came "like a clap of thunder from a clear sky" when Minnesotans heard that Abraham Lincoln had been shot on April 14th by an assassin. "President LINCOLN *is dead, and a nation weeps*," lamented the *Pioneer & Democrat* in St. Paul. "Seldom has the grief of a people for the death of their ruler been more sincere; never, probably, more universal."[13]

In that atmosphere of thanksgiving mixed with grief, Colvill went to his duties in Tennessee in May. There was little to do there, except to simply hold the forts and maintain a Union presence. He was at Chattanooga only about a month before his wounded shoulder "re-opened," and he returned home on leave to Red Wing. Colvill was honorably discharged from duty in July of 1865.

William Colvill, 1865 or 1866, when he was 35 years old.
Credit: Minnesota Historical Society.

William Colvill's law office in Red Wing, a brick building, downtown.
His earlier office was a wooden-framed building. "Col. William Colvill Law Office:
frame Greek Revival built 1856, moved from Bush between Main and Leech, 1861,
moved from 320 3rd St. ca. 1910." Red Wing Residential Hist. Dist.,
March 31, 1981, p. 7. This is brick, so it likely is the later office, circa 1870s.
Credit: Goodhue County Historical Society, Red Wing, MN.

CHAPTER TEN
Colvill, Minnesota Attorney General, 1868: The Hawkes Trial

Colonel Colvill finally came home to Red Wing in 1865, after all of his service in the war. He hung up his US Army uniform and put up his shingle as an attorney-at-law once more. After all, "he was a lawyer by profession," said a man who knew Colvill in Red Wing, "and a good one." Over the course of the next thirty years, Colvill worked as an attorney, for there was always a need for his skills, what with wills and contracts and disputes that needed settling.[1]

Colvill had learned so much about human nature and himself from his own suffering due to his severe wounds, the long span of recovering from his wounds, and the physical disabilities that never went away. All these gave him an empathy that made him an able attorney and advocate for others. "In the courtroom," said one of his law partners, "he fought for his client as he did for his country, with all the force of his genius." The same "qualities of mind that made him so great a soldier" made him a strong lawyer.[2]

"He was a striking personality," recalled Charles M. Webster, for he was "unusually tall" and "rawboned." Although "the wounds he received at Gettysburg so crippled him that he walked awkwardly," his strong and muscular physical makeup "would attract attention anywhere."[3]

Because Colvill had such a high profile of name-recognition in Minnesota, he was a logical choice as a candidate for state-wide office in 1865. As the most-revered of Minnesota's Civil War heroes, Colvill was a fine choice to vie for the office of Minnesota Attorney-General. In an effort to bring forth unity between some Democrats and the Republicans, Colvill ran for election as Attorney-General, and he won on what was called the Union ticket. Some called the Union ticket the "soldiers ticket," because it had a number of U.S. Army veterans, including Colvill (well-known as a Democrat) who were running under the "Union" title, even though it was actually the "Republican" label. Colvill won the election for the office of Attorney General, winning more votes than William Lochren, who was a fellow officer from the First Minnesota Regiment. William Lochren was the official Democratic Party nominee for the position. Colvill began his term of office in January, 1866, and served until January of 1868.[4]

Being Minnesota's Attorney General was not easy. Of course, Colonel Colvill's goal was to seek justice, but that not a simple task, because he had one especially-slippery case.

It was the Moses Hawkes case, and it was a sensational and controversial case. The very nature of what happened made it a national news story in 1866-1867. Attorney-General Colvill brought charges against this young man, who had been a Civil War veteran, and there were two big questions that had to be answered. Was there a murder? Or, was there a very tragic accidental shooting?

A young man named Moses A. Hawkes, a traveling salesman for a Chicago printing company, arrived in St. Paul in June of 1866. The 22-year-old Hawkes was establishing his territory in Minnesota, bringing samples of the company's work with him. Moses Hawkes was said to be a "number one salesman," though he had only been working for the company for less than a year. It appeared that Hawkes had plenty of "snap, grit, and 'git up and git' about him."[5]

Mr. Hawkes stayed at various hotels as he was actively establishing his sales-territory in Minneapolis and St. Paul and in the towns surrounding the Twin Cities. Hawkes rented a room at the Mansion House hotel in St. Paul on July 1, 1866, for a short time, then went about as a salesman, and then rented a Mansion House room again on July 17th. Mr. Hawkes sent a message for his wife, Lizzie J. Hawkes, to join him in Minnesota in early August.[6]

Moses and Lizzie Nichols had gotten married on January 13th in 1866, when both of them were, allegedly, students at Eastman's Business College in Chicago. Lizzie was about 21 years old. They had only known each other for a very short time, and they kept their marriage secret---supposedly "because it might embarrass them in their studies." When Moses Hawkes accepted the salesman job, he was at first very busy in Chicago in April and May, but then went to sell his wares in Minnesota. When Moses went north, Lizzie tried to get an acceptable place to stay in Chicago, but could not find one, so she went to stay with her mother-in-law, Mrs. Eliza Hawkes, who was the owner and operator of a boarding house in Kewanee, Illinois, located 130 miles west of Chicago. In their first seven months of marriage, Moses and Lizzie were apart from each other for about half the time.[7]

Lizzie Hawkes arrived in St. Paul on August 6th, and she and her husband had what was said to be their honeymoon. They took in all the usual tourist's highlights----taking "frequent excursions to Fort Snelling, St. Anthony's Falls," and to Lake Como. The honeymooners enjoyed some fishing at White Bear Lake and strolling along the breezy lakeshore there. Lizzie was described as being a "fine-looking, pleasant, agreeable woman," and she seemed be a "very intelligent woman." Her face and features were deemed to be "rather plain," according to one observer, but "when she was animated and interested, she became 'quite beautiful.'" The hotel-keeper, Alexander E. Etter, said that the young couple appeared to be "very kind to each other," from what he had witnessed of their public interactions. From the time of Lizzie's arrival in St. Paul, Mr. Hawkes was very attentive to her, so they were "believed to be a loving couple."[8]

The underlying problem with the whole scenario of a happy-ever-after marriage and honeymoon was concealed all the time in the seven months since the "secret" wedding of Moses and Lizzie.

The problem was the $10,000 in life insurance policies that Moses Hawkes had bought for his new wife, which appeared excessive for his income-bracket in that era. It was noted that "before the marriage," Mr. Hawkes had "consulted with insurance agents to know if a man could insure his wife's life for his own benefit," and soon after the secret marriage, Hawkes "commenced piling up insurances upon her life" and the newlyweds quarreled, at least once, over the policies.[9]

Moses Hawkes was a smooth salesman, both in selling engravings in his work and in selling the concept that he was a good husband.

Mr. Hawkes, with his "good appearance," his ease of conversation, and his gentlemanly manner, "won the good graces of those with whom he was brought in contact." His genial ways allowed him to cultivate some quick friendships in St. Paul, especially with the hotel-keeper, Alexander Etter; with William Walker, who worked as a steward/assistant-manager at Etter's hotel; and with Thomas T. Armstrong, who was staying at the hotel as a long-time boarder.[10]

All seemed well with Moses and Lizzie Hawkes for three weeks of vacationing in Minnesota.

The honeymoon ended abruptly on August 21, 1866.

Moses Hawkes started out on his busy morning by having an 8:00 a.m. breakfast with Lizzie in the hotel dining room.

Before they ate, Mr. Hawkes saw hotel-keeper Etter and he told Etter that he would pay his hotel-bill sometime that day, however, Hawkes said he "would have to go to the bank and get a bill changed" into smaller denominations in order to pay the lodging-bill.[11]

While at breakfast, Mr. Hawkes asked a question of the others who were at the dining-table. He said that he needed to clean his pistols, two revolvers made by Smith and Wesson, and inquired if anyone in the dining-room knew who might have some gun-oil. Hawkes used the term "sweet oil," referring to gun-oil. The waitress told Hawkes that Morris Fitzgerald, an employee who was in charge of the hotel's stable, had some of the desired gun-oil. Since Morris Fitzgerald was also eating breakfast nearby, Hawkes spoke to him about borrowing the gun-oil. Immediately after breakfast was over, Hawkes went with Fitzgerald to the stable and got the oil. Meanwhile, Mrs. Lizzie Hawkes went upstairs to their hotel-room on the third floor.[12]

Significantly, Moses Hawkes made sure that everyone he encountered that morning knew that he was going to clean his Smith and Wesson revolvers.

Mr. Hawkes took time to stop at the hotel's bar and bought some beers for about "half a dozen" men who were in the barroom. He treated them to the beers, paying the bar-keeper. Mr. Etter, the hotel-keeper, "saw him have some money" at that time.[13]

Hawkes then quickly stopped in at the hotel office, where he informed the steward/manager William Walker that he was ready to pay the bill for his lodging. Walker told Hawkes that the bill came to $14.00. Mr. Hawkes told William Walker that he had three big $100 bills, so he would get change from a bank for one of his $100 bills in order to make the payment.[14]

Moses Hawkes went up the stairs to the third floor, carrying the container of gun-oil, and there joined his wife in their hotel-room.

The chambermaid, Maggie White, was getting the dirty towels out of Hawkes' room just at the moment when Mr. Hawkes arrived at the room. Maggie White testified later that "he asked me how soon I could come up to clean his room," and "said his wife was going to sit down to sew and he wanted it cleaned before she commenced" with her sewing. Mr. Hawkes "had never before" asked Maggie White to clean the room in the time that she had been in charge of all services for his hotel-room. Nonetheless, Maggie White made up the room right away, making the bed and then sweeping the floor. There were three chairs lined up in a row, one was a rocking chair, the others were regular table chairs without arms. Oddly, Mr. Hawkes moved the three chairs out of the way, so Maggie White could sweep more quickly, then Mr. Hawkes carefully placed the three chairs in a row, "back again where they had been before." He put the "high-backed cane rocking chair" by the window so his wife could look out the window while sewing up holes in his stockings; and he arranged the two plain wooden chairs facing the back of her rocking chair.[15]

When Mrs. Lizzie Hawkes sat down in the rocking chair and started sewing, Mr. Hawkes also sat down--in the last chair, with the second chair in front of him. He placed his two pistols on the second chair and began cleaning the pistols with a cleaning-rag dipped in gun-oil. "He sat facing the back of the rocking chair" and "the other chair was between them."

Chambermaid Maggie White did a quick dusting, using her dust-cloth on the wash-stand and the dresser, a table at the foot of the bed, and the windowsills. As Maggie White was dusting the room, the hotel steward, William Walker, came into the room, and Mr. Walker and Mr. Hawkes began talking about the Smith and Wesson pistols.

Hawkes "showed to Mr. Walker a small revolver which he was cleaning" and then showed Walker the "larger one"----both pistols were "loaded with metallic cartridges."[16]

Maggie White "heard Hawkes say that one of them [pistols] would shoot through a [one] inch board.[17]

Maggie White left the room, closing the door, and began cleaning the other third-floor rooms.

After about five minutes, William Walker left Hawkes' room and went downstairs to work. At that time, Moses Hawkes sought out Maggie White nearby and asked her "to bring up a pitcher of water."

As Maggie White recalled the scene, she said: "I went in and got the pitcher, and came out; there was some water in the pitcher when I got it. I got the water; I was gone about five minutes. I went down immediately for the water and brought it right back."

Mr. Hawkes was sitting on the last chair and "Hawkes was kind of leaning over the chair," cleaning a pistol, and the other pistol was on the "chair between them." Mr. Hawkes was so close to Mrs. Lizzie Hawkes that "he could have reached her with his hand" while "she was rocking and sewing on his stockings."

Moses Hawkes had quickly cleaned and oiled one of his pistols and was loading it with bullets.

After chambermaid Maggie White placed the pitcher on top of the wash-stand, Maggie turned around and was looking at Lizzie Hawkes, when a loud explosion rent the air as the pistol blasted out a bullet.

After the "pistol went off," Lizzie Hawkes, in deep pain, stood up and said: "Oh, my God!" Then Lizzie "stepped toward the bed and fell down" upon the floor----dead.

The bullet from the pistol had gone right through her heart.[18]

The maid ran down the stairs to get help.

Moses Hawkes, who had been sitting in his chair, stooping down over the gun and the gun-oil and cleaning cloth on the chair in front of him, was shocked by the gun-blast, and he dropped to the floor beside his wife, not knowing if she was yet alive.

Placing his arm under her head and holding his bleeding wife close to him----"her life-blood" flowing onto him, Moses Hawkes was reportedly "overcome with grief and anguish, and in the midst of his unutterable woe, nearly lost his reason."[19]

The Mansion House hotel was in a "state of intense excitement over the terrible calamity" that was rapidly unfolding on the morning of August 21st.[20]

100

The steward/manager, William Walker, who had just re-turned to his downstairs office from the Hawkes' room, heard the pistol 'crack,' and "immediately ran upstairs." Then, "bursting open the door of the room," his eyes beheld a "horrible sight," Moses Hawkes was on the floor "on bended knees, with his left arm under the head of his dead wife," and he was pitifully calling her his "dear, dear, darling," pleading for "forgiveness for his carelessness."[21]

The stable-keeper, Morris Fitzgerald, was in the backyard of the hotel and someone told him to go and get a surgeon as soon as he could, so he went to get the nearest doctor. Fitzgerald quickly re-turned to the hotel, where there was much commotion.

The room of death was soon filled with an audience of "those drawn there by morbid curiosity, and others anxious to be of service," including passersby who observed all the uproar at the Mansion House hotel. "Hawkes seemed frantic with grief, and tore his hair and cried for revolvers with which to kill himself." He was raving and ranting frantically, and it took the combined efforts of two men to hold Mr. Hawkes and "prevent him from committing suicide."

One of those who held Hawkes to "keep him from destroy-ing himself" was the stable-keeper, Morris Fitzgerald, who had inno-cently given the gun-oil to Mr. Hawkes just an hour earlier. Fitzger-ald said that he "took charge of Mr. Hawkes" because Hawkes was "kicking and crying," and Hawkes "kept exclaiming: Oh, my God! My God! I have shot you, my dear Lizzie!"

The hotel-keeper and his wife sent messages to several nearby physicians in hopes of reviving Mrs. Hawkes. Dr. Brewer Mattocks (1841-1934) and Dr. Jacob Henry Stewart (1829-1884) rushed over to the Mansion House hotel to render assistance as needed, but they could do nothing, since Lizzie Hawkes was already dead. Dr. Stewart had been a surgeon in the First Minnesota Regiment in 1861 at Bull Run, so Stewart had seen plenty of dreadful wounds, and he exam-ined the body and determined that Lizzie Hawkes had been shot just under the shoulder blade and noted that the bullet had "passed com-pletely through the body" of Mrs. Hawkes. It was worth noting that Dr. Stewart knew William Colvill from their shared time in the First Minnesota from the first year of the Civil War.[22]

Dr. Brewer Mattocks observed all the ranting and raving of Moses Hawkes and "remarked that the grief of Hawkes . . . was too severe to be genuine."[23]

Because Lizzie Hawkes was dead, another call went to Dr. Alfred Wharton, M.D. (1835-1920), who arrived at the hotel about an hour or two after Mrs. Hawkes was shot, and he embalmed her body.

Dr. Wharton also evaluated the mental condition of Moses Hawkes. Dr. Wharton observed that Hawkes was lying "on the bed crying and sobbing," and Hawkes was "weeping and shedding tears profusely." Dr. Wharton administered morphine to soothe and stupefy Hawkes, and the doctor provided more morphine-doses that could be given to Hawkes later that day, as needed.[24]

Hotel-keeper Alexander Etter, eager to clear up this terrible situation in his establishment, helped arrange to get a "metallic coffin," and Etter spoke to Moses Hawkes about what Hawkes wanted to do next.

Hawkes told Etter that he wanted to have Lizzie's funeral in Illinois, however, the costs of the coffin and the costs of transporting the coffin would be expensive.

Hawkes then "said that he had plenty of money," but when he put his hand into his vest pocket where he kept his pocket-book full of currency-----Hawkes was shocked to discover that his pocket-book *was gone*. Hawkes said he must have been robbed.

A quick search of the hotel and premises produced his pocket-book in the hay that was piled in the hotel's stable, however, there was no money in it, only a few papers.

The accusation immediately arose that Morris Fitzgerald, the stable-keeper, who had provided the gun-oil to Mr. Hawkes and who had helped hold Hawkes to prevent Hawkes from hurting himself, had sneakily taken the pocket-book while Hawkes was consumed with frantic grief.

The police arrested Morris Fitzgerald on suspicion that he had taken advantage of Hawkes' condition and had stolen his money.

Because Hawkes conveniently had no cash on hand with which to pay for the coffin and for transportation of Mrs. Hawkes' coffin to Illinois, the hotel-keeper Etter paid for the coffin and he also agreed to pay for the railroad fare to transport the coffin to Kewanee,

Illinois. Hawkes said that he would pay Mr. Etter when he got to Illinois, if Etter would go with Hawkes and the coffin to Illinois.[25]

Because Lizzie Hawkes was dead as the result of a shooting, Ramsey County Sheriff Daniel Robertson rushed to the scene of her death "within twenty minutes" after Mr. Hawkes' gun had fired the fatal bullet. Sheriff Robertson (1812-1895) assessed the situation, noting that Lizzie was certainly dead and that Moses Hawkes "seemed to be in a violent agitation" about what had happened. In fact, Mr. Hawkes had kicked down the bed where men were trying to hold him down. However, the sheriff did not "remember any tears" flowing from the eyes of Mr. Hawkes, in fact, Sheriff Robertson stated "I don't think there was any [tears]."[26]

An official coroner's inquest was held that day, and there was "no suspicion . . . by anyone that the shooting was other than accidental, and the husband's apparent grief tended to confirm the impression."[27]

Mr. Hawkes returned to Illinois, accompanied by hotel-keeper Alexander Etter. Lizzie Hawkes' funeral and burial took place on August 26, 1866, in Kewanee. Moses Hawkes paid Etter part of the money, in the amount of $25.00, with the remaining $300 balance being covered by an IOU (I Owe You) signed by Hawkes and by Hawkes' mother.[28]

Everything seemed to be over. However, all the facts that seemed to be true about the death of Lizzie Hawkes began to unravel.

Mr. Hawkes wasted no time in contacting the life insurance companies about collecting the $10,000 in policies that he had taken out on his wife. Hawkes provided the necessary proofs of Lizzie's death, such as the official death certificate and coroner's report, reportedly on September 4, *only nine days after the burial*" of his wife.[29]

The life-insurance companies involved in this case, accustomed to instances of attempted insurance fraud, looked at Hawkes with suspicion, and delayed any payments to Mr. Hawkes. Instead, the companies hired private investigators from Chicago, agents of Turtle's Detective Agency, to uncover the truth in the Hawkes case.[30]

The head of Turtle's Detective Agency, ex-chief of police in Chicago William Turtle, wrote a note to his best detective, Mr. D. J. Page, telling him: "One Moses A. Hawkes killed his wife at the Mansion House . . . had insurances on her life; suspicion, investigate thoroughly."[31]

Although the work of the Turtle Detective Agency seemed to proceed at a snail's pace, the information about Mr. Hawkes and his life-insurance scheme emerged by February of 1867, six months after Lizzie's "accidental" death. The insurance companies contacted William Colvill's office as Attorney General of Minnesota, providing evidence of Hawkes' wrongdoing. Colvill reviewed the facts of the case and informed the Minnesota Governor's Office that Mr. Moses Hawkes of Illinois had likely committed a crime against Mrs. Lizzie Hawkes, the crime of murder. Accordingly, Governor William Marshall requested that the State of Illinois arrest Mr. Hawkes so that he could stand trial before a Grand Jury of Ramsey County in the city of St. Paul. Sheriff Robertson of Ramsey County traveled from St. Paul to make the arrest of Mr. Hawkes in Illinois.[32]

And so, Moses Hawkes, who had heavily insured the life of his wife and then shot her 'accidentally,' was arrested "on purpose."[33]

Attorney General William Colvill and Sheriff Robertson arranged a preliminary hearing in St. Paul before Justice of the Peace, Edward C. Lambert (1816-1870), in whose jurisdiction the alleged crime had been committed. Colvill brought the case of the State of Minnesota against Moses Hawkes, calling witnesses to testify as to the facts in the death of Mrs. Lizzie Hawkes. Most of the witnesses that Colvill presented were the people who had been present in the hotel on the day of the "accidental" shooting. However, the defense lawyers brought forth witnesses from Illinois who knew about the actions of Mr. Hawkes previous to the tragic demise of Mrs. Hawkes on August 21, 1866.[34]

It took quite some time for the witnesses to be gathered. And then it took eight days in the courtroom, on various days from February 26 through March 13, 1867, for witnesses to deliver their testimonies in this preliminary hearing.[35]

For Justice of the Peace Edward Lambert, the evidence as presented was enough to convince Lambert that this "accidental shooting case" was clearly a cold-blooded murder in the first degree. Justice Lambert concluded that Mr. Hawkes wanted to cash in on the life-insurance policies he had placed upon his wife. Lambert wrote that it was "unusual for a young man," aged 21, to secretly marry a young woman and to lie to his own family about having married her, and to have obtained thousands of dollars' worth of life insurance on a perfectly-healthy wife. Judge Lambert noted that Mr. Hawkes appeared to be an actor playing the part of a loving husband when he was honeymooning in Minnesota prior to his wife's death. The judge also concluded that Mr. Hawkes seemed to be very precise in informing the other people in the hotel that he was cleaning his pistols on the morning of the shooting and had cleverly maneuvered the maid, Maggie, to be present during the time of the 'accidental' shooting of Lizzie Hawkes. Justice Lambert said that the actions that Mr. Hawkes had taken while cleaning and oiling his pistol were unsafe, in that Mr. Hawkes "would first load a pistol and then oil and clean it in the manner which the defendant did this, keeping it in the meantime pointed at his dearest friend," his newly-wed wife, Lizzie. An innocent man would have cleaned and oiled the pistol and *then* would have loaded it with live bullets.[36]

The judge perceived that Mr. Hawkes' financial dealings appeared to be part of a preconceived plan. Moses Hawkes had been careful to tell everyone that he had plenty of money for all of his expenses while on his honeymoon vacation in Minnesota, but his wallet pocketbook conveniently was 'stolen' when his wife died, and then the empty pocketbook-wallet was found in the hotel's stable and he had no money to buy a funeral casket or to transport his wife's corpse to Illinois. And when Hawkes and his wife's casket arrived in Illinois, Mr. Hawkes paid only $25 for the costs, with the remaining $275 to be paid back later, most likely when Mr. Hawkes got the life-insurance money in his hands.

"Under these circumstances," ruled Judge Lambert, "I can but believe from the testimony in the case, that there is *probable cause* to believe that the pistol which the defendant was pretending to clean was criminally and purposely discharged with the intent to take the life of his wife," and it was Lambert's solemn duty to order Mr. Hawkes to be locked up in jail to await a murder trial when the next term of the District Court opened in late May.[37]

Mr. Hawkes was released on $3,000 bail, with the bail-money supplied by seven individuals, among those were the hotel-keeper, Alexander Etter, and Thomas T. Armstrong, who was staying at the hotel at the time of the death of Mrs. Hawkes and had been present in the turmoil of that August 21 morning at the hotel.[38]

The actual trial of Moses A. Hawkes for the murder of his wife began on May 27, 1867, in St. Paul, about seven weeks after the preliminary hearing.

Because Attorney-General William Colvill's Office was responsible for the Hawkes case, Colvill brought the charges against Hawkes into the Ramsey County courtroom. Colvill wrote that "it was exceedingly difficult to obtain a jury" because the Hawkes murder case was of such "great public interest." It took just over two days of wrangling in order to find the required twelve jury-men from among 300 potential jurors.[39]

The general rule for jury-selection in that era was that the only acceptable jurors were those "who had formed no sort of opinion" as to the "guilt or innocence" of Mr. Hawkes.[40]

The way the law was written in those days was that if a potential juror had "even a very vague idea" about whether Mrs. Hawkes died by accident or if she had been murdered, then that man could be rejected by either the defense attorneys or by the prosecuting attorneys.[41]

As Colvill observed: "It is impossible that men of character and intelligence should not have some idea of a case when statements concerning it," were "in general circulation" in Minnesota newspapers and when the sensational events of the Hawkes preliminary hearings were widely-discussed in common conversations.

This meant that finding the best "men of character or independence of judgment" who happened to know nothing about the Hawkes case was next to impossible, because the defendant's lawyers could challenge and reject the best and brightest jurors. The defense could then accept "illiterate or unreading men" who obviously had no opinion about Hawkes and who might be "in sympathy with the criminal if not the crime."

The end result of the jury-selection process, according to Colonel Colvill, was that the court was "deprived of that class of minds which of all is most capable of reasoning dispassionately and deciding correctly."

After countless challenges by the Hawkes' defense team, attorneys E.C. Palmer and Lorenzo Allis, the court finally had its "illiterate twelve," as one observer called them, who would decide the Hawkes case.[42]

It was the State of Minnesota that brought the charges against Mr. Hawkes, so Attorney General Colvill was in charge of presenting the evidence in the trial. Colvill was assisted by the prosecuting attorney for the Ramsey County District Court, Mr. Samuel Minot Flint. It was Flint (1818-1881) who made the opening statements for the prosecution, in which Colvill and Flint would show the jury the evidence that Mr. Hawkes had committed a premeditated murder of his wife, all the while making it look like an accident while he was cleaning his gun, which was pointed at his wife all the time that he was cleaning and oiling his pistol. The prosecution would prove that Hawkes had "told different stories about the manner of the explosion" of his pistol after his wife was dead with a bullet in her heart. Colvill and Flint would attempt to prove that Mr. Hawkes "had no money" with which to pay all of his accumulated bills and that he threw the empty wallet/pocketbook into the haymow of the hotel's stable in order to throw suspicion onto an unsuspecting stable-keeper. The prosecution would show that the murder of Lizzie Hawkes was "one of the coolest and most deliberate murders on record; that is was all coolly concocted and carried out with the utmost deliberation as a speculation" designed to cash in on the life-insurance money.[43]

The evidence was carefully laid out in the trial by Colonel Colvill and Attorney Samuel M. Flint, with testimonies of the maid, Maggie White, and the stable-keeper Morris Fitzgerald, regarding the peculiar actions of Mr. Hawkes on the day that Mrs. Lizzie Hawkes died.

Colvill, who knew all about pistols and rifles and bullets that tore into flesh from his several wounds at Gettysburg and at the Seven Days' battles in the Civil War, arranged for a gunsmith, William Golcher, to testify concerning the pistol that Hawkes had been cleaning and oiling on that fateful August morning in 1866. Unfortunately, gunsmith Golcher's testimony ended up being ambiguous as to how the Smith and Wesson revolver should properly be cleaned and loaded, leaving the jury uncertain about what actually had happened with Hawkes' pistol.[44]

However, the defense attorneys, E.C. Palmer and Lorenzo Allis, confused the jury by bringing in the witnesses who were on "friendly terms" with Mr. Hawkes, namely, the hotel-keeper Alexander Etter; the assistant-manager William Walker; and the fellow-hotel-guest Thomas T. Armstrong---all of whom were sympathetic to Mr. Hawkes and who spoke dramatically of the deep travail and grief expressed by Mr. Hawkes after he had accidentally killed his beloved wife. The attorneys brought Mrs. Eliza Hawkes to the witness stand, the "elderly and respectable-looking lady" who was a widow-woman and the loving mother of Moses Hawkes, and who could speak movingly of the innocence of her loving son whose wife had died while on their honeymoon trip of a lifetime. The defense expertly played upon the sympathy of the jury to overwhelm the contrary evidence that clearly pointed toward murder for money.[45]

A major factor in the defense of Mr. Hawkes was the way in which his defense lawyers put a focus on the life-insurance companies and how these companies worked together to hire Turtle's Detective Agency to investigate the case. The defense attorneys provoked resentment towards the insurance companies and the refusal to pay Hawkes for the tragic loss of the wife that he loved so much.

The biggest factor in this case, however, was the simple fact that the jurors liked Moses Hawkes. The personal qualities of Mr. Hawkes that served him so well as a traveling salesman also played out well during his criminal trials in St. Paul. He was a young man who was well-dressed, wearing a suit and tie, and who had an innocent-looking face, indeed, according to one account, there was no "maliciousness or guilt in his expression." Mr. Hawkes would sit attentively in the courtroom with a "remarkable coolness and composure," especially "considering the awful crime" of murder, for which he was being tried.[46]

The jury was made aware of the fact that Mr. Hawkes was a Civil War veteran, having served in the 124th Illinois Regiment from 1862 through the end of 1863. His regiment had been engaged in the Battle of Vicksburg, and Moses Hawkes had spent time in a military hospital recovering from a severe illness contracted while in the army.[47]

After all the witnesses had been examined and cross-examined, the closing arguments for the defense and for the prosecution were elemental---the death of Lizzie Hawkes was either an accident or a murder.

Colonel William Colvill gave the closing argument for the prosecution: clearly this man was guilty, he had everything perfectly lined up---including the chairs in the room, the witnesses, the newly-made friends, the dramatic suicidal scene---so that his wife would die and he could cash in the insurance policies.[48]

Attorney Lorenzo Allis was masterful in the closing argument for the defense. He made a "complete review of the entire case, and all the evidence bearing thereon," with a focus on the events of that fateful day in August of 1866.

Attorney Allis described "the beautiful morning," when Lizzie and Moses Hawkes were busy with simple tasks----darning socks and oiling pistols. The accidental gunshot changed all of that in a moment, and the "sudden startling of the community" of St. Paul "with the announcement of Mrs. Hawkes' death," and the sad "circumstances surrounding it."

At least once during Attorney Allis' narrative, Moses Hawkes, "giving the closest attention to every word" being spoken, "shed tears and seemed much moved."

The Hawkes trial had consumed the public interest of the citizens of Minneapolis and St. Paul for several weeks, and "almost every one" was eager to hear the verdict. It was said that Minnesotans held an "almost universal belief of his guilt."[49]

However, some just felt sorry for him.

To many, it seemed that Moses Hawkes had lost his wife so heartbreakingly, in an accidental shooting.

It did not take long for the jury to deliberate the Hawkes case, in fact, it was only after a "very few minutes" of consultation that they came back to the courtroom and "returned their verdict in the following words: *Not guilty of the offence charged in the indictment.*" Very obviously, the jurors had sympathy for Mr. Hawkes as a man who projected grief for the death of his wife.

The acquittal was immediately "followed by congratulations, shaking of hands, and a general rejoicing among the friends of the prisoner and his relations." The writer for the *Minneapolis Tribune* summed it up: "We hardly know who appeared the happiest, the prisoner in being honorably acquitted by a jury of his countrymen, or the family of the prisoner in receiving back the son and brother;

the attorneys who have been successful, or the jury who were just released from so long, tedious and responsible a trial."

The newspaperman summed up the feeling of half of the citizenry of Minnesota by scolding "those parties who have spent so much time, labor and money in trying to hang an innocent man."

Moses Hawkes went back to his former life in Chicago. Available evidence indicates that Hawkes cashed in on the life-insurance policies and then continued his work as a traveling salesman. Mr. Hawkes settled down, he married a new wife, and had several children. If he had committed misdeeds, he had to face judgment in the afterlife, because he had not been found guilty in his earthly life in the dramatic trial in St. Paul. [50]

For Colonel William Colvill, the "case of Moses A. Hawkes" was extremely troubling because of the "startling character" of this murder trial wherein Hawkes collected the "spoils" of his crime and had remained "unpunished." Accordingly, Colonel Colvill, in his official report to the Legislature of Minnesota, recommended a change in state laws, whereby attorneys in criminal cases could have only a "limited number" of challenges to prospective jurors, rather than being able to eliminate jurors who seemed to be the most impartial and who would logically examine the evidence and give a correct verdict.[51]

Attorney-General Colvill also asked the Minnesota Legislature to write a law forbidding newspapers from publishing the "evidence taken in preliminary examinations on a charge of murder," so that the public would not know every detail of a prosecutor's case against an alleged murderer.

The legislature immediately heeded Colvill's call for change in the jury-selection process in early 1868, allowing prosecutors to challenge and reject seven jurors in murder cases, and permitting a defendant to challenge and reject 20 unacceptable jurors.[52]

Colvill had been upset that a seemingly open-and-shut prosecution of Mr. Hawkes for a willful murder had gone the way that it did. Yet he was more upset by an incident that took place right after the Hawkes trial had ended.

The not-guilty verdict had been delivered in St. Paul on Monday, June 10, and William Colvill was in St. Paul's Merchants Hotel conversing about the outcome of the Hawkes case with Detective Page, of Turtle's Detective Agency. The time was "between seven and eight o'clock," maybe an hour or so after leaving the courtroom. In the front hall of the Merchants Hotel, two of the witnesses in the trial, William Walker, who had been intimately involved with the death-scene of Lizzie Hawkes; and Thomas T. Armstrong who had provided money for bailing Moses Hawkes out of jail; were visiting cordially with prosecuting-attorney Samuel M. Flint.[53]

As Colonel Colvill and Detective D.J. Page were ascending the nearby stairway, Mr. Armstrong said to Prosecutor Flint: "You are a gentleman," but "them two are no gentlemen. Them two are damned rascals."

Colvill, a well-educated man with a great sense of dignity, heard the "insulting words," and reacted immediately.

Colonel Colvill turned around and said to Mr. Armstrong: "What remark was that you made about me, you damned little puppy?" Colvill, being angered by the lack of respect from Armstrong, used the word 'puppy,' which when applied to a man, was a "name expressing extreme contempt," and Colvill came back down the stairs as fast as he could, clutching his cane for good balance. And to make himself perfectly clear, he repeated to Armstrong what he had said a moment before: "What remark was that you made about me, you damned little puppy?"[54]

Mr. Armstrong, seeing Colvill's commanding figure moving toward him with an upraised hand held high, poised to strike, said that he "had made no remark to him."

The powerful Colonel Colvill, having heard what he had heard, then "slapped Armstrong in the mouth with the back of his hand."

The intensely-offended Colvill had made his point and promptly left that scene.

But that was not the end of it. Armstrong, smarting from his comeuppance, from having been put in his place by Colvill, simply went home that night. However, the next day, Thomas T. Armstrong, co-sponsored by William Walker, took an official complaint to the Ramsey County Justice of the Peace.

Unfortunately for Mr. Armstrong and Mr. Walker, the Justice of the Peace who heard their complaint was none other than Justice William Lambert, who had adjudicated the charge of murder against Moses Hawkes.

Lambert did his duty and called all five of the men who had taken part in the conversations and insults, and who had witnessed the mouth-cuffing, into his courtroom and heard the testimonies of each one.

Justice Lambert "sagely remarked that the case had taken a different turn from what he had anticipated from the complaint."

Judge Lambert judged "that there had been no assault by Colvill, under the statutes" of law, for Colvill had only responded as any self-respecting man would respond after having been "provoked by the insulting words of Walker and Armstrong."

Instead, in a major about-face, Justice Lambert found Armstrong and Walker to be guilty of "disorderly conduct," and he "fined Armstrong and Walker $5 and costs each."

The $5 fine and court costs punishment "was an unlooked-for eye-opener" to the two men.

Furthermore, Justice Lambert informed Armstrong and Walker that "there was no appeal from his court," so that those two miscreants should not even *try* to appeal the verdict, telling the men the even the President of the United States or Minnesota Governor William Marshall "could not get an appeal from his court."

Judge Lambert "immediately ordered the two young men locked up" for 3-days, or until the fine and costs amounting to $7.50 each was paid.

The judgment was "enforced on the spot," and Armstrong and Walker decided to pay the penalty rather than go to jail. So the Lambert court collected $7.50 from each man.

Colvill's honor as an officer and a gentleman had been upheld.

But that was not all that transpired from the incident of bad language used in the Merchants Hotel. Mr. Armstrong and Mr. Walker, knowing they would not be able to appeal their punishment to Justice Lambert's court, instead took their petition of appeal to the City Council of St. Paul. The City Council referred the matter to the City Attorney, and the City Attorney ruled in their favor; so Armstrong and Walker got their money refunded. Likely they had learned a lesson: "Respect your elders, respect the Attorney General of Minnesota, and, most certainly, respect the 'Hero of Gettysburg.'"[55]

CHAPTER ELEVEN
Colvill's Later Years

Colonel Colvill served two years as Minnesota's Attorney General, 1866 to 1868.

But attitudes in Minnesota changed dramatically. The idea of the "Union" party, with an emphasis on electing Democrats who had fought for the Union and who ran as Union Army veterans, faded away. Statewide, voters wanted real Republican Party candidates, as the party of Abraham Lincoln, rather than Democrats such as Colvill. In fact, Colvill's allegiance to the Democratic Party became a political liability, and voter sympathy for Colvill dissolved. And so, when Colvill gained the Democratic nomination for U.S. Congress in 1866, he lost to Ignatius Donnelly, one of Minnesota's political luminaries of the 19th century, who was a Republican at that time.[1]

Colvill was in the political wilderness for another decade, because Minnesotans linked the Democrats with the South's attempt to destroy the Union in the Civil War and also with the racist actions of the Ku Klux Klan after the war. Finally, in 1877 Colvill again got elected to the Minnesota House of Representatives, despite running in the "strongest Republican county in the state." Goodhue County voters revived their memories of this wounded former officer and Civil War hero, as the Red Wing newspaper described him: "He was Colonel of the First Minnesota Regiment, and *as brave a man as ever led men to battle*," and "the honorable scars which he bears, are ample evidence in that regard." The voters honored this soldier, and supported him in this election, but he only served for one term. During that time he was on two House committees---Judiciary and Military Affairs, which fitted his experience.[2]

Colonel Colvill, while in the state legislature, became the Democrat's candidate for Minnesota Railroad Commissioner in the fall of 1879, but it was a "hopeless" run for office, for the state-wide Republican ticket was a sure thing that year.[3]

Life for William Colvill turned away from war and politics, for he got married to Jane Elizabeth Morgan in 1867. A man who had known Colvill "personally for years," said that Jane had been Colonel Colvill's 'angel of mercy' in the time when he was recovering after his grievous wounds in the Battle of Gettysburg. It was Jane Morgan who had helped nurse Colvill back to health, and William and Jane had formed a deep bond of love from that time in Forestville, NY. After the wedding, Jane moved from her home in upstate New York to Red Wing to begin their life together. Jane was 32 years old and William was age 37, so neither of them was very young at the time of their wedding.[4]

The Colvill's first house was located within the Red Wing city limits, on "Third Street, between Bush and Plumb streets." They also acquired 98 acres of land, situated just a mile east of downtown Red Wing, land located along the Mississippi River.[5]

Location of the farm of William and Jane E. Colvill on the banks of the Mississippi River, east of Red Wing. 1894 Goodhue County plat map, "East Part of the City of Red Wing, Minnesota." Credit: Goodhue County Historical Society, Red Wing, Minn. Jane E. Colvill [misspelled on the map], and William Colvill farm.

In 1875 or 1876, Mr. and Mrs. Colvill bought a house from Nils Freeman, on east edge of town, on Seventh Street (807 East 7th Street). This house overlooked their 98 acres of land, which was listed on county plat-maps as being owned by "Jane E. Colvill," likely for tax purposes. There, together, William and Jane tended their farm acreage, taking care of their plants and animals.[6]

William and Jane Colvill's farm was in a lovely location, situated as it was along the banks of the Mississippi, with a "large grove of black walnut timber, which bore a bountiful crop of walnuts in the fall of the year." The famous Barn Bluff highland loomed, ever-present, above their trees and fields and pasture-land, catching their eyes and attention as they tended their vegetable garden there.[7]

Colonel Colvill was blessed with a "green thumb," and he was "always" a "great lover of trees, fruits, and flowers," along with garden-vegetables.[8]

The Colvill garden had pumpkins and cucumbers with long vines, along with radishes, beets, and rhubarb. Of course, there was a potato patch.

The Colvills also had an orchard of apple trees and crabapple trees there alongside the Mississippi River. The colonel's Spitzenburg apples were said to be the "best of those famous old apples" grown in the vicinity of Red Wing. The Spitzenburg variety was considered to be "about the best" apple for eating and was rated as "very good" for making apple-pies.[9]

Mr. Colvill planted oats and barley, albeit with the help of a hired man, due to his physical difficulties with his war-wounded leg. When Colvill needed additional help with working the fields or with harvesting crops, he oftentimes hired men from the Dakota tribe, of the nearby Prairie Island community.[10]

The Colvills had livestock on the farmland, so they had some pasture-land and a hayfield. They needed a modest-sized hog-barn and pigpen for Mr. Colvill's "Chester White boar," a breeding sow, and the resulting piglets.

There was enough space out there for a small barn to shelter a cow and a couple of horses. In later years, Colvill had two horses for his carriage, one called "Pinch," of a bay (reddish-brown with black mane) coloring, and "Don," an all-black one. In winter, he used one or the other for pulling his one-horse-open sleigh.[11]

Colvill also had a chicken coop on his farm, to shelter his flock of chickens, safe from varmints. When he needed a chicken for supper, he would "look over his flock after having scattered some corn," and "when a big rooster got too close," he would "stun the bird" "with one quick rap" upon the head with his "trusty" walking-cane. By this means, "there was chicken on the table" at the Colvill house that day because the clever Colonel scattered corn kernels that way.[12]

For several years, Mr. and Mrs. Colvill enjoyed entering their produce, livestock, and goods in the Goodhue County Fair. In 1868, Jane took 1st prize for the "best three pumpkins," winning the $1.00 premium. She also got 2nd prize for her bushel of beets. Her hand-crafted crochet work garnered another 2nd prize award.[13]

1869 was the best year for the Colvills at the Goodhue County Fair, held in October. Jane won first prize for her bread and first prize for butter (that she had churned), and the local newspaper wrote that "Mrs. Colvill's butter was very nice." She got 2nd prize for her plum jam and cucumber pickles. Their radishes got the 50-cent 1st prize. William brought some "fine young cattle" to the county-fair, and he swept first-prizes for his boar and breeding-sow and litter of baby pigs. The Colvills got 2nd prizes for a "bushel of potatoes" and for barley; and won 3rd Prize in the "Display of Apples" category.[14]

Their showing in the 1870 Goodhue County Fair was not too bad, either. The cow won a $4.00 prize as the "2nd Best Cow;" and her heifer calf was awarded $1.00 as the "2nd Best" in that class. Their apple trees had a good year, bringing a runner-up award as "2nd Best and Largest Variety." Jane Colvill had not only the "Best Crabapple Preserves" and "Best Rhubarb Wine," but she came home with the "Best Display Artificial Flowers" and "Best Woolen Blankets" awards, and also the "2nd Best Display Artificial Flower" and "2nd Best Woolen Blankets" prizes.[15]

The Colvills settled into a pattern of life in Red Wing. William worked at his law office, and Jane took up the responsibilities of being a homemaker.

According to a neighbor, Colonel Colvill "enjoyed taking a hand in the cooking now and then." Occasionally, Colvill could "be heard singing battle hymns" as he fried some "beefsteak for breakfast."[16]

116

Jane and William Colvill also worshipped God in their church in Red Wing. William Colvill had been active in the Episcopal church when he first arrived in Minnesota in the 1850s, in fact, Colvill was heavily-involved in the very first Episcopal worship-service in Red Wing, held on the "third Sunday in November, 1855." The twenty-five people who made up the congregation needed a place to gather together, so Colvill provided his law office as the place to meet. In fact, Colvill made an improvised podium for the preacher "by piling up law books upon the table until the requisite height was attained," so that the pastor could use the *Book of Common Prayer* to conduct the worship service. The *Book of Common Prayer* was the beloved treasury of Bible verses and prayers for all occasions---for baptisms, funerals, for communion and other sacraments; for healing, renewal and strength, for congregations and for individuals, and for Mr. and Mrs. Colvill throughout their lifetimes.[17]

William Colvill was a founding member, along with a host of other Red Wing Episcopalians, of Christ Church in Red Wing on Christmas Day, 1857. He became a vestryman during the following year, making him one of those who were the legal representatives of the church---responsible for helping to carry out the church's mission to spread the Gospel and conduct worship-services; as well as managing the finances and resources of the church. In 1859, Vestryman Colvill assisted his fellow church-people in constructing their first Christ Church building.[18]

The congregation of Christ Church quickly outgrew its first building, so they completed a big, majestically-designed, new church edifice in 1871, and the renowned Minnesota Bishop Henry Whipple came to bless and consecrate it, delivering the dedication sermon. Notably, the new Christ Church included a stained-glass window in the central nave, placed there to honor the memory of Colvill's fellow First Minnesota Regiment soldier, Major A. Edwards Welch. Ed Welch was the one that Colvill had raced against to be the first to enlist from Red Wing, way back in April of 1861. Welch was the son of Judge W.H. Welch (who became a church warden at the same time when Colvill became a vestryman), and young Welch had been wounded in the Battle of Bull Run in 1861, never recovered fully, and died of diseases later, in 1864, much beloved by his regiment.[19]

Welch Window, 1871, Christ Episcopal Church, Red Wing. The stained-glass window honors the memory of Abram Edwards Welch, the second man to volunteer for the 1st Minnesota Regiment in April of 1861. Welch, born in 1839, died in 1864 of disease complications after having suffered several battle-wounds. The village of Welch, nearby, was named after him.
Credit: Britni Nordine; Daryl & Joan Hoffbeck. Taken Nov. 26, 2024.

Mrs. Jane Colvill was active in congregational life at Christ Church throughout her years in Red Wing. Colonel Colvill was less active in the organized church in his later life.[20]

The church was assuredly a haven for Mrs. Colvill, a place of peace and harmony with brothers and sisters with faith in Christ.[21]

The outside world tested that faith plenty of times.

William Colvill faced a challenge that came his way, unexpectedly, in 1871----a crisis that revealed some elements of his character and, certainly, gave evidence of his stubborn refusal to give up when he believed his cause was just.

It was in the time period when railroads began to build their main railway lines in Minnesota, and the St. Paul and Chicago Railroad sent its representatives to negotiate a right of way for a route that ran very close alongside the Mississippi River between Winona and Red Wing. The problem for William and Jane Colvill was that their farm was situated right smack-dab in the path of where the railway wanted to lay its tracks, and the railroad would cut off access to the Colvill farmland closest to the river. It would be very hard to keep crossing the tracks, especially when trains were barreling through their land.

The railroad negotiators wanted to pay for the sliver of land where the railroad tracks crossed the Colvill farmland, just down the line from Barn Bluff. Colonel Colvill wanted the railroad to pay a fair price for the land he was losing, but also to make a considerable payment for the damage caused by his reduced access to the river. A trifling amount was not acceptable.[22]

The railroad negotiators would not budge.

Therefore, William Colvill was determined to stand his ground.

Colvill hired carpenters to build a small house directly in the path of the rail-line so that he could live there during the negotiations with the railroad company. No one was going to "oust him before a compromise" could be reached whereby the railroad would pay him properly.

The Colonel stated that he would "protect that house at all hazards," and that he was armed and ready to defend his property.

It looked like a skirmish was brewing, pitting the railroad against the former-Civil-War officer that would "send the yells of battle echoing over the top of Barn Bluff."[23]

Anyway, on a Saturday morning in June, after the railroad tracks had been laid right up to the door of Colvill's little house, an eleven-man work-crew of strong and tough-looking men approached the house. Colonel Colvill was inside the house and he was ready and waiting for them.[24]

Mr. Colvill "had a revolver in his belt" as he "went out and ordered them to leave."

The workmen refused, so Colvill simply "went back into the house." He really did not want to shoot anyone, but he did want to see what the workers would do next.

Taking matters into their own hands, the "brawny fellows" ordered Colvill to get out of his little house, and the workers proceeded to "pull the house down," starting at the end nearest the railroad tracks.

The men carefully removed all the contents of Colvill's house and piled them up, alongside the boards and shingles of his house, so that he could rebuild it away from the tracks, if he wished to do so.

In the end, Colvill backed down and got out of his disintegrating house, and decided to depend upon the laws of the land to give him justice. So he immediately drove his horse-and-buggy into Red Wing and had the authorities arrest the entire work-crew of eleven men for trespassing on his land.

The workmen got out of jail, with bail money from the St. Paul and Chicago Railroad Company and the men completed the job of laying tracks across the Colvill farm.

But that was not the end of it.

Colonel Colvill brought a lawsuit against the railway.

Colvill pointed out, in District Court, that Minnesota's State Constitution stated that when private property was condemned in order to be turned over to public uses, the property-owner was to get a fair price for the land and that the landowner would get "just compensation for damages" caused by the loss of the land.

Colonel Colvill won the case. The court ordered the St. Paul and Chicago Railroad Company to pay $1,600 in damages to Colvill. However, the railway appealed the case to Minnesota's Railroad Commission, and the commissioners changed the damage award from $1,600 to the more-appropriate total of $750.[25]

The railroad company got Colvill out of its way and completed its river-route connections from the Twin Cities to Winona in 1872 so that trains could run all the way from Minnesota to Chicago. Thus ended what Minnesota's newspapers referred to as "The Colvill Railroad War," or his "War On The St. Paul And Chicago Railroad."[26]

The episode left no doubt that Colvill "was a born fighter."

The "railway war" put Colonel Colvill's name in the news in the 1870s, but did not change his political fortunes as a Democrat in a state dominated by Republicans.

The big change came after Grover Cleveland, the Democratic governor of New York, became U.S. President in the 1884 election, becoming the first Democratic president since the Civil War. It was Grover Cleveland's administration that appointed Colvill to a federal job in Northern Minnesota.

Colvill's appointment in 1887 to become Register of the Federal Land Office in Duluth brought him a prominent position and a good salary. The job came to him because he was a loyal Democrat and because he was a well-known veteran.[27]

William and Jane established a second home 'up North' in Duluth after he got the job with the Duluth Land Office. Both had gotten old, for he was now 57 years old and she was 53.[28]

Both of them faced more health problems.

Colonel Colvill had limited mobility because of his old Gettysburg ankle wound, and that gave him big trouble on a June day in 1886. On that day, he was gored by a bull. The trouble came when Colvill entered the pastureland on his farm in order to lead the bull to get water. The bull attacked him.[29]

Colvill knew well the dreadful-power of a bull from the years of his youth.

After all, his father William had a 151-acre farm at Forestville, New York, where he grew some wheat and potatoes. He had several horses and a couple of milk-cows, with pasture-land and hay-fields sufficient for his livestock. When breeding time came around, he needed a bull in his bullpen.[30]

All who had a connection with a farm knew that a mature bull was dangerous. At eighteen-hundred-pounds, a bull could charge and knock down any perceived-threat when the bull felt threatened, or was angry, or even when unprovoked. If a farmer was knocked down by the bull, the powerful animal would pummel its victim until someone rescued him, or until the victim was dead.

A farmer could never completely trust any bull.

A farmer could never turn his back on a bull.

Colonel Colvill made a mistake and "nearly lost his life." When leading the bull to water, Colvill turned his back on the animal, and got gored "severely." The bull knocked him down and then "gored him in the thigh" and pummeled Colvill in his chest area.[31]

Due to Colvill's difficulties in walking, he had trouble getting "away from the brute." Crawling for his life, as best he could, he moved far enough to roll under the lowest board on the wooden pasture-fence. Providentially, Colvill had recently "removed the lower board of the fence" to enable his dog to "get out when chased by the cattle."

The hired man, hearing the commotion, soon arrived on the scene to help him. Colvill was taken to a local doctor who treated his bruises and his thigh wound, which were judged to be "very serious, but not fatal." The physician was of the opinion that the Colonel had suffered "no internal injuries," although Colvill complained of "severe pain in his lung."[32]

Surprisingly, Colonel Colvill recovered quite quickly, but the attack by the bull certainly took a toll on his well-being and mobility that year.

Jane Colvill also suffered from a decline in health. The cold winters of Minnesota became more difficult for her and she spent the winter of 1887-1888 in Florida, with expectations that a warmer climate would be of benefit to her.[33]

In the summer of 1888, Jane Colvill left Duluth again, traveling to "California in the hopes of bettering her health." Still, she struggled with her physical condition for several years.[34]

Colonel Colvill was very busy with his work as the Register of the Federal Land Office in Duluth. He worked with land claims at a time when land claims were numerous, because money-makers were getting lumber from lucrative timber lands; and iron-ore lands were furiously sought after by those who were looking to make a fortune after the Merritt brothers discovered the Mesabi Iron Range.

Fairness and accuracy in dealing with land-claims was the big focus in Colvill's work as Duluth Register from 1887 through 1891. According to the *St. Paul Globe* newspaper, Colvill had done his duties in an "able, conscientious" manner and he supervised an "honest administration." Colvill resigned from his position in 1891, shortly before his term expired, and immediately opened his own law office in Duluth, located in the "Old Masonic Temple on the northeast corner of Superior Street and Fourth Avenue West." Due to his experience in the Land Register office, Colvill specialized in real-estate cases.[35]

Just after getting out of the land office, Congress passed an act to provide Colonel Colvill with an increased veteran's pension of $50.00 a month, which was a good-sized amount for that time.[36]

For William, Jane's struggle with poor health was a deep concern. The couple had been childless, but they were certainly not friendless. Jane Colvill gained many friends in Duluth during the seven years they lived there, for she was quite a "leader in church work," despite being "greatly hindered by feeble health."[37]

Colonel Colvill enjoyed the company of those who had served in the First Minnesota regiment and he faithfully came to as many of the yearly reunions as he was able to get to. Jane had made "hosts of friends" in Red Wing.[38]

The couple had close relationships with William's two sisters and their husbands and families, for his sisters lived in Cannon Falls, 21 miles from Red Wing. Colvill had acquired land in Cannon Falls way back in 1854, and Colvill's property became part of the townsite. Seeing the opportunities in Minnesota, two of Colvill's older sisters and their families moved to join him there. Colvill's sister, Jane Colvill Wheat (1823-1904), had married John Dewitt Wheat (1817-1878) back in New York State, and the Wheat family journeyed west to Cannon Falls in 1857, where they established a new home. The other of his sisters who came to Minnesota, in 1856, was Elizabeth Colvill Tanner (1824-1898), who with her husband, William P. Tanner (1821-1883), also made their home in Cannon Falls.

One of the Tanner daughters, Kate (1856-1946), was especially dear to Mr. and Mrs. Colvill. Kate never married and was a schoolteacher in Cannon Falls. When Jane Colvill went to California for health reasons, Kate accompanied her.[39]

Kate's father, William Tanner, had died under sad circumstances at age 61, in 1883, either from "strangulation of the intestines," or from an accidental dose of poisonous 'nux vomica,' mistaken for his medicine. Tanner's wife, Elizabeth, was devastated by his death, and it was said that her "consternation and grief . . . were beyond expression."[40]

As for Colonel Colvill's wife, Jane, her health, always a concern, became more difficult for her in the 1880s and she became an invalid. It is hard to know the nature of her infirmities. Yet in that era, before penicillin and antibiotics and advanced medical care, a whole host of chronic conditions could result in limited energy and could trouble her in everyday life. Her health problems could have involved diabetes or arthritis or lung-problems or hypothyroidism or high blood pressure, or Lyme disease from tick-bites, or prolonged depression. The available information does not specify her particular health disabilities.

Whatever the nature of her chronic conditions, the infirmities of her body worsened in the years of the 1890s. She died in November of 1894, when she was only 60 years of age, in their home in Duluth, and her funeral service was held in their church in Duluth.[41]

The burial place for Mrs. Colvill was in Cannon Falls, *not in Red Wing*, because Colvill and his two sisters and their families had bought burial plots in the Community Cemetery. The two sisters, Elizabeth Tanner and Jane Wheat, and their husbands were all, eventually, buried in the Cannon Falls cemetery.[42]

Shortly after Jane died, Colonel Colvill quit his law practice, retiring in 1895 from his forty-year-long career as a Minnesota attorney.[43]

By all accounts, the widower William Colvill was a sympathetic figure in his later years. This gray-bearded former-giant-of-a-man hobbled around in his everyday world and at home, sometimes using one cane and sometimes using two canes to help him walk.[44]

Colvill had come to love the North Shore of Lake Superior and he put in a homestead claim declaration on 160 acres of property located seven miles east of Grand Marais in 1892, but did not complete all of his paperwork for it at that time. After his wife died, Colvill filed his homestead application and he hired carpenters to build a house for him, "nearly all made of log material hewed out of the nearby forest," there on a "beautiful spot on the lake shore," in 1895. Soon thereafter, he added a "large two-story addition to his house" (in 1896). He gained full title to what turned out to be 167 acres of land, located east of Devil Track River, when the paperwork was finalized in 1902.[45]

The old colonel supervised a little bit of farming there, with the farmwork being done by a younger neighbor named John Hussey (1855-1931). John and Anna Hussey (1864-1957) and their four sons----John, Michael, Francis, and Leo---provided company for him at the Grand Marais property for about six years, from 1895 through

"Sketch of Col. Wm. Colvill's Homestead on North Shore of Lake Superior & 7 Miles East of Grand Marais, Cook Co., Minn." Expanded log home "sketched Aug. 10, by George Durfee, (Geo. H. Durfee)," of 1st Minnesota Regiment. Credit: Cook County Historical Society, Grand Marais, MN.

1901. The Hussey family was like Colvill's extended family in his last years of life. For a time, Colvill also had a housekeeper named Annie McCormick; and his niece, Kate Tanner, visited him frequently.[46]

Colvill also had two old friends from the First Minnesota regiment living in Grand Marais, the brothers George Durfee and Chester Durfee. It seems likely that George Durfee, who moved to Grand Marais in 1886, had gotten Colvill interested in getting some property along Lake Superior's shore near the town, and Colvill later set up a law office in George Durfee's business building in Grand Marais. Still, no one had to point out the obvious beauty of the North Shore and getting 167 acres almost for free through the Homestead Act was a commonplace way of gaining land ownership back in those days.[47]

So, for a few years, Colvill enjoyed two of Minnesota's most beautiful spots----summers along the Lake Superior shore, and fall, winter, and spring in Red Wing in the bluffs country.[48]

At the turn of the century in 1900, Colonel Colvill left his large log-cabin home at Grand Marais, and "never returned to Cook County." He spent his last five years of life in Red Wing.[49]

The family of John and Anna Hussey accompanied Colonel Colvill to Red Wing in his last years of life, from about 1901 to 1905, at Colvill's 98-acre farm. The address of Colvill's house on the farm was listed as either 787 7th Street East, or 856 East 7th Street in East Red Wing. John Hussey did the farmwork and Anna Hussey cooked and performed all the household tasks that needed to be done. Anna was the primary caregiver for Colonel Colvill in the years after Colvill's wife had died, and she was devoted to making "his last years comfortable for him."[50]

In fact, there was a memorable occasion, likely in 1903, when Colvill's housekeeper Anna Hussey invited some neighbors to Colvill's house for a birthday dinner for the old Colonel, when he turned age 73. The neighbors, Mr. Gust Freeman, his wife, and family, came over for a "wonderful meal of goose stuffed with oysters," prepared by Mrs. Hussey.

Colonel Colvill, with a characteristic humor, likely from his growing-up years in upstate New York, said to Anna: "You did not spoil this," which was his way of saying "it is delicious."

William Colvill and the children of John and Anna Hussey, circa 1900, in the woods near Colvill's home located east of Grand Marais near Lake Superior's shore. Credit: Cook County Historical Society, Grand Marais, MN.

Summer Colvill Red Wing home. William Colvill, the large man with a cane, standing on the porch of his home in Red Wing, MN, circa 1900. Dutch Colonial Revival style (gambrel roofline) house with Queen Anne porch detailing. Credit: Goodhue County Historical Society, Red Wing, MN.

The Freeman family returned the invitation the following Christmas, asking the old Colonel and the John and Anna Hussey family to their home, located next-door, for a big dinner. Among all the dishes served, Colvill "seemed to prefer lutefisk above everything else, and partook liberally of it." He informed the Freemans that "it was his first taste" of lutefisk. Lutefisk, of course, was the peculiar lye-soaked codfish, traditionally "eaten by Scandinavians in general and Norwegians in particular."[51]

By 1905, the Hussey family had expanded to include four sons and a daughter named Katharine; and William Colvill was like a grandfather to three-year-old Leo and baby Katherine. Whenever Colvill went on his short walks around the farm, and when going to Red Wing, some of the Hussey children were likely to go along with him.[52]

Everyone in Red Wing knew the name of William Colvill, for he was the hometown hero. And a large boulder made his name

Wintertime. William Colvill with horse and sleigh in front of his house in Red Wing, MN, circa 1900. Credit: Goodhue County Historical Society, Red Wing, MN.

and fame spread even wider than before. As the story goes, a crew of workmen was opening up a quarry for limestone to be used for buildings and blasted the soil off the top of a bluff "about a mile up the river" from Red Wing, and a huge rock came loose. The boulder "rolled down the ledge," bounced over the "railroad track at the base of the bluff," and landed in the river. It was so large that it stuck out of the water. A local artist painted a "large picture of Colonel Colvill . . . upon the side of the rock facing the steamboats as they plied up and down the river." It is hard to become more famous than that---to have your face and fame known by all who traveled along the Mississippi River past your hometown.[53]

The idealized portrait of Colvill on the big rock showed the Colonel in his prime, however, when he turned age 70 in 1900, his face *looked old*---and "he was in poor health." By all accounts, Colvill was an elderly man, no longer vigorous, with some very distinctive old-man ways.[54]

"In his later years," wrote Judge Bert Fesler, Colvill was so pitifully disabled "in body and foot that he walked with difficulty, leaning heavily on a high cane," so that "no one could pass [by] him for the first time . . . without turning to watch him lumber along."[55]

Colonel Colvill had several walking-canes. These were "heavy canes to take care of a big, heavy man," recalled William M. Ericson, and the canes were "big and strong and rugged . . . . you might say just like the Colonel."[56]

Colvill was unforgettable, for he was a "huge, burly man," who was "over six feet five inches tall, massive in every aspect," with long white hair and a full white beard.[57]

Red Wing's citizens knew him as "intrepid" and "gigantic," as a "rugged figure, deep-chested, with beetling brows and shaggy beard." And they knew that he was truly a "giant in his youth."[58]

Colvill "usually dressed in black, wearing a Prince Albert coat and a small black tie," and "he always used a stout cane" to help him walk.[59]

When William Colvill "limped along the streets" as he walked in Red Wing, he attracted attention.

Children, especially, wondered about what had happened to Colvill in his past, for they saw him getting out of his horse-drawn

William Colvill at a reunion of the First Minnesota Regiment, at Fort Snelling, in June 1902. White-bearded, Colvill was a distinctively-old man, age 72, who walked slowly, with the use of a cane.

buggy and hobbling along the sidewalk to get to his office located in downtown Red Wing. They couldn't help but stare at him when he went up the eleven steps of the front stairway to Red Wing's Carnegie Lawther public library to get a book.[60]

The younger generation saw him as a "strange figure, huge of body, [with] bristling brows," and with "serious mournful eyes that pierced the soul" of anyone who met his gaze.[61]

When children asked their parents about Colvill, they were told that he was the "Hero of Gettysburg." They would hear of him as "one of the legends of days long past," for "they have all heard the stories of his wars with abated breath." They could see with their own eyes that "few men in history were ever so shot to pieces as this man." Colvill became the hero of stories told at the fireside on a winter's night, for he had made it through the battle, against all odds.[62]

No matter that Colonel Colvill was naturally an intimidating-looking big man, the children learned that he was kind at heart. All they had to do was to approach him and ask him politely for a coin and "he would hold out his open hand with whatever change he had and say: 'Help yourself.'"[63]

Colvill's neighbors in Red Wing also knew him as a "good and helpful man," who was always as "generous as his income would allow." One winter in Red Wing, "when the snow lay deep over the countryside," the Colonel was passing by the home of Nils Freeman (1824-1917), and noticed that Freeman's woodpile was getting low. Colvill said to Mr. Freeman: "I see that you need some firewood. I will have my man draw you some." And that was done----his hired man brought over a "generous supply" from Colvill's woods.[64]

At his farm, his farmhand John Hussey planted a large "melon patch" with plenty of watermelons and muskmelons, and when Colvill "was told by some busybody at Red Wing that the children were robbing his melon patch, he replied that he was raising them for the children."[65]

"If a friend or neighbor was in need," recalled Gust Freeman, "he was always glad to share and help out."[66]

Colonel Colvill, despite his physical limitations, was also noted for being a "man of great energy and many varied interests."[67]

Colvill knew the law; he studied Civil War history; he delved into the geology of his beloved Goodhue County; he studied to understand the history of the Native American tribes in Minnesota; and he conversed with many about these very subjects throughout the years. Some said that when Colvill spoke, he was "always short and to the point," however, others said that the old Colonel could talk "by the hour," about serious topics like "religion, philosophy, and, of course, politics," not to mention his observations about "people in different walks of life, with plenty of stories and anecdotes." He was both "very entertaining and well informed" on a host of subjects.[68]

According to Judge Bert Fesler, Colvill was "an omnivorous general reader." And there seemed to be "no field of knowledge in which he was not interested." Interestingly, there was an instance when one of Colvill's neighbors loaned two books to the Colonel on a certain day, and then "he returned them the next morning, having sat up all night reading them." Maybe he had trouble sleeping at night, maybe he so engrossed in reading these books that he could not put them down.

Regarding the books he kept in his library, a number of them are notable.[69]

Colvill had a six-volume set of the works of Charles Dickens.

He kept Ralph Waldo Emerson's Essays, six volumes.

The Colonel had Shakespeare's *Works* in two volumes.

Beside Shakespeare on his bookshelves were two volumes of Thucydides; six volumes of the works of Josephus; along with the "Memoirs" of U.S. Grant, and William Tecumseh Sherman, and Philip H. Sheridan (2 volumes each).

For poetry, Colvill owned *Poems* by Robert Burns in one volume.

As for the involvement of Mr. and Mrs. Colvill in the Episcopal church, their library included the *Book of Common Prayer* and a "Psalms and Hymns" book, along with *The Altar At Home*.

The *Altar at Home* had prayers for times of "Affliction and Adversity," and prayers with topics that included "The Brevity of Life," "Dependence Upon God," and, importantly, "Help Thou Our Unbelief."

Two fascinating books were like two sides of the coin: Friedrich Nietzsche's *Ecce Homo*, a disturbing book written just before he went to a madhouse; and *A World Without Souls*, by J.W. Cunningham, in which a future government banned religion and belief in a human soul.

The Colonel also had a copy of Izaak Walton's *Compleat Angler*, which gave him a real sense of his place in the universe because he was known for catching trout in the streams near Red Wing.

Seriously, Colvill had a copy of "Lincoln's Stories and Speeches," and it would appear that Colvill and Lincoln had a number of factors in common.

Significantly, in the last year of his life, Colvill was reading *Paradise Lost*, the epic poem of John Milton, "for the *sixth* time."[70]

Passages from *Paradise Lost* clearly related to Colvill's life with his past difficulties involving health problems for his wife and for himself.

When Milton wrote: "Chase anguish, and doubt, and fear, And sorrow and pain, from mortal or immortal minds," these words likely resonated deeply for Colonel Colvill.[71]

Similarly, in reading about how a "spear" or the "tallest pine," when held in the hand of a gigantic, Leviathan-like created-being, would serve as "but a wand, He walked with to support uneasy steps," Colvill could apply the words to Colvill's own walk in this troublous world.[72]

Concerning the death of his wife, Jane, the lines that read: "Tears, such as angels weep, burst forth," and "Words interwove with sighs found their way," reverberate for anyone who has suffered loss.[73]

The cosmic battles described by John Milton sound similar to Colvill's agony at Gettysburg, when reading these stanzas:

"And on the perilous edge of battle when it raged,

In all their assaults their surest signal,

They will soon resume new courage, and revive,

Though now they lie groveling and prostrate on yon lake of fire."[74]

Colvill, who had been pulverized into the ground, gravely wounded, at the bottom of Cemetery Ridge, had been in need "of hope in fears and dangers, heard so oft in worst extremes."[75]

As poet Milton wrote: "War, then, war, open or understood, must be resolved."[76]

The resolution of the fiery nightmares of combat experiences, after the Civil War was long over, had to happen inside of Colvill. In *Paradise Lost*, one of the most-profound insights read:

"The mind is its own place, and in itself

Can make a heaven of hell, a hell of heaven."[77]

Colvill had to come to grips with his own mortality and with the mental burden of being the commander who had led his Minnesota soldiers into a dreadful place in the bloody-glorious

"Charge at Gettysburg." In his own Christian faith, Colvill had been orthodox through his childhood years and when he was among the leaders of Christ Episcopal Church in Red Wing before the war. After the Civil War, it was not hard to notice that Mrs. Colvill was a regular church-goer, but that Colvill was considered somewhat of a "heathen" for often staying at home. Still, an observer would have to wonder at the fact that Colonel Colvill would actually read *Paradise Lost*, a "Poem in Twelve Books," *six times*, when the majority of readers would not have read it even *one time*.[78]

The great John Milton wrote that it was the calling of a poet "to **celebrate** in glorious and lofty hymns **the throne and equipage of God's almightiness, and what he works**, and what he suffers to be wrought with his providence in his church; to sing the victorious agonies of martyrs and saints, the deeds and triumphs of pious nations."[79]

Alas, it is impossible to know exactly what went on in the mind of William Colvill, and no one could fathom what he was thinking about faith and life, or, really, anything.

Yet his behavior and demeanor spoke volumes, even if he would seldom speak of himself, or write about his own life.

Those who knew him, said that it was hard to coax him "to talk of Gettysburg." He "would seldom speak" about the "great event in his life" in that immortal charge at Cemetery Ridge. However, Colonel Colvill had plenty to say about his war experiences when he was conversing with his old First Minnesota comrades, reminiscing at the annual reunions of the regiment.[80]

At those gatherings, he thrived, and his heart was always beating for those who were there at the reunions with him, for they all were remembering those that they lost along the way in wartime and thereafter.

Sadly and realistically, those who saw the elderly Colvill walking slowly along, knew they beheld a living legend who did not have a long time to live. If an observer squinted his eyes, one could imagine that "his cane was a sword, and shadowy soldiers rose from their mouldering graves and followed him" along his pathway.

In June of 1905, the Colonel traveled from Red Wing to Minneapolis to participate in the annual reunion of the First Minnesota Regiment, to be held at the Old Soldiers Home, the nursing home for veterans, located near Minnehaha Falls and just north of Fort Snelling. Colvill loved these reunions, it was his true joy to talk of their shared experience in the Civil War. As each of them got older and grayer, Colvill and his comrades-in-arms held truer to the red, white, and blue as each year went by. The held each other in deep mutual-esteem.

Needing a place to stay overnight, Colvill was given a room within the Old Soldiers Home on June 12th. That evening, Martin Maginnis arranged to visit with his old friend. As Maginnis related the story to a reporter, "I met Col. Colvill at the Minnesota Soldiers' Home, and we sat up until 11 o'clock talking."[81]

Colvill "was in good spirits," said Maginnis, "and happy at the thought of meeting his comrades again."

Chester S. Durfee Trefoil Badge, 1st Minnesota Regiment, Company K, worn during the war, and afterwards to reunions with his comrades. The trefoil (meaning "three leaflets, like three leaf clover; or a shamrock) badge of the Second Army Corps, worn by Chester S. Durfee, (1845-1929), and others, was a "thing of pride" to show that they had been in the Second Corps of the Army of the Potomac in 1863. Some soldiers wore a white trefoil made of cloth and sewn onto the uniform. Credit: Stephen & Wendy Osman Collection.

"We were discussing war events," Maginnis recalled, "and speaking of the happenings of the following day."

"I bade him good-bye," Maginnis said, "little thinking it would be our last meeting."

As a Minneapolis newspaper reporter wrote: "Never had he appeared in better spirits." Colvill had been enjoying "fairly good health considering his many old wounds," although he "had been troubled some with his heart."[82]

When Colvill was ready to go to sleep, he said 'good-night' to Freeman L. McKusick, another old friend from the war days, who worked at the Soldier's Home, and had the room next to Colvill's room. Colvill also said that he felt sure he would get a "good night's rest."

McKusick had his door open in case the old Colonel called him for help in the night. Not a sound was heard through those night hours.

Early in the morning of June 13th, at 6 a.m., McKusick was going to awaken Colvill for breakfast, so that he could get ready for the big reunion day.

Freeman McKusick entered the room and spoke to his old commander.

There was no answer.

As McKusick approached the bed, he saw that Colvill was laying naturally on his left side, with his head resting on his hand----his facial features calm. However, McKusick was "startled by the pallor that had spread over Colonel Covill's features," and, as he looked closer, he could see that the "gallant old soldier was dead."[83]

Colvill had "evidently gone to sleep" only "to wake no more in this world, and had passed the great divide without a struggle and without pain," for the bed sheets and blanket were "unruffled."

At once, McKusick summoned the Soldiers Home physician, who judged that "death had come several hours" earlier, from heart failure.

At about 10 o'clock that morning, Martin Maginnis and others of the First Minnesota were gathering near the pavilion of the Soldiers home, and McKusick informed Maginnis of what had happened. Whereupon, Maginnis went with McKusick to the "little room where Colonel Colvill lay."

Maginnis felt the loss, and then took charge----contacting Colvill's relatives in Cannon Falls, and then helping to arrange the funeral in Cannon Falls, where Colvill and his other relatives had their gravesites.

On the day of Colvill's death, the reunion proceeded, anyway. The veterans, many of whom had brought spouses, children, and grandchildren with them, were deeply saddened by the Colonel's death. What was supposed to be an enjoyable day of a fulfilling reunion of old soldiers turned into a day of mourning.

After the "midday dinner, the memory of Colonel Colvill was honored" by means of sharing recollections and memories of the times the soldiers had spent with Colvill in former days.

Martin Maginnis, as a "lifelong friend of Col. Colvill," paid tribute that afternoon to his old friend and mentor:

"Unless our beloved colonel had died on the field of battle . . . he could not have chosen a more appropriate spot or time than that which fate fixed for his passing.

"At Gettysburg," continued Maginnis, "he well knew the desperate nature of any charge upon . . . the enemy but he instantly obeyed General Hancock's orders and led the sortie in which he received wounds from which he never fully recovered."

"I can confidently call upon those whom he commanded," concluded Maginnis, "to say that no man who served his country's cause at the time had more indomitable will or more heroic heart than our dead chieftain."[84]

The next day, June 14th, was Flag Day, and Colvill's body lay in state in the new Minnesota State Capitol building, where hundreds paid homage to "Minnesota's war hero."

The funeral service for William Colvill, age 75, followed, on Wednesday, June 15th, in Cannon Falls, at the Episcopal church, Church of the Redeemer, the church of the Colvills who lived in Cannon Falls. Nephew William Tanner was a warden there at that time, serving as a leader of the congregation in all matters of the ministry of the church.[85]

Reverend Thomas Crump delivered the funeral sermon for Colonel Colvill, on the Bible verse from 2nd Timothy 4:7: "I have fought a good fight; I have finished my course; I have kept the faith."

Colvill had persevered----through battles, war wounds, sufferings, disabilities, childlessness, and other infirmities over time. He had fought a good fight and kept the faith, as Pastor Crump told the mourners on that day.

This was no ordinary preacher, for Thomas G. Crump was known at the "Fighting Parson," having served in the Civil War, joining the 8th Minnesota Regiment as a private in 1862, before attending Seabury Seminary in Faribault and becoming an Episcopal missionary in the Minnesota frontier in the 1870s.[86]

It was no ordinary funeral service, either, as 'Parson Crump' asked the congregation "to unite in the familiar hymn, 'Jesus, Lover of My Soul,'" an old Charles Wesley classic. And Crump related a story of the First Minnesota Volunteer regiment, wherein "after one of the battles of the Civil War in which the old First Minnesota had borne a conspicuous part, a religious service was being held."

"When it was found that no one was able to lead the singing," continued Parson Crump, then Colonel Colvill told his men that he knew a good hymn and Colvill "immediately struck up 'Jesus, Lover of My Soul,'" with one of its verses bidding for Divine mercies:

"Hide me, O my Saviour, hide,
Till the storm of life is past;
Safe into the haven guide;
O receive my soul at last."

Parson Crump intimated to the war veterans, including Martin Maginnis and a number of his companions in arms from the Minnesota First, and to the mourners from Cannon Falls and Red Wing and the Twin Cities there assembled: "If our comrade knows anything of what is going on here today, I think he would like to hear us sing that same hymn," the one that he had led in the battle's aftermath.

At the end of the funeral service inside the church, all the members of the First Minnesota who were present were "gathered around the casket and a flash-light photograph was taken." The six pallbearers surrounded Colvill's casket in the photo: Richard L. Gorman.; Christopher B. Heffelfinger; Thomas Pressnell; Freeman L. McKusick; Martin Maginnis; and Henry T. Bevans.

Colvill's coffin was draped with a large, silk, American flag and a wreath of immortelles, given by the men of the 1st Minnesota, as a sign of resurrection, and immortality.

At the gravesite in the cemetery, where Colonel Colvill was to be buried in the plot beside his wife, Jane E. Colvill, Pastor Crump read the concluding prayers and then Martin Maginnis, "one of the first men to enlist in the company of which Col. Colvill was captain," delivered a few parting words before the coffin was committed to the earth, "ashes to ashes, dust to dust."[87]

The rifled muskets fired a volley and "taps" was sounded by the bugler of the Grand Army of the Republic post of St. Paul.

Colonel Colvill had written a will, dividing his estate into twelve shares. Because William and Jane Colvill didn't have children, he directed one share each to his nieces and nephews and to the children of his nieces and nephews, along with one share to his sister, Mary Colvill Sherman back in New York. So niece Kate Tanner, who had moved away to California by this time, got one of the equal portions of the money and lands, as did Kate's sister, Mary, and Kate's brothers---William and Walter Tanner.[88]

William Colvill funeral in Cannon Falls, Minnesota, June 15, 1905. Members of the First Minnesota Regiment posed next to Colvill's casket, from left to right: Richard L. Gorman; Christopher B. Heffelfinger (1834-1915); Thomas Pressnell (1843-1915); Henry A. Lowe (1832-1914); George H. Durfee (1838-1928); William Lochren (1832-1912); Chester S. Durfee (1845-1929); preacher in back was Thomas G. Crump (1841-1918); David Schweiger (1844-1912); Freeman L. McKusick (1841-1912); Martin Maginnis (1841-1919); and Henry T. Bevans (1839-1913). Note the trefoil badges (3 leaf clover) badges placed on the wall. Credit: Minnesota Historical Society.

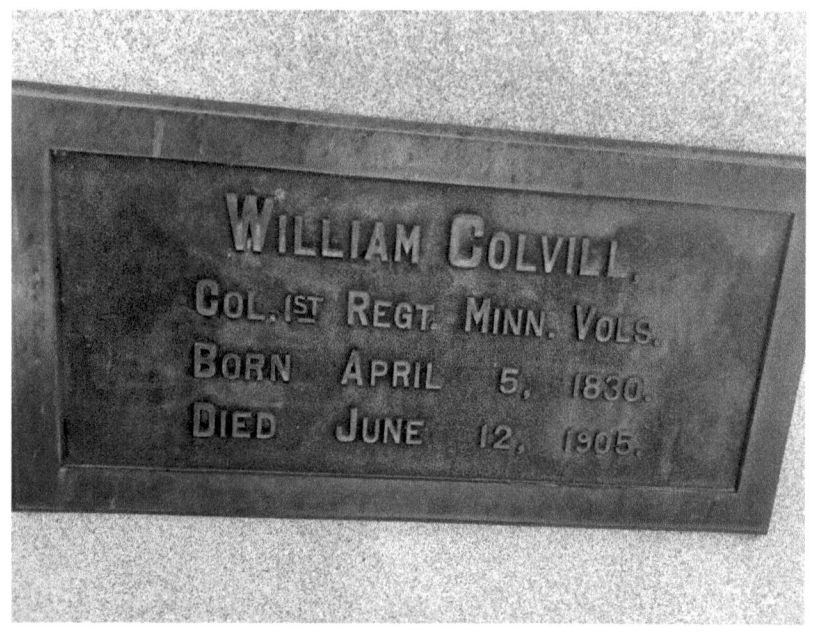

Cannon Falls, Minnesota. Author's photo.

CHAPTER TWELVE
The Story of Martin Maginnis: Rising To Montana Heights

After the body of his old friend and mentor Colvill had been laid to rest in Cannon Falls, Martin Maginnis returned to his home in Helena, Montana.

It was in Montana that Maginnis had made a name for himself above and beyond his reputation as a good soldier in the Civil War, having first served as a sergeant, before rising in the ranks to lieutenant, and then to major.

When the First Minnesota regiment disbanded in May of 1864, Maginnis had time to decide what to do next, and time to see his family near Red Wing and to process in his mind all that had transpired during his sojourn to the east in the Army of the Potomac. His decision was to continue his military service, joining up with the Eleventh Minnesota regiment which was looking for volunteers that summer.

Appointed as the Quartermaster in August, 1864, First Lieutenant Martin Maginnis had work to do---to procure equipment and supplies for the new regiment.[1]

As the command structure formed, there was an opening for a promotion for Lt. Maginnis and he became "Major Maginnis" in September, just before the Eleventh Minnesota regiment left Fort Snelling on September 20th of 1864. When they started out from St. Paul, a band played the classic tune "The Girl I Left Behind Me," as the men were leaving Minnesota for duty in Tennessee. The soldiers of the Eleventh were sent to guard the railway link to Union forces at Nashville.[2]

Arriving at Nashville, orders came to spread out the 1,000-man-strong regiment along the tracks of the Louisville &

Martin Maginnis with his fellow officers of the Eleventh Minnesota Regiment, 1864. L to R: Lt. Col. John Ball of Winona; Col. James Gilfillan of St. Paul; Major Henry Mc-Mahon, surgeon, Sauk Rapids; Major Martin Maginnis, Red Wing. 1864 photo. John Ball (1835-1875); Gilfillan (1829-1894); McMahon (1826-1877); Maginnis (1841-1919). Credit: Minnesota Historical Society.

Nashville Railroad, a stretch of about 30 miles, with the responsibility of "guarding tunnels and bridges" from attacks by guerrilla forces, which they did from October on through the end of the war, occasionally killing or capturing some of the guerrillas.[3]

Major Maginnis fulfilled his duties from a base at Gallatin, Tennessee, and successfully kept the railway supply line free from enemy attacks, due to his regiment's strong presence. Although there were battles near Nashville, the Eleventh Minnesota was not called into action at the Battle of Franklin (November 30) or the Battle of Nashville in December, 1864, both of which were Union victories. They "heard the thunder of the battle of Nashville from afar."[4]

Maginnis was unscathed by this duty in Tennessee, and he and the Eleventh Regiment got to come back home to Minnesota in July of 1865. His town and his family received him as a hero. After his honorable discharge from the U.S. Army, Martin Maginnis was free to find his own destiny.[5]

Working as a newspaperman in Red Wing once again, at the *Argus*, enthused him for only a short while. He found himself changed by the war, so deeply affected by what he had experienced, by the danger of death, the sheer adventure, and the awareness of having lived through one of the great moments of history at Gettysburg, that he was unable to resume his life in his old hometown. After only six months, he "grew tired of the monotony of the life," and he considered new ventures in the West.[6]

And so when Hezekiah Bruce, one of his Red Wing friends and who had been elected as a sergeant alongside Maginnis at the organizing meeting of the First Minnesota in April of 1861 and served with him in Company F in battle after battle, told him of gold-mining opportunities available in Montana, it struck a nerve---he wanted to make a fortune in gold.[7]

Hezekiah Bruce (1832-1911), had gone to Montana Territory in the summer of 1864 after the 1st Regiment had been decommissioned, crossing the plains of Dakota Territory and then getting a "good claim in Last Chance" Gulch. Hezekiah was one of those who discovered "Nelson Gulch" and "made money there." Soon after, Hezekiah Bruce suggested calling the nearby town "Helena," and the other miners approved the name.[8]

Major Maginnis caught the 'gold fever,' with a mindset to seek gold, pan for gold, dig gold, find gold, in golden daydreams of a promised land. So he organized a wagon train expedition to join Hezekiah Bruce at Helena in the summer of 1866, venturing through Dakota Territory with forty wagons and about 150 travelers, including several men from the First Minnesota regiment. Even though such a venture was considered highly dangerous at that time, there really wasn't much that Major Maginnis would be afraid of. After all, he had survived being wounded three times in battle; he had lived through the Charge of the First Minnesota at Gettysburg, on the second day of the battle; and outlasted Pickett's Charge on the following day.

There might be marauding warriors, grizzly bears, and perilous travel, but he had outlived warfare and endured all kinds of weather in the long marches of the Civil War. He knew how to shoot and march and ride and hunt and fish with the best of them.

The overland wagon train made it safely to Helena on September 5th, 1866.

At once, Major Maginnis prospected for gold at Mitchell Gulch, situated twelve miles due east of Helena, panning for gold, digging for gold, sluicing for gold. And then he joined a stampede of gold-miners working at Indian Creek, located 35 to 40 miles from town, using his muscles and a shovel, seeking paydirt. And then he tried Tucker Gulch, where a man named "Mr. Belcher," had "rocked

Martin Maginnis, age 24, near the end of the Civil War, in 1865.
Credit: Minnesota Historical Society.

out nearly six hundred dollars, amongst which was a beautiful nugget" worth $174.00. It didn't pan out for Maginnis----either in the fall, winter, or spring, so he turned back to journalism, as editor and part-owner of the *Rocky Mountain Gazette*.[9]

His personal life took a big turn, getting engaged to marry Louise Elvira Mann in Michigan and he journeyed there for their 1868 wedding. She was not really young, being about 29 years old, a bit older than Martin, who was 26.[10]

Maginnis brought his new bride west to Montana and they built a home in Helena, where he became publisher/editor of the *Rocky Mountain Gazette*.

Martin Maginnis was as fearless a newspaperman as he had been as a soldier under fire, in fact, he had a close call in the fall of 1871 when the other local newspaper, the *Helena Herald*, had its building go up in flames. Maginnis hurried to the scene to help his competing editor retrieve some equipment from within the blazing office-building. Several times the two men went into the inferno and each time the swirling smoke and heat sent them running out. The two editors made one more futile attempt, scurrying out the door just as a "sudden, terrific explosion of smoke and flame burst through the upper rear door and windows," propelling them forward, "knocking Maj. Maginnis with great force to the ground, severely burning his luxurious locks, and nearly obliterating his eye-brows, eye-lashes, and whiskers." Both men "picked themselves up and hastened out of harm's reach," alive and thankful.[11]

Major Maginnis worked at newspaper-editing in Helena for about another year, until an 1872 fire swept through a portion of the city, destroying his newspaper office and printing-press.[12]

At that point, he had already jumped wholeheartedly into politics, for there was always plenty of excitement to be found in vying for office. Maginnis was described as a "picturesque character," being a Civil War hero whose "record as a soldier was brilliant." Besides, "he was called the handsomest man in Montana," with a distinguished look about him and an air of command that came from his time as an officer, having risen from sergeant to lieutenant to captain and to be a major.[13]

And so, Martin Maginnis was elected to be Montana Territory's delegate to Congress. He was a Democrat and the Democratic Party predominated in Montana throughout territorial days. He won the 1872 election because he was well-known as an early settler, a miner, and a newspaperman. There were many miners of Irish ancestry and they faithfully voted for their fellow Irish-American politician---Major Maginnis.[14]

"The miners and pioneers," Maginnis said, "mostly knew each other," and they voted for the man, not necessarily the party, for in that era, "there was no corporate influence."[15]

When he got to Washington, D.C., "he was said to be the handsomest man in Congress," for others could not help but notice him.[16]

Montanans re-elected Maginnis for five successive two-year terms. Despite having no vote, because he represented a territory, Maginnis was "a most successful and efficient delegate." He worked masterfully with the U.S. House of Representatives and U.S. Senate to pass bills that were good for Montana. Maginnis understood human nature so well due to his wide experience in journalism and in wartime service.[17]

Martin Maginnis of Helena, Montana, circa 1875. Maginnis was Montana's delegate to Congress when it was a territory, so he did not have a vote. Montana became a state in 1889. He served in Congress from 1873 to 1885. Credit: Library of Congress.

The list of accomplishments for Maginnis in his twelve years as congressional delegate, dating from 1872 through 1884, was notably long, including getting legislation to stimulate railroad development across the vast reaches of Montana. He got federal money for the maintenance of military posts at forts named Missoula, Logan, Custer, Keogh, Assiniboine, and for a new one named after him, Fort Maginnis. Major Maginnis helped get "land and timber laws" passed by Congress for the benefit of farmers and ranchers in the territories. Significantly, he got land grants for the state university and other institutions, and finally, even after he was no longer a delegate, assisted in getting Montana's admission to the Union as a state in 1889.[18]

Major Maginnis, as he was known in Montana, witnessed the rise of monopolies in the "Gilded Age," as his state, and all of the U.S., changed rapidly from being an agricultural society into an industrial society, dominated by wealthy tycoons. In the rise of 'Industrial America,' from the end of the Civil War in 1865 through 1900 or so, big business 'trusts,' developed----the railroad trusts; Standard Oil trust; steel trust; banking trusts; coal trust; and, significantly for Montana, the copper trust. Butte became world-famous for its copper ore found in the "Richest Hill on Earth," with mining outfits in the 1880s producing riches for a few men. Three "Copper Kings" arose in the vicinity of Butte, and one of them, William A. Clark, became a political ally of Maginnis within the state's generally-dominant Democratic party. Clark probably had the "biggest mining income of any man in the entire world," and he was so rich that he was "a multi-millionaire in Montana, a millionaire in California, New York, New Jersey and Mexico, and in Arizona he had a mountain of money."[19]

William A. Clark had quickly gained money and status through mining and investments, and he sought recognition as U.S. senator. Martin Maginnis already had recognition as a Civil War hero, newspaperman, and office-holder, and he was willing to serve as the second senator from the newly-minted state. Strangely, the state legislature, which chose the senators at that time (prior to the 17th Amendment, providing for direct election of U.S. senators by the voters in a public election), was divided in a seemingly-impossible 50/50 split. Unable to agree, the two parties separately chose their own two men in early 1890 and sent them to the national capital.

So all four men went to Washington, D.C., and there the Republican-controlled Senate decided, not-surprisingly, to accept the two Republicans (Thomas G. Power and Wilbur F. Sanders), and sent Democrats Clark and Maginnis back home to Montana. Maginnis knew that his claim would be rejected, but he seemed to enjoy the 1890 controversy.[20]

To make money, Major Maginnis accepted the position of U.S. Mineral Land Commissioner for Montana, a political appointment that gave him a good income from 1890 to 1893. He got a little money from his own gold-mining, having invested in some mining properties. Unfortunately, more than once he "had a piece of land lying right between two points" where others were "getting out gold and silver," but their good fortunes eluded his grasp.[21]

Maginnis had another close brush with the fame of becoming a U.S. Senator from Montana ten years later. Again, in 1900, it was millionaire William A. Clark who helped write another convoluted election story. Clark wanted so badly to become senator that he bribed as many of Montana's state legislators who were willing to take Clark's cash. In this period of corrupt politics, big money talked, for some referred to the U.S. Senate as the "Millionaire's Club," whereby any man who could buy a state legislature could control his own election to the Senate. In January, 1899, when Montana's state legislature met to choose a senator, the going price for a vote was $10,000, placed in a plain envelope and delivered by hand by Clark's people to Democrats and Republicans alike. The bribery worked, because it was possible that the vote of a legislator could be bought by ten pieces of paper-money, if each of the ten pieces of paper was in the form of a one-thousand-dollar-bill. Clark won election, getting 54 votes of a total of 93 votes. Clark traveled to Washington and took the oath of office to gain his Senate chair in December of 1899. It seemed clear, as some humorous observers believed, that the Montana state legislature was *the best that money could buy*.[22]

However, an official protest came immediately upon Clark's seating, alleging big bribes by this "Copper King," and a Senate investigation commenced. Witnesses testified that Clark had, indeed, gained election by having his operatives give cash to Montana legislators, and a senatorial committee uncovered other acts of brazen bribery done on his behalf. The bribes ranged in value from $240 to $100,000. Besides cash, Clark's agents had "paid mortgages," and had "purchased ranches" for the legislators. Clark's people had also paid debts owed by the legislators and had "financed banks" in order to give kindly assistance to the members of the state legislature, and all they wanted in return was a vote for Mr. Clark. The report was written in April of 1900, and it was clear that the evidence was overwhelmingly against Copper King Clark. On May 15, 1900, the Senate was ready to vote on Clark's case, and Clark spoke to the Senators, telling them that the investigation had been unfairly carried out and had been rigged against him. Aware that the Senate would punish him, Clark resigned from his Senate seat rather than face further humiliating publicity.[23]

Wishing to have a senator, Montana again turned to Martin Maginnis. Governor Robert B. Smith appointed Maginnis to fill the vacant Senate seat on May 18, 1900, but the Senate tabled this plea until Montana could hold another election.[24]

So Maginnis did not get the senatorial honor----he was knocking loudly on the door, but the Senate did not let him in. Oddly, the Montana legislature held another election in January of 1901 and chose the same Copper King, William A. Clark. This time, there were no allegations of bribery and Clark went to D.C. and served one term as a U.S. Senator.

No doubt, formulation of the 17th Amendment to the U.S. Constitution, providing for direct election of U.S. Senators by voters, was advanced by public knowledge of the bribes and corruption of William A. Clark, who reportedly had said: "I never bought a man who was not for sale." The American public wanted to clean up the corruption of politics by 'big money.' The Montana fiasco of Senator Clark helped bring forth the Progressive Era (1900-1914), with its 'good government' leagues; the furtherance of secret ballots in elections, and primary party elections so the people could help choose candidates for public offices. The federal government began to regulate big business, attempting to limit the power of big business monopolies.[25]

For Martin Maginnis, his time in politics was over, due to his advancing age. However, he continued to be a "well-known Soldier-Orator-Statesman," and was in demand as a speaker for any occasion, especially on a Memorial Day or on the Fourth of July. He was known all across the U.S. as "Maginnis of Montana," for the "name of the man and [name] of the state" had become "inseparable." Those who liked him called him a "speaker of rare power."[26]

Oratory in his era was an art, even though in modern times it became a big bore, or a series of trivial 'sound bites.' His reputation as an orator came from several speeches from 1879 through 1883, in notable places.

War-hero Maginnis was "the Orator of the Day," in Washington, D.C., on Decoration Day (now called Memorial Day), May 31, 1879, at the Soldiers Home cemetery, fourteen years after the Civil War ended. Major Maginnis painted a powerful word-picture of the Gettysburg battle and honored those soldiers buried at Soldiers Home cemetery, giving an "eloquent Tribute to the Living and the Dead." He especially remembered his fellow-soldiers of the First Minnesota who died at Gettysburg and he said that he "began to realize that the war was a long time ago; that its incidents were being confused amid the throng of occurrences that crowd our busy lives, and that its memories began to pale as seen through the medium of accumulating years."[27]

Yet, the gravestones in that cemetery were a "never-failing reminder of the comrades who had fallen---those with whom we had shared the march in heat and cold, on nights of rain and tempest, and on nights when the soft moon and stars above shone down on the rivers of steel that flowed through the forest paths of Old Virginia; on days of darkness and defeat; and of brightness and hope, when the heart swelled at the glory of the martial scene, and the soul stirred at all the magnificent panoply of war; those who shared with us feast and famine, bivouac and battle, sorrow and joy, hardship and danger, until they were linked to our hearts with that spirit of comradeship which passes the love of brothers."

A *Philadelphia Times* reporter praised this Montana delegate to Congress, stating forthrightly that "there is not in either house of Congress a finer speaker than this young orator from the far West."

A greater honor came to the "Honorable Martin Maginnis, of Montana Territory," in 1883, when he accepted the invitation to

Martin Maginnis delivering a speech, drawing from The Anaconda Standard,
October 21, 1902. Maginnis was considered to be a tremendous speaker,
stylish yet solid.

deliver the "annual oration" at the reunion of the Army of the Potomac in Washington, D.C.

Notably, Major Maginnis pointed out the fact that Washington, D.C., was "strategically weak," having been destroyed in the War of 1812 by British forces and vulnerable to encirclement. It was the difficult duty of Maginnis and his fellow soldiers in the Army of the Potomac to save the city from being conquered by the C.S.A.'s Army of Northern Virginia. "The line of conflict---in ten campaigns and twenty battles," Maginnis said, was "everywhere spotted with blood." These two "struggling armies" had fought "stubborn battles;" through the "roar and smoke, summer's heat and winter's cold," with "appalling loss" of killed and wounded. The Union soldiers and officers had shared "together dangers and pleasures, sorrow and joy," and became bound together "forever by the ties of comradeship" in war.[28]

National recognition of the name of Maginnis also came from Democratic Party national conventions, because he went to those as the most-prominent Democrat in Montana.

The best story of how Major Maginnis became more wide-ly-known came from the Democratic national convention in St. Louis in 1888. He was now 47 years old, and his body was under-standably thicker than when he was a slender Civil War soldier in his youthful days when he had a mustache and goatee. When the convention leaders were getting things organized in the great hall, Maginnis stood up and tried for some time to "catch the eye" of the Temporary Chairman, Stephen M. White of California. Finally, Mr. White, seeing this well-dressed, "short, squarely built, full-whiskered, large-eyed man," who was known as the "handsomest man in Mon-tana," paused, and then asked: "Will the gentleman [please] state his name and delegation?"[29]

An "unexplainable, temporary" hush had "fallen upon the hall," and the Major's answer rang out, spoken in his powerful voice, with his typical "resonant tone," filling the hall to its farthest cor-ners, in his rich Irish-tinged brogue: "MAGINNIS . . . OF MON-TANA!"[30]

Awakened from routine boredom by the power of Magin-nis's voice, the other delegates cheered and laughed and applauded and chanted: "MAGINNIS OF MONTANA!; MAGINNIS OF MONTANA!," again and again with a mighty roar, echoing "from gallery to gallery," so impressed were they with his visage and his vo-cal power.[31]

For the next three days of the convention whenever there was a lull in the proceedings and nominations, "when there was nothing else to cry," someone would joyously shout: MAGINNIS OF MON-TANA!, and others took up the chant that "fairly shook the build-ing." Thereafter, it was said, "the name and the man won a national reputation."[32]

CHAPTER THIRTEEN
Maginnis, Aging

In 1901, when Martin Maginnis turned age 60, his bid for a seat in the U.S. Senate was turned to dust, and he turned his face towards his twilight years.

Maginnis had a very real vitality, tempered always by a long-lasting concern for the health of his wife, Louise.

Martin and Louise were childless, and Louise's health became an issue within six years after their 1868 marriage. The couple had to travel from Montana to Washington, D.C., from the time when Major Maginnis became the territorial delegate to Congress after his 1872 election. Delegate Maginnis wrote a letter in 1874 telling of his trip from the U.S. capital-city back to Helena, stating that he would go part of the way in a stagecoach, but that his wife "was not able to stand the stage ride and so will go by boat."[1]

When Louise Maginnis was about 39 years old, in 1877, she was "prostrated by sickness" for quite some time.[2]

The following year brought a major health crisis for the forty-year-old Mrs. Maginnis, for she was sick for "several months" with a "continued severe illness" in that year with only a slow improvement in her condition.[3]

Martin and Louise traveled together less frequently in 1879, when her health was described as "delicate," so much so that she remained "in the East for medical treatment" in the summer of that year, rather than return home to Montana.[4]

Despite Louise Maginnis's years of delicate health, she had a generous and fascinating personality. She was active in social life in the times when she and her husband were in Washington, D.C., from 1872 through 1884. A *Washington Post* writer referred to Mrs. Maginnis as an "accomplished and brilliant lady," and "the center of a coterie of cultured and refined society." A favorable commentator remarked that Mrs. Maginnis had been a "prominent and popular factor in Washington circles," during her years there.[5]

A writer for a society column in D.C. described the nature of Louise Maginnis in 1887 in a most-flattering way: "She is not only a woman of uncommon mental gifts, but she is personally most attractive. Her face is beautiful in contour and coloring, and gives earnest of the clever brain and winning womanliness that serve to make her equally admired and loved."[6]

The Maginnis home in Helena was alive with the social life of the city, and Louise was at the "head and front" of "wonderful, polished and charming interactions. "Major and Mrs. Martin Maginnis," wrote Mary (Sheehan) Ronan (1852-1940), "were both intellectual, cultured, clever, and distinctly different." The Major "was witty and scintillating," recalled Ronan, while "Mrs. Maginnis was astonishingly frank, a kindly but keen observer upon life who expressed those observations with a dash of cynicism that was spicy rather than bitter." Mary Ronan had known Martin Maginnis from the times when her father, James Sheehan, had been a partner with Maginnis at the Helena newspaper from 1867-1872.[7]

The Maginnis home," according to Mary Ronan, was "charming" due to "its interesting and unusual pictures and books," and "every detail of its furnishing, reflected the rare personalities of the owners." Mary Ronan spent many evenings "in that delightful atmosphere."

"On Sunday evenings," Martin and Louise Maginnis accompanied the young Mary Ronan to vespers services at the Catholic Church in Helena.

Martin Maginnis had been a good Catholic all his life, and Louise became a Catholic in the 1880s. The music within the church and the mass, the confession and the sacraments were a fountain of constant spiritual refreshment for them both.

And Louise's health was always an issue through the years, with ups and downs. In the winter of 1894, she and Martin spent "several months" in southern California, and she returned "home in improved health," due to the Los Angeles sunshine and the mild air of Santa Barbara.[8]

In the last fifteen years of his life, in his twilight years, Martin Maginnis spent much time in travel, and his Montana-based world got bigger.

In fact, Maginnis got the opportunity to circumnavigate the globe, starting in Montana in late November of 1901. He went around the world in 214 days (7 months). Taking off from Montana he traveled to New York City, and thence across the Atlantic to Gibraltar; across the Mediterranean to Malta and to Egypt; then through the Suez Canal; over the Indian Ocean past India, onward to the Philippines and Japan; and finally, crossing the wide Pacific to San Francisco. It was a trip of a lifetime, some of it difficult, what with the voyage across the Atlantic being "an exceedingly rough passage;" some of it magnificent, for the Mediterranean travel from Malta to Egypt was "over water as smooth as a millpond and all dark blue."[9]

Major Maginnis got to see the Pyramids near Cairo; to walk in the streets of Singapore; to visit Japan, and to tour the Philippine Islands. Maginnis was "highly impressed with Japan," which he regarded "as one of the most beautiful countries in the world." He witnessed the "ingenuity and industry of the Japanese," and concluded that Japan assuredly would "cut a great figure in the future . . . in the affairs of the world at large."[10]

Maginnis traveled from New York to Manila on a U.S. troopship, the transport *"Crook"* (named for General George Crook); carrying soldiers to the Philippines, along with regular passengers, as the guest of Brigadier General Alfred E. Bates (1840-1909), U.S. Army paymaster, who also brought his daughter, Henrietta (1878-1967). This was not a luxury cruise, for there were only 71 regular passengers who went along with 766 soldiers who were headed for duty in the Philippines. After Manila, Maginnis and General Bates and Henrietta Bates and 72 other passengers traveled home on a better boat, the *"City of Peking,"* a Pacific Mail steamship.[11]

Mrs. Maginnis did not go around the world, instead, she visited with old friends out East and then met Martin in Olympia, Washington, before they went home to Helena in the first days of July, 1902.[12]

On the next big trip, Mr. and Mrs. Maginnis went to Europe together for a period of 15 months from the springtime of 1907 through the summer of 1908. They were accompanied on this tour

Martin Maginnis, in his maturity, was considered to be a distinguished-looking man who had been a Civil War hero and Montana's man in Congress in territorial days. It was said that Martin Maginnis looked much like King Edward VII of Great Britain.

of the continent with several nieces from Louise's side of the family, and these nieces would attend to the care of Aunt Louise, for her health was not the best. Taking a steamboat from New York City, they "went to the North of Ireland first," in order for Martin to connect with his Irish roots. "I have some relatives in Ireland," he said, "and I spent some time with them."[13]

Maginnis, his wife, and his nieces went at a slow pace from place to place, stopping long at legendary highpoints along the way--after Ireland, they were touring Scotland and England. Then, on the continent, starting in Brussels, Belgium, then traveling up the Rhine River to German cities---Cologne, Frankfurt, Nuremberg, and Munich.

They took a train through Switzerland, taking in the Swiss lake vistas, and the Alps where Brown Swiss cows in pastures chewed their cuds and rang their cowbells as they grazed on clover. Montana's Rocky Mountains equaled Alpine heights, yet Swiss villages and slopes held centuries more of history than those in the state of Montana, a new state in 1889.

A winter's stay in Italy helped Mrs. Maginnis's health, and she was strong enough to see the sights of Florence, Venice, and Rome. The breezes of Spring of 1908 carried them to Naples before the Maginnis party toured Monaco, where Major Maginnis refused to gamble away any money. Then they enjoyed going through southern France, "a beautiful, vine-grown country," as Maginnis described it and thence onward hesitatingly to Paris, for Louisa was only "improving slowly." The Maginnis travelers had begun to turn their faces homeward, towards America, and made their way, gradually, "enroute home." In hopes of finding medical help for her delicate health, Louise visited "an expert in Paris."[14]

While in France, Major Maginnis made a side trip to Belgium to visit the battlefield where Napoleon met his final defeat in 1815 at Waterloo. As he "studied some of Napoleon's battles," and as he examined the history of Waterloo, Maginnis "found nothing in their history showing greater valor than that of the Old First Minnesota, July 2nd, 1863," at the battle of Gettysburg.[15]

Next came London and views of Big Ben and Parliament and Windsor Castle and Buckingham Palace. England's ruler was the handsomely-bearded King Edward the 7th, who was 67 years old at that time. People from Montana thought that Martin Maginnis looked a whole lot like King Edward. And it was most certainly true, because Maginnis had the same body shape, having become a "stout, stockily-built man," five-foot-eight-and-a-half-inches tall, who had "iron-gray hair and beard," along with "grayish-blue eyes and a pleasant face and voice." Their body sizes and shapes and facial expressions were remarkably alike. In fact, some observers believed that the resemblance was the other way around---namely, that Martin Maginnis looked more like England's King Edward than King Edward looked like King Edward. Humorously, when Edward VII was crowned in

1901, a Montana observer wrote: "Besides bearing a striking resemblance to Major Maginnis of Helena, King Edward is said to be a royal good fellow, too."[16]

Plenty of people remarked on the close resemblance of Maginnis and King Edward, especially when Major Maginnis traveled overseas, and the frequent comments were "sometimes quite embarrassing to the major."[17]

By May of 1908, after 15 months abroad, Martin Maginnis was "tired of sightseeing and traveling," and he and Mrs. Maginnis

King Edward VII, Great Britain. Martin Maginnis had a strong resemblance to the looks of King Edward VII (who was born in 1841, and died in 1910). Credit: Library of Congress.

made one last stop at the Emerald Isle of Ireland before boarding a steamship at Belfast, headed for home. They crossed the wide Atlantic to Quebec, Canada, and went on a train to St. Paul, onward to Denver, and then northwest, at long last, to their house in Helena.[18]

In their last years, Martin and Louise Maginnis spent summers in Montana and winters on the Pacific coast in sunny Pasadena, California.[19]

His "health had been failing" for several years and Major Maginnis died on March 27, 1919, "after a lingering illness," in California, in Los Angeles. Mrs. Maginnis was with him when he died.[20]

The Catholic funeral mass for Maginnis was held in Helena, with the sermon given by Bishop John P. Carroll, in the magnificent Cathedral of Saint Helena. "Hundreds of citizens who had known and loved Major Maginnis during his lifetime" came there "to pay a last tribune to his memory." The church chimes played "Lead Kindly Light" as the first hymn, with "Nearer, My God To Thee" as the closing hymn.[21]

Bishop Carroll's sermon was a "glowing tribute to the sterling qualities" of Martin Maginnis. "Montana and the nation mourn with us today," the bishop said, "for he . . . not only ranked high among the founders and noblest benefactors of the treasure state, but as a soldier, statesman, and orator his career is interwoven with the history of our country."

His remains were laid to rest in Resurrection Cemetery.

After the funeral, Mrs. Louise Maginnis moved away from Montana, going back to Martin's Minnesota hometown of Red Wing, where she lived with her wealthy sister, the millionaire widow Evalyn Lawther (1842-1932), in her brick octagon house. Louise was in Red Wing only for a few months, for, in the same year that her husband had passed away, Louise Maginnis also died, on November 27, 1919. Her casket was taken by railway to Helena for a December 1, 1919, requiem mass, with burial beside her husband's grave at Resurrection Cemetery.[22]

Brick octagon house of James and Evalyn Lawther in Red Wing. James was a real-estate investor who became a millionaire. Evalyn was the sister of Martin Maginnis' wife, Louise. Martin and Louise were frequent visitors at the Lawther home through the years. Credit: Library of Congress (by Carol M. Highsmith).

CHAPTER FOURTEEN
Legacies of the First Minnesota: "The Regiment Is Their Home"

It has often been noted that soldiers who had put their lives on the line for each other, charging shoulder to shoulder in battle, would become as close as brothers. The men of the First Minnesota kept locked in their hearts the memories of their Civil War army service and the unbreakable bonds of friendship that bound them to their regiment.

Shakespeare wrote in 1599, in *Henry V,* about English soldiers who had lived through battles and got to "see old age," and a soldier who remembered "what feats he did that day" on the battlefield and would remember his comrades in arms. "From this day to the ending of the world, But we in it shall be remembered---We few, we happy few, we band of brothers, For he today that sheds his blood with me, Shall be my brother."[1]

Martin Maginnis wrote something in 1883 that echoed the words of Shakespeare: "There grows up in every army a body of men who . . . in good soldiership and . . .

in good fellowship . . .

sharing together dangers and pleasures,

sorrow and joy,

become bound forever

by the ties of comradeship,"

for they had become like brothers.[2]

Of the First Minnesota, noted Maginnis, "their regiment is their home."

The army had become "their sanctuary."

They were willing to "die to save" their country, and, for those who survived the "hardship of battle, march and camp," their brotherhood was cemented in their souls.[3]

The First Minnesota Volunteer Regiment had "made its record in blood" having "left its dead upon twenty battle fields."[4]

This concept of "their regiment is their home" was likely not original to Martin Maginnis, for he met with so many Civil War veterans and spoke at so many Memorial Day commemorations, that this universal truth within men of war would enter his consciousness. Oddly enough, when *War And Peace*, oftentimes regarded as the greatest novel of all time, was finally translated into English in 1886, Leo Tolstoy reinforced the ideas of interrelationships of war and soldiers and family.[5]

"The regiment," wrote Tolstoy, "was a home . . . and a home as unchangeably dear and precious as the parental home." Nikolay Rostov, a fictional soldier in *War and Peace*, upon returning to his regiment after time spent away from it, had a secure "feeling of peace and of moral support and the same sense of being home . . . and in his proper place, as he had once felt under his father's roof."[6]

"In the regiment everything was clear and simple," for the "whole world was divided into two unequal parts:" one was the "regiment, and the other---all the remainder. And with all the great remainder one had no concern."

"In the regiment," wrote Tolstoy, everything was well known: this man was a lieutenant, that one a captain; this was a good fellow and that one was not; but most of all, every one was a comrade."

The fictional Rostov resolved to be a "thoroughly good soldier and officer, that is, a good man, a task so difficult in the *world*, but so possible in the regiment."

For the First Minnesota Regiment, those who had lived through the Civil War remained loyal to this 'regiment as family in a home' for the rest of their lives, making great efforts to be with their brothers in arms at their annual reunions. At the 8th annual reunion, held in Minneapolis in 1875, Lieutenant William Lochren said that the blood they had shed on many fields of battle "had converted them into a brotherhood whose bonds time cannot break until the last survivor stands alone."[7]

For Colvill and Maginnis, their bonds were incredibly strong with Company F of the First Minnesota because these men had been neighbors and friends in Red Wing, and some had been college-class-mates of Maginnis at Hamline, so they knew each other well even before the war. They had lost so many along the way that they would cling to those who remained, for as long as each would live.[8]

The veterans of the First Minnesota Volunteer Regiment remembered those individuals "who took his life in hand and marched with the heavy musket on his shoulder, through mud and rain and snow, leaving his loved ones around the hearthstone."[9]

How few came back.

In 1900, Martin Maginnis, who had accomplished much in his life after the war, spoke of his feelings for his battle-scarred 'band of brothers' when he movingly said: "You may call me sergeant or major or senator, as you please, but the proudest title I can boast is that I was a member of the old First Minnesota."[10]

Close up of Welch Window, 1871, Christ Episcopal Church, Red Wing.
The stained-glass window honors the memory of Abram Edwards Welch, the second
man to volunteer for the 1st Minnesota Regiment in April of 1861. Welch, born in 1839,
died in 1864 of disease complications after having suffered several battle-wounds.
Credit: Britni Nordine; Daryl & Joan Hoffbeck. Taken Nov. 26, 2024.

CHAPTER FIFTEEN
Legacies of the First Minnesota: The Statues

The First Minnesota regiment earned a revered place in the hearts and minds of Minnesotans because its story of enlisting and serving and dying at Gettysburg was so compelling.

The idea arose in Minnesota that the heroic sacrifices of the regiment should be taught in every school, written in every history of the state, and imprinted upon the memory-banks of all Minnesotans for all time.

When the soldiers of the First Minnesota came home from the war, in 1864, they got a hearty welcome in Winona, and a *Winona Daily Republican* newspaper writer wrote: "The First Minnesota has not been forgotten in their own State, and **never will be**. They are welcomed to the hearts of the people as no other body of men ever can be." Though other Minnesota regiments were recruited and fought in the Civil War, "the First has always been the favorite."[1]

John W. Willis (1854-1925), of St. Paul, a Minnesota native and former district court judge, expressed his admiration for the First Minnesota in a 1905 speech.[2]

"When I was a boy of 6 years," he said, "I saw the First Minnesota march away, 1,140 strong, and three years later *I saw **what was left of the regiment** come back*, 309 men. Out of that gallant host 831 fell on the battlefield or were stricken with malaria" [or other diseases]. The numbers of those who died overwhelmingly-exceeded the numbers of those who lived through the years of battles, bullets, and illnesses.[3]

"The fame of the First Minnesota is assured forever, and in generations to come and when deeds of heroism are mentioned, the

Drawing of the Minnesota Soldiers' Monument at Gettysburg, located at the place where the famous 'Charge of the First Minnesota' began on Cemetery Ridge on the second day of the 1863 battle. The onrushing soldier in bronze, with an earnest face and a fixed-bayonet, was heroic. The monument was constructed and installed in 1893, then dedicated in 1897. Minneapolis Daily Times, September 10, 1893, p. 7.

First Minnesota regiment will be ever discussed. Men will say a hundred years hence, 'My grandfather was a member of the First Minnesota.' The fame and glory of this gallant regiment *will never fade*, and the pen of the historian can never trace the history of the nation without inscribing in letters of gold the name of the First Minnesota regiment and an account of its glorious deeds."

One way to permanently remember the 'charge of the First Minnesota' was to place a statue honoring the regiment at Gettysburg, right on the very place where the men started their desperate charge on July 2, 1863, on the slopes of Cemetery Ridge. The monument features a "heroic bronze soldier figure in the act of a double-quick forward move with level bayonet," ready to plunge into the Confederate forces massed in front of the regiment. The top of the soldier's head rises 32 feet above the ridge.

Built in 1893 and finally dedicated on July 2, 1897, the First Minnesota monument at Gettysburg will forever stand as long as bronze and granite endure.

Both William Colvill and Martin Maginnis were seated on the speaker's podium on that dedication day.

Maginnis "made [by] far the most effective speech of the occasion," according to one observer. He spoke of the famous charge of the 1st Minnesota on a hot and "murky afternoon" when he and his fellow Minnesotans came to know that the battle of Gettysburg "was the great infantry fight of the world," and they were called upon to play their vital role in it. "The roll of musketry, the crash of cannon filled the world," and "the flood and foam of fire" washed over them, and they "went through it" and their actions paid honor to the state of Minnesota on that day, for Maginnis and his regiment had met the "highest standard of discipline, devotion, death, success and necessary military sacrifice." On that blood-stained soil, they had done their necessary duty.[4]

Colonel Colvill was right in the middle of the speaker's platform on this dedication day. As always, he was conspicuous because he was such a large man and had such a fulsome gray beard. All eyes were on Colvill when he was on the podium and curiosity arose regarding a woman sitting right next to him. Colvill was sitting next to a "gray-haired lady, and many were the inquiries among his old comrades as to who was the lady to whom the gallant colonel was so attentive."[5]

It should not have been a surprise that this mysterious lady was none other than Tillie Pierce, who had looked after the wounded Colonel Colvill in her parents' house, in the days immediately following the last day of battles at Gettysburg. Known now as Mrs. Matilda "Tillie" (Pierce) Alleman (1848-1914), she had given "a cup of cold water" to the colonel and "cared for him until he was taken to his friends in New York" on his long recovery path to getting back on his feet.

Colonel Colvill spoke briefly to the assembled crowd and his fellow old soldiers and the others who were there cheered his introduction and his spoken words---for he "gave all honor to the enlisted men of the Civil War."[6]

Colvill posed for a photograph in front of the First Minnesota monument, a moment etched in time for all time.

Gov. D.M. Clough (pronounced "cluff," 1846-1924) delivering his speech to dedicate the Minnesota monument at Gettysburg on July 2, 1897. William Colvill, with his big gray beard, was seated in the middle, sitting next to Tillie (Pierce) Alleman, likely in white dress (but hidden behind the man with the full mustache), the kindly girl who had helped care for Colvill after he was severely wounded at Gettysburg in the famous charge. William Lochren was seated below the flag with the trefoil clover on it. Martin Maginnis was on the podium but not visible in the photo.
Credit: Minnesota Historical Society.

William Colvill, July 2, 1897, at monument dedication. Colonel William Colvill, age 67, standing at the foot of the First Minnesota monument at Gettysburg, where the famous bayonet charge occurred on July 2, 1863. Colvill has a very sturdy cane. Near the top of the monument, just under the charging bronze soldier are engravings of the trefoil, (shamrock or three leaf clover), symbol of the Second Corps of the Army of the Potomac. Credit: Minnesota Historical Society.

CHAPTER SIXTEEN
Two Colvill Statues, Also

After William Colvill's death in 1905, Samuel Van Sant, recently-retired Minnesota governor and a Civil War veteran himself, voiced a proposal to honor Colvill with a monumental statue. The proposal caught on with newspaper editors and with veterans of the First Minnesota. The new State Capitol building had just been completed in that year, and the idea of placing a bronze likeness of Colonel Colvill somewhere inside would be a fitting memorial to Minnesota's greatest Civil War hero.[1]

The monumental Colvill sculpture concept grew, but it took a while.

The Minnesota legislature allotted $10,000 for a suitable statue in 1907, and, in 1908, a number of sculptors submitted miniature clay models portraying the hero of Gettysburg.

It made sense that a sculptor from Minnesota might win the competition, to keep the allotted money within the state. However, Cass Gilbert, the genius-level home-grown architect who had designed Minnesota's magnificent Capitol, expressed doubt. "There is no one in Minnesota," he said, with his nose figuratively in the air, "who can make a statue suitable for the capitol."[2]

Despite the opinions of Cass Gilbert, there was a talented entrant who had begun working in Minneapolis. Her name was Catherine F. Backus, a gifted sculptor, and she won the competition. The wife of George Joseph Backus (1858-1944), Catherine had studied sculpture at the Art Institute of Chicago (taught by Lorado Taft); at the Minneapolis School of Fine Arts; and in Paris (in 1906).

Born in Toledo, Ohio, in 1863, the very same year of the Gettysburg battle, Catherine was the daughter of John and Martha Fallis. John Fallis (1831-1897) "operated flour mills at Toledo, Ohio" for many years.[3]

Catherine moved from Ohio to Minneapolis when she was a young woman, and there met George J. Backus and these two then got married, very romantically, joining together their "hearts and lives" on Valentine's Day, February 14, 1894.[4]

George Backus was wealthy because he was associated with his brother, Edward W. Backus (1860-1934), who built his fortune in the white-pine lumber business in its Minnesota heyday in the 1880s. The sawmills of E.W. Backus & Company (1885 and onward) were buzzing through the 1890s and into the early 1900s. So much so, that a Minnesota town located between Brainerd and Walker was named "Backus" after the family. George started as a bookkeeper for the Backus company and then became a salesman for his brother's company before starting up his own enterprise, namely, the George J. Backus Lumber Company. Both of the brothers had grown up just outside the Red Wing city limits, in rural Featherstone Township, Goodhue County, so they had always known and revered Colonel Colvill, their home-town Civil War hero.[5]

Because the Backus family had come from Red Wing, Catherine had connections in the town and she had a vision of making a sculpture of William Colvill. Accordingly, Catherine contacted Mr. Colvill and arranged to "make a number of sketches" of Colonel Colvill "at his home in Red Wing," in 1904, the year prior to Colvill's death. Catherine "planned to make a bust of Colonel Colvill."[6]

In fact, Catherine Backus had made an appointment to meet with Colonel Colvill and complete more sketches of him---on the very day of his death, June 13th, 1905.[7]

Instead of drawing images of Colvill's face, Catherine Backus was authorized to make a death mask of his facial features that evening. After spreading oil or grease upon his face, she applied plaster over his visage and lifted the plaster cast soon thereafter. The plaster mask became a mold to be filled with wet plaster or wax to make a positive model of Colvill's face, as it was on the day of his death. The death mask captured every feature of his face, providing a true likeness as others saw him in his old age, and as he would have seen himself in a mirror when he was alive.[8]

Catherine Backus used her real-life sketches and Colvill's death mask to make a small-scale model of the Colonel of the First Minnesota regiment, showing Colvill's body almost in his prime, yet showing the effects of the terrible wounds Colvill had suffered in his wartime service. So the image that Backus created was to show his body-frame some time *after* the 1863 Gettysburg battle, in essence, making him appear to be *both* 'whole' and 'wounded.' She made several models for a Colvill statue in the years from 1905 through 1908, hoping to be chosen to be the one to cast his form in bronze.[9]

She was chosen.

Sculptor Backus also interviewed Colvill's friends from the First Minnesota regiment, in order to get a better sense of his character, personality and life-force. Colonel Colvill "never showed fear," according to William Lochren, in fact, Lochren told Catherine Backus in these powerful words: "No braver man ever lived than Colonel Colvill." Regarding Colvill's battle-wounds, Lochren understood that Colvill had "suffered excruciating pain and never gave a sign to even those of us who knew him best."[10]

The figure of Colvill, as sculpted by Catherine Backus, showed the fearlessness for which Colvill was known. The sculpture portrayed him with characteristic broad shoulders, straight and strong, which "were his pride." After Colvill's ankle and foot had been shattered at Gettysburg, he had difficulty in standing upright, so the statue realistically shows his left hand "braced against his hip," while his right hand was outstretched in order to keep his balance, holding tightly to a sword. The sword was in place of the walking-cane that he had to use in real life just to stand up. Colvill's face had a full beard and his eyes seemed to be "looking far away, as though he were reviewing his troops." The overwhelming effect of the monumental form was one of great height, being 8 feet tall, which corresponded to Colvill's towering stature, for at six-foot-five-inches, he was considered to be "an unusually tall man" in that era. Altogether, the sculpture of Colonel Colvill "showed dignity, spirit and strength."[11]

Catherine Backus finished her work on the Colvill statue in 1909 and then she went to Chicago, where she forged it in bronze. She made two identical statues while she was there.[12]

The first of these larger-than-life-size sculptures was placed in a dignified alcove niche in the second-floor rotunda in the Minnesota State Capitol building on March 31, 1909.[13]

The second Colvill bronze figure, also 8 feet tall, was put on the top of a knoll in the Cannon Falls Community Cemetery to mark his gravesite. It was dedicated on Memorial Day, on May 29. Governor John A. Johnson, with no exaggeration, said it was "the greatest Memorial Day ever held in the state of Minnesota," because it marked the day of unveiling of the magnificent Colvill statue.[14]

Martin Maginnis was unable to be in Cannon Falls that day, but he wrote a memorial address, which was read to those assembled there. Maginnis lauded Colonel Colvill as the "undaunted leader of undaunted men," who had been willing "to take the chances of wounds or death." Colvill had "faced death so often on the open field," at Bull Run, at Antietam, at Chancellorsville, and, especially, at Gettysburg, where he was horribly wounded and within an inch of dying. "The colonel," wrote Maginnis, "was one of those who, after a desperate struggle with his wounds, was left alive, but to be a wreck of one of the finest and strongest physical forms into which a man was ever moulded," making him "a cripple and a constant sufferer from many long years."[15]

Maginnis was extremely proud that the State of Minnesota had authorized the two statues of Colvill to be made by sculptor Catherine Backus, so that "the heroic form" of Colonel Colvill could be "reconstructed" to once again appear as strong as he had once been in July, 1863, when he had stood on Cemetery Ridge on the second day of the Battle of Gettysburg, just before the charge when Confederate bullets "shattered" his body.

The bronze statue was a fitting memorial to the leader of the old First Minnesota, who had truly been "the gallant leader of gallant men."

One would suspect that awareness of the Cannon Falls statue of Colvill would fade somewhat with the passing of time, however, the city of Cannon Falls revived the Colvill memories with a new feature added to the Colvill Memorial in the cemetery in 1928,

Sculptor Catherine Backus created two statues of William Colvill, one placed in the State Capitol in St. Paul, and one situated in Cannon Falls at the gravesites of William and Jane Colvill. Each bronze statue stands 8 feet tall, and the Colonel is portrayed as being in his prime, yet also with the infirmities from the wounds he suffered in Civil War battles. Both statues were installed in 1909. Dianne Hoffbeck photo, Cannon Falls, MN, 2023.

nineteen years after the statue was unveiled. The officers and soldiers of the 135th Infantry, being proud of its history as the direct successor of the First Minnesota Regiment, donated their own money to make a small memorial just a short distance below the Colvill statue in the cemetery in Cannon Falls. They installed a bronze tablet, embedded in stone, that spelled out the succession:

"1861, 1ST MINN. VOL., 1865 (Civil War);

1898, 13TH MINN. VOL., 1899 (Spanish-American War);

1916, 1ST MINN. INF., 1917 (Mexican Border Service);

1917 135TH INF., 1918 (World War I)."

"TO THE LAST MAN."

135TH INFANTRY MINNESOTA NATIONAL GUARD. Dedicated July 29, 1928."

The officers of the 135th Infantry, knowing that President Calvin Coolidge and his family were in Wisconsin at their Summer White House, invited the president to speak at the dedication of the enhanced Colvill Memorial on a Sunday at the end of July. Coolidge was in the middle of a three-month-long vacation, getting away from the broiling heat of Washington, D.C., to the coolness of Cedar Island Lodge, located on the trout-filled Brule River in northern Wisconsin, just east of Duluth.[16]

Remarkably, President Coolidge accepted the invitation. In Coolidge's time as president, he "had never traveled anywhere to make a public appearance on Sunday," in order to go to church and keep the Sabbath Day holy. Not only that, Coolidge had pledged to refrain from giving speeches while on vacation, which made perfect sense---being known as "Silent Cal," stereotyped as a 'sour man weaned on a dill pickle,' the fact that he was "speechless" fit his public persona. Cal wanted to go fishing for trout, using worms for bait, rather than go anywhere or speechify anywhere away from that Wisconsin trout stream.[17]

However, upon the urging of Minnesota's Governor Theodore Christianson (1883-1948) and Minnesota's Congressmen, Coolidge decided it would be worthwhile to honor Colonel William Colvill's Civil War heroism by speaking at the memorial dedication in Cannon Falls.[18]

First Lady Grace Coolidge unveiled a new, smaller, memorial near the Colvill statue in Cannon Falls on the day when President Calvin Coolidge spoke of the fame of Colonel William Colvill and the First Minnesota Regiment at Gettysburg. Colonel Otto Ronningen on the right, with the bronze Colvill looming over all, on July 29, 1928. Minneapolis Journal photo, July 30, 1928.

President Coolidge, his wife, Grace, and son John (age 21), took an early morning train from Wisconsin, arriving on time in Cannon Falls for the Colvill event.[19]

15,000 men and women, including both the "great and the humble," gathered around Colonel Colvill's towering statue, on a swelteringly-hot July day for the dedication. First Lady Grace Coolidge unveiled the new memorial tablet, gracefully taking hold of the flag that covered the bronze plaque, lifting it and holding it aloft "at arm's length," in a red-white-and-blue pose for the newspaper photographers. The assembled crowd could not help but cheer, for "it was a brilliant picture." The First Lady looked perfectly cool, being dressed all in white; with a wide white hat to hold off the sun, and a white dress with white shoes and stockings.[20]

President Coolidge was not as cool as his wife that day, wearing "formal clothes" with a "tall silk hat," and he "appeared very nervous and tired" upon his arrival in Cannon Falls. Still, that weariness did not prevent Coolidge from delivering an eloquent speech of tribute to Colonel William Colvill, commander of the First Minnesota on that fateful day in 1863 on the Gettysburg field of battle.[21]

Calvin Coolidge took out the "little black book from which he reads his speeches" and spoke his speech.[22]

"The story of Col. William Colvill and the First Minnesota Volunteer Infantry," the president said, "was an exhibition of the most exalted heroism against . . . Confederate forces" on the second day of the Gettysburg battle. By holding the Rebel soldiers in check at the decisive moment until reinforcements came forward, "Colonel Colvill and those eight companies of the First Minnesota are entitled to rank among the saviors of their country," because their immortal charge "probably saved the Union Army from defeat."[23]

Regarding his decision to speak on a Sunday afternoon, President Coolidge said: "It is altogether fitting that should assemble on this Lord's day to reconsecrate ourselves by dedicating a memorial to one of the heroes of the Battle of Gettysburg," asserting that it was an act of Christian devotion to reverence Colvill and his soldiers who believed in "the reality of right and truth and Justice." Coolidge trusted that Divine Providence had called Colvill to lead the First Minnesota in the Civil War. Was it not an infinite power, Coolidge asked, "which set these men as its sentinels on that July day to guard the progress of humanity?"[24]

This was a deep question to ask. It was clear that Coolidge, being true to his strong Christian faith, concluded that the North's victory over the South, and the actions of the First Minnesota fit with the "Words of Holy Writ that 'the judgments of the Lord are true and righteous altogether.'"[25]

President and Mrs. Coolidge and son John went back to Wisconsin, the throng of people went back to their homes, and Cannon Falls had experienced its biggest day in its history, for the nation's Chief Executive had visited their town, and the band had played "Hail to the Chief" on that hot July day at Colonel Colvill's gravesite.

CHAPTER SEVENTEEN
Colvill's Name on Minnesota's Maps

Red Wing honored William Colvill as a native son by creating a city park and naming it "Colvill Park." The park land was part of Colvill's 98-acre farm, his homestead located along the Mississippi River, just a short distance east of Barn Bluff, in fact, the farm and its nearby Colvill Bay lay in the evening shadows of the historic hill that looms over Red Wing's skyline.[1]

The park became a reality, but bringing it into reality was not an easy process. In 1906, the year following Colonel Colvill's death, Red Wing's leading citizens petitioned the city council to buy Colvill's farm as a public park and swimming beach. Surprisingly, the city council rejected the project and did not purchase Colvill's land.[2]

But the wish for a swimming area became an urgent need in 1908, after a 16-year-old Red Wing high-school student named George B. Hauenstein drowned in the unsafe waters of the Mississippi River, and so the concerned women of Red Wing formed the Colvill Park Organization.[3]

Several other swimmers had perished in the perilous waters near the city---in fact, the young Hauenstein's father, George W., a local jeweler, age 49, had also drowned in the river, in the summer of 1905. The elder Hauenstein was watching boat-races in the river, having gone out by himself in a rowboat that he anchored in the river-current. Unfortunately, Hauenstein was standing up, and a wave suddenly rose up and capsized his rowboat. Hauenstein was instantly pitched into the water and yelled, "Help!." Before he could utter another word, the swirling swift currents of the Mississippi swallowed him up, for its "water was deep" in that spot. Hundreds of fellow spectators watched him fall, unable to help, mouths agape, and the races came to a sudden end.[4]

Too many had died in the hazardous waters, so the members of this all-women's organization vowed to make a safe swimming area along the river. Mrs. Alice A. (Purdy) Neill (1851-1938), as president of the group, led the way in raising enough money to purchase the old Colvill farmstead for $1,500 and the organization used the portion of the property that edged upon the river as a picnic grounds and supervised swimming area.[5]

Colvill Park remains as a recreational area for Red Wing's residents who use the boat launch, playground structures, tennis courts, swimming pool and waterpark, and marina areas, largely oblivious of the historical marker telling of Colonel Colvill. The spacious park, located just off Highway 61, one-and-one-half miles east of downtown Red Wing, and situated adjacent to the Minnesota Correction Facility, gets plenty of use. Birdwatchers from all over travel to the park to see the bald eagles who spend winters there and to view the spring and fall migrations of the wild ducks that pass over the park.[6]

Northeast of Grand Marais, the land surrounding Colvill's property was organized and named "Colville township," (misspelled with an "e" at the end), in 1906. A village arose there, also. Almost nothing of Colvill village remains today, except for a Highway 61 wayside sign that reads: "Colvill. In 1906 this community was named in honor of Colonel William Colvill, commander of the First Minnesota . . . Colvill's summer homestead was in this community."[7]

Another memorial on the Minnesota landscape, is "The Colvill Memorial Highway," which is the stretch of Minnesota Highway 19 that meanders to the north and west from Red Wing through Northfield, New Prague, and Henderson to its end-point at Gaylord (in Sibley County). The route has been largely forgotten, for many years have passed since the establishment of this memorial highway back in 1933[8].

Located on the shoreline of the Mississippi River, Red Wing boasts of its Colvill Park, just off Highway 61, on the land that formerly had been the Colvills' 98-acre farm. Birdwatchers flock there to see wintering bald eagles, and to admire migrating ducks in the spring and fall seasons. Dianne Hoffbeck photo, 2024.

Barn Bluff -- Red Wing, B.F. Upton. N.Y. Public LIbrary Digital Collections.

CHAPTER EIGHTEEN
Legacies Of William Colvill, Regimental Reunions

Those researchers and historians, who like me have looked into the life of Colonel William Colvill have reported that they were unable to really know the deep essence of the life of this man because he left only a handful of written items. Colvill was really good at writing about the Battle of Bull Run, and he eventually gave his own account of the Second Day of Gettysburg and the "Charge of the First Minnesota." His actions told more about him than did his words----because he did not write much about himself and did not leave a written record of his inner thoughts. It appears that Colonel Colvill did not write introspectively because he did not wish to boost his own fame. But then, the terrible nature of combat with the resultant blood and gore combined with the sadness that came with the deaths of those he was leading into battle could bring nightmares, and by leaving those horrors of warfare in the past, Colvill could ease his mind.

For example, when the First Minnesota Regiment held its fourth annual reunion in 1870, the men called upon Colonel Colvill to give a speech, but "he declined making any extended remarks." Instead, speaking cryptically, he said "that if we were in some places where we have been," meaning that if he were with them on a major battlefield of the Civil War, then "I *should* have a speech to make, and it should be to tell you to 'advance,' and I should follow not far behind."[1]

His former-soldiers gave him "cheers," for this. They cheered because whenever the First Minnesota was called upon to advance upon Confederate troops on those battlefields, the privates and corporals and sergeants formed the front line, and the Colonel and other field officers were positioned *BEHIND* the battle-line. At Gettysburg, as explained by Civil War historian Wayne D. Jorgenson, Colonel "Colvill was thirty paces behind" his men so that he could "see what was happening with the regiment" and could give orders to adjust the direction or speed of the charge in real time.[2]

While this position behind the front line could seem to be a safer place, it was not. The Rebel soldiers would deliberately look for the officers and aim at them, in order to remove the leadership. Wearing an officer's uniform made each one a target for enemy fire, and the fact that Colvill, at six-foot-five-inches tall, stood taller than the rest of his regiment made him a *big* target.[3]

Even though Colvill did not write much about himself, there were plenty of lifelong friends and fellow Civil War soldiers who *did* write about him.

And so it seems that the greatest legacy of Colonel Colvill was the esteem that was expressed by the men in his regiment, for Colvill knew how to treat people the right way. Expressions of appreciation came to the Colonel from his men through the years, especially at the annual reunions of the regiment. Colvill, like many others, was "never more at home than when attending a reunion" of the old soldiers."[4]

The First Minnesota Volunteer Regiment held reunions every year from the year 1867 until about 1930, when there were only a few of the "Last Men" remaining.[5]

One of those regimental reunions, the 17th annual reunion, held in Minneapolis in 1884, provided a perspective on Colvill and his fellow soldiers. The officers and enlisted men, these veterans, lined up at Lake Calhoun and then marched to the banqueting hall at the Lyndale Hotel. As always, the Colonel was at the "center of an admiring group of old fellow fighters," and "his giant form" made him a "marked figure anywhere." His clothing and the way that he acted showed very "little of the pomp and pride of war," instead his appearance was "plain and unpretending."[6]

When the veterans of the First Minnesota began to march from the lakeshore to the hotel, Colvill was with them, but not in the forefront. His bad leg made it hard for him to go as fast as the rest of them. It was a sentimental sight for those who saw him limping, with his walking-cane, "bobbling bravely along, trying hard to keep the step."[7]

Clearly, there was a deep devotion of the soldiers of the 'Old Minnesota Regiment' to Colvill and his popularity among his men "almost amounted to worship," and they looked "toward him with the affection a son should bear to a father." He was their hero, their idol, because he had led them through those three perilous years of war from 1861 through 1864.[8]

They trusted that he would not put them into situations of needless danger. And when the emergency situation arose at Gettysburg on that fateful day of the 'famous charge,' they did it because Colvill was willing to do it with them.

This is what they had to say about the man regarding his courage and his leadership, and, sometimes, about how his gruff exterior masked his warm heart.

"I remember a dozen incidents," recalled Martin Maginnis, "of what seemed a want of comprehension of danger, so absolute was his indifference when duty called on him to take the chances of wounds or death." At the battle of Bull Run, Colvill had gone "forward further than any of our men, into a woods that was filled with the enemy and . . . escaped capture on that ill-fated field which he was one of the very last to leave. It was always the same, in the battles of the Peninsula, at South Mountain and Antietam, Fredericksburg, Chancellorsville," he had "faced death . . . on the open field."[9]

"How well was he fitted," wrote Maginnis, "to lead the regiment at the supreme moment . . . at Gettysburg." The 'Charge of the First Minnesota' was a "feat of arms" that had "gone on into history," and was considered to be "most useful to our country, most glorious to our state, and *most destructive* to our regiment." Colonel Colvill "was left alive" after being shot twice at that battle, and "after a desperate struggle with his wounds," but was "a wreck" of what had been "one of the finest and strongest physical forms into which a man was ever moulded," turning his "heroic form" into being a "constant sufferer for many long years."[10]

Admiration for Colvill also came from Charles L. Hubbs, who wrote a letter in 1928, long after the events, but written with sincere devotion. "Colonel Colvill," recalled Hubbs, "came nearest to a god-father I ever had."[11]

William Colvill and his soldiers had more drudgery than perilous action during their war service. The Colonel was revered by his men for guiding the regiment through the Civil War from 1861 to 1864. Illustration entitled "Army of the Potomac, Sleeping On Their Arms," Harper's Weekly, 1864 (formerly attributed to Winslow Homer).
Credit: Metropolitan Museum of Art. Public domain.

"It was only through his great personality and determination," wrote Hubbs, "that I was permitted to become a member of the First Minnesota," back in May of 1861, when Charles Hubbs (1843-1931) tried to enlist in Colvill's Company F, when more volunteers were needed due to a change in term of service.[12]

When Assistant Surgeon Charles Le Boutillier was examining Hubbs and about a dozen other volunteers for inclusion in the regiment, the surgeon was looking him over, and he declared that Hubbs was "too small and too young for service and could not or would not be accepted" because he was only 18 years old and was only "five feet eight inches in height" and was too skinny.

At that moment, "Colvill, whom I had never before met," remembered Hubbs, "protested, saying he wanted me in his company," and "a hot argument ensued."

"To my delight," wrote Hubbs, "the assistant surgeon lost in the count." And "from that hour on," William Colvill and Private Hubbs were forever bonded in a "real" friendship, as far as Hubbs was concerned.

Hubbs also recalled a "few minor incidents . . . probably not now remembered by any now living aside from myself." He said that "at the first 'Bull Run' where the 'First' received its baptism of fire, James Imeson" and Hubbs "brought in a prisoner" from the Confederate lines.

Private Imeson and Private Hubbs reported to Colvill while the First Minnesota was "hotly engaged with the enemy."

Imeson said: "Captain, I have a prisoner. What shall I do with him?"

Captain Colvill "cooly replied, 'Oh, I guess we'd better kill him.' (Of course with no intention of so doing.)"

Then, immediately "following his remark, he drew a very small revolver from its holster and fired a shot about a foot to one side and past the prisoner's head."

As Hubbs related the story: "If that Johnny [Rebel] was not plenty scared, then his actions failed to indicate his feelings." Captain Colvill ordered him to the rear of our line with the injunction to 'keep going.' The last seen of him he was breaking the record for speed."

Mr. Hubbs, filled with admiration and gratitude for all Colvill had done for him, wrote about another incident at Bull Run in June of 1861, when Hubbs gave Colvill a gift.

"Up to the time of this battle," recalled Hubbs, "the captain had never possessed an officer's sword," although "he did have a non-com's (non-commissioned officer) little 'toad sticker' . . . which he carried under his arm instead of suspended from the belt. The weapon . . . was decidedly out of proportion to his massive size."

"I happened," wrote Hubbs, "to come into possession of a good-looking cavalryman's sabre with a bright metal scabbard. I took my find to the captain and as I handed it to him remarked, 'Captain, I think this more becoming than the one you've been carrying.'"

"Receiving it with apparent pleasure and thanks," Colvill "attached it to the belt with no apparent concern of the bullets which were thickly whistling by in close proximity. Breaking the apology for a sword over his knee, he cast it from him."

Hubbs marveled: "At all times under fire," the captain's "coolness and poise amounted to almost indifference, and that coolness, considering his exterior surface, was very reassuring to us little fellows who presented so much less" size for stopping passing bullets.

"With Colonel Colvill, the care and comfort of his men was a first thought. He was justly proud of his command and so far as able saw to it that it had 'first place' in every important undertaking," including the "second battle of Fredericksburg, ... Colvill was proud of the fact that his regiment had a part in accomplishing all . . . that was expected of it" throughout the Civil War.

For Mr. Hubbs, he held dearly to his memories of Captain Colvill because Hubbs was wounded and captured at Bull Run. Hubbs was imprisoned for ten months, first in Richmond, Virginia, at Libby Prison, thence sent to Parish Prison in New Orleans, and, finally, to Salisbury, North Carolina, before being paroled and returned to his regiment. At Gettysburg, Hubbs and his Company F were not in the famous charge on July 2, 1863, but Charles Hubbs was in the thick of things with Company F as skirmishers nearby; and, the next day, July 3rd, Hubbs served in the "face of Pickett's great charge." Hubbs "fought until he fell," being wounded twice at Cemetery Ridge.[13]

Hubbs was put in the field hospital the night of July 3rd, "with two bullets in his body," one in his leg and one in his arm, near his wrist, "but not seriously wounded." Hubbs recalled that the rain was "pouring down in torrents" in the night. Private Hubbs remembered that he "lay not exceeding four feet" from Colonel Colvill who had been "critically wounded" on July 2, and Colvill had not yet had medical attention.[14]

A number of soldiers from the First Minnesota regiment lay there "all night long on the bare ground without cover," and "although suffering intensely," Colvill "was solicitous as to the comfort of his men." There was "not a word from him as to his own greater wounds----no word of complaint---just words of cheer and encouragement to the many others about him" and when "morning came he asked that others be cared for before himself."

"I mention this . . . . from personal knowledge," wrote Hubbs, "as indicating his unselfishness and his fortitude."

Colvill was "ever brave, gentle, kind and tolerant."

All of these uplifting things that have been written about Colvill are like the two large statues of the man, showing the surface of his personality, but what about was underneath the bronzed, hardened skin?

Within Colvill, and within each of the men of the First Minnesota, were 'invisible wounds.'

Seeing so much death in a battle gave each of these Minnesotans varying degrees of what was then known as the 'Soldier's Heart.'

To witness the sudden death of your friend in the blue uniform, or to carry your gravely wounded brother-in-arms to the field hospital was like a thorn in his heart that could not be pulled out, that, try as you might, a pain that would never go away.

Colvill and his comrades could talk about the war and the battles with each other, and they needed to meet together, but they could not speak of the depth of what they had experienced at Gettysburg or Antietam or Bull Run with those who had not been there with them. There were some things that happened that not everyone could understand. War was filled with blood, suffering and death. The worst time was at Gettysburg, which had been "such an awful universe of battle."[15]

When Martin Maginnis wrote home to Red Wing in June of 1862, he said the 1st Minnesota "fought a bloody battle Saturday and yesterday" at Fair Oaks, and "conquered gloriously." Yet "the field is a *most terrible sight,*" he wrote, "covered with *10,000 dead and wounded, beside what were buried and cared for.*"[16]

The glory and the ghastly were all somehow mixed together, so that Maginnis made sure to write home so that he could "write to relieve Red Wing people of anxiety" for their loved ones in the battle.[17]

Two themes predominated in the years of the Civil War: Love and Death. No one could be sure how long life would last in wartime. Artist Thomas Nast depicted a soldier and his family on Christmas Eve of 1862. Homesickness; worry; a shipwrecked Union, frozen graves, and St. Nicholas were in the minds of soldiers and families alike, "praying for one another." Title: Christmas Eve, 1862 (from Harper's Weekly, 1863). Credit: Metropolitan Museum of Art. Public domain.

As a song of that war put it---written by Stephen Foster:
"Was My Brother in the Battle?"

Tell me, tell me weary soldier/
From the rude and stirring wars/
Was my brother in the battle
Where you gained those noble scars?/
He was ever brave and valiant,/
and I know he never fled,/
Was his name among the wounded/
Or numbered with the dead?/

Was my brother in the battle/
when the tide of war ran high?/
You would know him in a moment/
By his dark and flashing eyes./

Tell me, tell me, weary soldier/
Will he never come again/
Did he suffer with the wounded/
Or die among the slain?/

Was my brother in the battle/
When the noble Highland host/
Were so wrongfully outnumbered/
On the Carolina coast?/
Did he struggle for the Union/
Mid the thunder and the rain,/
Till he fell among the brave/
On a bleak Virginia plain?/

Oh, I'm sure that he was dauntless/
And his courage never lagged/
By contending for the honor/
Of a dear and cherished flag./

Tell me, tell me, weary soldier,/
Will he never come again/
Did he suffer with the wounded/
Or die among the slain?/

Was my brother in the battle/
When the flag of Erin came/
To the rescue of our banner/
And protection of our fame,/
While the fleet from off the water/
Poured out terror and dismay/
Till the bold and wearying foe/
Fell like leaves of Autumn day?/

When the bugle called to battle/
And the cannon deeply roared,/
Oh! I wish I could have seen him/
Draw his sharp and glittering sword./

Tell me, tell me, weary soldier/
Will he never come again,/
Did he suffer with the wounded/
Or die among the slain?[18]

In regards to the aftermath of battles, another soldier wrote about the supposed glory of war, twenty years after his heart was wounded by his combat experience. Before the Civil War he had read about "many battle scenes . . . and . . . the impressions they made upon my mind----impressions and visions of glory" that inspired the "desire to 'go in on a rush and clean out the foe," by being "in a 'brilliant charge'" and come out alive---- "covered with glory . . . for our dear country's sake."[19]

This soldier wrote that war was presented as glorious and that young men were "taught to "believe that it is fun to take part in a battle."

These "notions of war" got obliterated by experience in a battle. There was a dreadful "difference between a battle on paper" when the reader was "seated in an easy chair reading of 'charges'" and actually taking a place in the front lines and staring face-to-face with the "chances of one in two or three to get out alive" and unharmed.

It was a jolting shock for the Minnesotans in the first battle at Bull Run to witness the death of Captain Lewis McKune, when he was "shot through the heart and fell dead instantly." Later, in 1863, it was a frightful sight to see that Private Isaac Taylor of Company E had been killed by an artillery shell that struck him on the "top of his head" and then went out of his body "through his back, cutting his belt in two," during the famous 'Charge at Gettysburg.' When one of the Minnesotans wrote home about battles, they left out the details of dying, leaving out the "unutterable horror" of it all.[20]

The "sober truth" of the Union and Confederate soldiers clashing at Plum Run creek bed with point-blank shooting and piercing-bayonets and close-range pistol shots and clubbing of rifle-butts, with cannonballs and exploding shells and canister shots thudding into bodies, was that it was a "murder-mill," and those who managed to live through it would "never be able to get the terrible picture out of their minds."[21]

When these soldiers saw hundreds around them being punctured or mangled by weapons of war, the images of the battles "got jammed into that wedge that stuck in our lives and remained there."

Every time that Colonel Colvill or another man of the First Minnesota would have a "restless dream," whether from going to sleep "while lying on his back," or being "delirious with fever," or "whenever his mind is disordered, night or day" after the time of the battle-shock, especially in a 'glorious' charge down the slope of Cemetery Ridge, it all could come back into mind. It could be the "visions of disfigured faces, with the black blood spouting out of their mouths; a crushed skull---or a rent side, or head crushed; arms and legs torn off---shrieks----groans----yells----every noise that agonized and terrified men," the visions----suddenly appearing, "like every woe on earth----it all returns, more terrible than any nightmare;

-------because it was real."[22]

In Old Testament times, David, the psalmist and warrior, wrote:

"How long must I wrestle with my thoughts

and day after day have sorrows in my heart?" (Psalm 13:2, New International Version).

This was the reality of "soldier's heart," as experienced in the Civil War and in other wars from time immemorial. The same thing today is known as "Post-Traumatic Stress Disorder," or "Shell-Shock" from World War I, or "Battle Fatigue" in the time of World War II. The First Minnesota had "marched down to the battlefield, the hospital, the grave," all the way to 'Death's Door.'[23]

For William Colvill, there was a great need for healing after the war, yet it seems that just like his foot and ankle never fully healed, maybe his mind had to put away the images of battle in order to live each day without staring into the past.

It would appear that his marriage to Jane was a way to get healing, by means of her love and companionship through their shared life.

Likely his time on the land near Grand Marais was a form of healing for him.

Doubtless he loved the lands and scenery surrounding Red Wing, for he had written about the meadows and prairies and woods just outside of the town, back in the year 1859, prior to the turmoils of wartime: "Up on the prairies, they say, the breeze is rustling over the wheat fields and thro' the corn. How beautiful is the grand swell of the green sward, rolling off until far away it mingles with and is lost in the sky."[24]

The groves of oak trees and maple trees, wrote Colvill, were "like islands floating beautifully on the sea," and the clouds above were "other islands."

He loved the "sweet-scented harvest fields" where he could hear the scythe-cradles "sliding gracefully thro' the grain."

The sounds of the "tinkling cowbells" and the "ceaseless hum of the bees and flies," along with the "gently rippling brook" were "all befitting, and harmonizing with, a tranquil frame of mind."

"So if you are tired and listless and depressed," advised Colonel Colvill, "betake yourself to the lovely prairies." Then you would "experience the miraculous and happy change . . . in all your feelings and sentiments" among the "wonderful harmonies of nature."

Civil War veterans like William Colvill wished to return to their former lives, but sometimes their thoughts remained on the battlefield. The wheat fields near Red Wing were alive with the sounds of scythes in the late summer of 1865 and Colvill saw the golden harvest that contrasted with the bloody battles in some wheat fields out east during the war. Winslow Homer captured the hope and regret of "The Veteran in a New Field" in his 1865 painting. The reaper could mow wheat or he could mow clover for hay. Either way, the aftermath of the war spoke of love and loss. The word "aftermath" meant "after the mowing," when the clover would grow back anew, just like after the battle, the soldier might recover from his wounds.
Credit: Metropolitan Museum of Art. Public domain.

CHAPTER NINETEEN
In Closing

The purpose of this book is to preserve in one volume what might reasonably want to be known about William Colvill and Martin Maginnis, with a focus of these two as representatives of the 1,000 men of the First Minnesota Volunteer Regiment.

It might be useful to find out what they had learned along the way to Gettysburg.

It might be good to know what they came to understand about war and life and death and faith and brotherhood. They had seen so much death and the war had bound them together.

As these men from Minnesota grew older, they became aware of their own place in U.S. history as writers compared the deeds of the First Minnesota Volunteer Regiment to other classic tales of courageous resistance against seemingly-impossible odds.

Some writers noted similarities with the famous 1854 "Charge of the Light Brigade," when a British cavalry unit, "*the six hundred*," made a hopeless advance against the Russians at Balaklava in the Crimean War. The Light Brigade responded to ill-advised orders by commanders who sent them to be decimated by artillery.[1]

The bravery of the 600 was commemorated by Alfred, Lord Tennyson (1809-1892) in his poetry:

""Forward, the Light Brigade!"
Was there a man dismay'd?
Not tho' the soldier knew
Some one had blunder'd:
Theirs not to make reply,

Theirs not to reason why,
Theirs but to do and die:
Into the valley of Death
Rode the six hundred."

Another common comparison was with the ancient Spartans, when Sparta and the other Greek states blocked the advance of the Persians at a narrow passage at Thermopylae, (480 B.C.). King Leonidas and his 300 Spartans delayed the Persian hordes of Xerxes but could not withstand their overwhelming numbers. These powerfully-fierce, skilled warriors made a heroic stand against great odds as recorded by Herodotus, the historian, and, much later, as graphically filmed by Zach Snyder in "*300*," memorably, in 2006. "Go tell the Spartans," Herodotus wrote, "that here we lie, faithful to their orders," informing the world that Spartans would not retreat. The Greeks were inspired to unite to deter Xerxes and eventually placed a stone marker at the battle-site with the defiant message inscribed upon it. Centuries later, Greece built a stone lion monument there to honor Leonidas.[2]

The U.S. Senator from Minnesota, Cushman K. Davis (1838-1900), gave a speech in 1897 at Gettysburg, wherein he declared that the soldiers of the First Minnesota who had "died in defense of the laws" while making their famous charge should be glorified "with equal justice," as the 300 Spartans of ancient time. The 300 at Thermopylae had died to defend Greek democracy, while the 262 from Minnesota had fought to uphold American democracy (the republic). The fact that Gettysburg was a major turning-point in the Civil War, also ensured that slavery, the worst curse in U.S. history, would end, because the South had lost its hopes of winning the war.[3]

Martin Maginnis said, in 1882, that the Gettysburg 'Charge of the First Minnesota' was, "indeed, the Thermopylae of the Regiment," in its "heroic daring."[4]

Some who have studied the Civil War might downgrade the significance of the "Charge of the First Minnesota," in the sense that other regiments assuredly could have responded to General Winfield S. Hancock's order in the same obedient way that these Minnesota soldiers responded. However, Hancock had placed the Minnesota regiment in a strategic location so that the 1st Minnesota would be there when he needed them.

When General Hancock was asked why he had put the Minnesotans into the famous charge, sending them to "be slaughtered," he said (according to widely-published newspaper articles published in 1885 and 1886): "I would have done it if I had been morally certain that every man of them would be killed. They were put there because I knew they were fighters. I wanted just five minutes to get my line [of reinforcements] up, and they gave me just that. It was the best fighting of the whole war."[5]

The well-trained soldiers of the 1st Minnesota obeyed like a "living machine" when Colonel Colvill responded to General Hancock's orders on that day, and this "living machine" went into "instant action, and the column was deployed into the line of battle."[6]

One of the Minnesota men, Samuel Lilly of Company G, was able to go back to Gettysburg in 1913 for the 50th anniversary of the battle. Mr. Lilly stood again on Cemetery Ridge, and he spoke about his experience in the famous "charge." He said: "As I look down the field where we charged, I can almost hear again the command to start, forward march, trail arms. And then after the first plunge, the impact with the enemy----we were but a handful, and there seemed to be no earthly chance for us; but we went on because Minnesota had sent us. All we wanted was to fire a volley that would throw the enemy into temporary confusion. We fired and the confusion was a fact. Before they had recovered, we were reinforced, although the sacrifice had been pitiful. *I dropped wounded.*"[7]

"When I think of that day," continued Samuel Lilly, "when 262 First Minnesota men stood here, and twenty minutes later there were 215 of them dead or bleeding from wounds . . . . It was an awful sacrifice, but we are all glad that Minnesota had a chance to show the stuff its men were made of; *and we would do it again if we had to.*"[8]

General Winfield S. Hancock, who gave the order to charge there at the Battle of Gettysburg on July 2, 1863, was reported to have made this famous statement about the 1st Minnesota; and it must be included in this book:

"There is no more gallant deed recorded in history. I ordered those men in there because I saw that I must gain five minutes' time. Reinforcements were coming on the run, but I knew that before they could reach the threatened point the Confederates, unless checked, would seize the position. I would have ordered that regiment in if I had known every man would be killed. It had to be done, and I was glad to find such a gallant body of men at hand, willing to make the terrible sacrifice that the occasion demanded."[9]

Some visitors to the Cannon Falls cemetery place a coin on the gravestone of Colonel William Colvill and his wife, Jane E. Colvill, as a sign of respect and to honor the lives of these revered Minnesotans.

APPENDIX
Questions That Remain To Be Answered

In writing about William Colvill and Martin Maginnis, there were many issues that had to be faced, many rabbit-holes to hop into, and some questions that had only partial answers.

How much can be known about two men from the past?

The sources of information were plentiful in numbers, yet limited in scope.

Why did Colonel Colvill smile in the middle of the Battle of Gettysburg when he and his regiment were ordered to charge towards the Confederate forces on July 2, 1863?

There was nothing humorous happening at that moment, so levity would not be the answer.

Maybe Colvill thought that marching forward with his men was his fate.

The smile might have been more of a painful grimace, with his teeth showing, or, most likely, Colonel Colvill's brave face.

Bravery.

Those in the regiment said he was powerfully brave, as William Lochren said: "he was cool and imperturbable in battle and never showed any evidence of fear." A smile of any sort, with his men watching, would be the exact opposite of a fearful face.[1]

As quoted before in this volume, John Milton wrote about "victorious agonies," a phrase that applies to Colonel Colvill and his First Minnesota Regiment on that day at Cemetery Ridge.[2]

Most likely, no one can ever know why "Colvill smiled."

I began the "Prologue" with an Old Testament quotation, and I end with an Old Testament quote, one that best explains the unknowns in Colonel William Colvill's life:

"Each Heart Knows Its Own Bitterness,
And No One Else Can Fully Share Its Joy."
Proverbs 14: 10.

The whole story of what was in the heart and mind of William Colvill will never be completely known, just like the sketch of an unidentified officer at Gettysburg leading an advance is incomplete. Colvill was on foot during the charge at Gettysburg, but, as an officer, he rode his horse much of the time. Artist: Alfred R. Waud (1828-1891). Credit: Library of Congress. Public domain.

EPILOGUE

It has been said that war comes to every generation in U.S. history. For my Baby Boomers generation, it was Vietnam and before us, there had been the Korean War; World War II; World War I, the Spanish-American War of 1898, basically, endless wars because men will always get into fights with other men. Men will offend neighboring men, they will dispute, fuss, feud, and throw elbows at minimum, and, as things worsen, threaten, kill, and destroy.

The Civil War was the biggest event in U.S. history. Would the U.S. remain as a nation? Would this experiment in democracy, this republic, endure?

The young men in Red Wing answered the questions, believing that the U.S.A. was worth fighting for. So they volunteered in 1861.

At what price? Their lives.

In researching the story of Colvill and Maginnis, I came upon an obscure newspaper article from the *Red Wing Advance Sun*. Written in 1890, and then printed on paper for circulation in the city and in Goodhue County, this article might have been saved by a few people, and then the newspaper was thrown away. Copies of that particular newspaper were kept in the local archives and in the Minnesota Historical Society's collections and, ultimately, microfilmed and unlikely to be easily found. Recently, however, the Red Wing Public Library digitized some old newspapers, and it was relatively easy to search and find this article, just by looking for the search-term "Colvill."

Here is the article, describing Red Wing in 1861 and telling about the raw emotions with the onset of war; the vital enthusiasm of Colvill and Maginnis and Welch in volunteering; and the bitter-

C. C. WEBSTER.

As an eyewitness to the events of April 1861, Charles C. Webster later wrote about his friends and neighbors volunteering to be in Company F, the Goodhue County Volunteers, of the First Minnesota Regiment. Eloquently, he described what it was like to see the Red Wing 'soldier boys' going away to Fort Snelling in the springtime of that fateful year, leaving their loved ones at home. (He wrote his recollections in 1890).

sweetness of the goodbyes at the town's riverfront, as the steamboat left Red Wing to take the men upriver to Fort Snelling.

C.C. Webster wrote it. So I looked up the information, on-line, about Charles Carroll Webster (1824-1893). Born in Vermont, and a graduate of the University of Vermont, class of 1851, he came to Minnesota, to Zumbrota, in 1856. Webster was a lawyer, admitted to the bar in 1858 and he moved from Zumbrota to Red Wing to become the Register of Deeds for Goodhue County in 1860. When the war began in 1861, C.C. Webster was 37 years old with a wife, Elizabeth, and three young children, ages 3, 5, and 7.

This is what he wrote, beautifully, in my estimation.

"Reminiscences of Early Days." [By C.C. Webster.] *Red Wing Advance Sun*, Nov. 26, 1890, on page 7. [All words by Webster, hence, no quotation marks.]

The tidings of the attack on Fort Sumter, and the defense made by the gallant little band within, flew upon the wings of lightning to every part of the land. Throughout the North there was a general uprising of the people. Patriotism triumphed over party. Red Wing and Goodhue County were no exception.

Republicans, Douglas Democrats, and Breckinridge Democrats vied with each other in patriotic expressions of indignation at the warlike attack upon the integrity of the union and at the dishonor to the flag.

War, grim war, by this act of the rebels was now an assured fact.

President Lincoln's call for 75,000 men to repair to Washington at once for the defense of the capitol, came simultaneously with the news of the fall of Sumter.

When I went down town in the morning, men were running to and fro with blanched faces, clenched fists, and teeth set in determined indignation.

. . . . The evening came and the court room was crowded to overflowing.

Judge Welch was made chairman of the meeting. He took the chair and opened the meeting with a patriotic speech, urging the raising of a company in Goodhue County at once.

His gifted son, A.E. [A. Edwards, "Ed," told about earlier in this book] Welch, after whom the Grand Army of the Republic Post at Red Wing is named, made one of the most eloquent speeches of the evening.

Hamline University was there in the person of its students and faculty and helped raise the spirits of the meeting to fever heat. Lengthened details cannot be given.

It was resolved to raise a company in Goodhue County. A committee was appointed to solicit enlistments. Little solicitation was necessary.

I happened to be one of that committee. Early next morning, I started for Zumbrota, my old home. The news of the fall of Sumter and the call for volunteers preceded me. I conferred with the leading men there. A public meeting was called for the evening. Runners were sent into all the country round about.

A crowd assembled in the public hall in the evening. It required little effort to arouse them. They were already full of patriotic enthusiasm. Six young men came forward and said they would accompany me to Red Wing next morning.

Next morning came. The young men kept their word.

I reached Red Wing about noon. Nearly one hundred men had already offered their services.

Captain A.D. Whitney, who had been connected with a military organization at the east, was the only man in Red Wing who had knowledge of military tactics and drill. He was already drilling squads of volunteers.

Before night, the company had reached a full hundred and more.

The governor was telegraphed, offering the services of the volunteers. The offer was accepted.

The whole town was converted into a busy hive of preparation. The women vied with the men in fitting out the volunteer soldier boys.

Meantime squads continued to drill under Capt. Whitney, and, after a little, tried it on their own account.

The volunteers were to take the steamboat for Fort Snelling on Sunday.

The company had organized by electing officers. William Colvill was elected captain and A.E. Welch one of the lieutenants. I have forgotten the other officers.

Saturday night the volunteers met at the court house, together with the citizens. Speeches were made by both citizens and soldiers.

The next day, about noon, I think, Co. F., of the Minnesota First, marched to the levee in their motley uniforms, or without uniform.

Nearly the entire population of the city and many from the country gathered there on the banks of the Father of Waters to bid adieu and God-speed to the soldier boy.

There were tears and sobs in that assembled throng.

War was a new experience.

How many agonizing hearts were there.

The brave boys themselves turned away their faces that the trickling tear might not be seen.

The volunteers were drawn upon the levee. Solemnity pervaded every heart. Prayer was offered. "America" was sung.

Matthew Sorin mounted on a dry goods box. He had been selected to make the parting address, and for half an hour poured out a strain of eloquence, mingled with patriotism and pathos that I have never heard surpassed, rarely equaled.

The steamer's whistle was heard behind Barn Bluff. Heart throbs became stronger, and tears flowed more freely.

Wives and sisters and mothers and sweethearts flew to have a final hand shake and to imprint a parting kiss.

The steamer came along side of the levee. With a light step but with heavy hearts the boys embarked.

The plank was drawn in. The huge wheels of the steamer began to move. The vast crowd on the levee stood as if transfixed, waving hats and handkerchiefs, which salute was returned by the boys by the waving of hats and by rousing cheers, till the steamer passed out of sight.

No more thrilling scene occurred during the war.

It was the first experience in that dreadful contest, the prelude to the awful scenes which were to follow in the succeeding months and years.

ACKNOWLEDGMENTS

I want to acknowledge those who have helped me to write this book about two men from Red Wing, Minnesota. May the legend of the epic charge of the First Minnesota never die.

My deepest gratitude goes to my wife Dianne for contributing to this work in so many ways, through proofreading, and through her love and support, and her sense of humor. Together we went to Cannon Falls and Welch and Red Wing and St. Paul, and had fun along the way.

My thanks go to Stephen Osman, retired manager of Historic Fort Snelling and author of *Fort Snelling and the Civil War*, for sharing his expertise and photographs. I also say "thank you" to Wayne Jorgenson, author of *Every Man Did His Duty: Pictures and Stories of the Men of the First Minnesota*, for his insights into Colonel Colvill's story.

I am greatly indebted to Kevin Clementson, my old friend from Erskine via Bemidji State University, who earned his Master of Divinity at Gettysburg Seminary and who gave a personalized tour of the battlefield for me (and Dianne & John W. Hoffbeck, and aunt Muffy Dickinson) back in 2017.

I owe special thanks to Kip Johnson, truly a godsend, for his graphic design work to masterfully tie this book together for self-publishing.

Thanks, too, to Rich Iverson, Nathan Peterson, Todd Lenz, and Jon Iverson, my fellow book-club friends, for their careful reading and editing of this manuscript.

I sincerely appreciate research-assistance given me in Red Wing at the Goodhue County Historical Society by Robin Wipperling, Bethany Nelson, and Liz Schmidt. Thanks, also, to Laura Durenberger-Grunow, at Grand Marais' Cook County Historical Society, for help with photographs from up north.

Special thanks go to Daryl Hoffbeck, and his wife, Joan, of Legacy Hill Farm near Welch, Minnesota, and Britni Nordine for their help with stained-glass window photos; and their encouragement for this book project. Thanks, also, to Brad Tengesdal for informing me of the Welch window's location.

And I thank God for giving me life and health so that I am able to write about Minnesota's history as I get older and older.

BIBLIOGRAPHY

Books

Alleman, Tillie Pierce. *At Gettysburg Or What A Girl Saw And Heard Of The Battle.* New York: W. Lake Borland, 1889.

A.N. Marquis & Company's Handy Business Directory of Chicago. Chicago: A.N. Marquis & Company, 1886.

Blegen, Theodore C. *Minnesota: A History of the State.* Minneapolis: University of Minnesota Press, 1975.

Curtiss-Wedge, Franklyn. *History of Goodhue County, Minnesota.* Chicago: H.C. Cooper, Jr., & Co., 1909.

Curtiss-Wedge, Franklyn. *History of Rice and Steele Counties, Minnesota*, Vol. I. Chicago: H.C. Cooper, Jr., and Co., 1910.

Dawes, Rufus R. *Service with the Sixth Wisconsin Volunteers.* Marietta, Ohio: E.E. Alderman & Sons, 1890.

Dodge, Theodore Ayrault. *Great Captains*, Vol IV. Boston: Houghton, Mifflin and Co., 1907.

Donald, David Herbert. *Lincoln.* New York: Simon & Schuster, 1995.

Folwell, William Watts. *A History of Minnesota*, Volume II. St. Paul: MHS Press, 1961.

Fox, William F. *Regimental Losses in the American Civil War, 1861-1865.* Albany, NY: Albany Publishing Co., 1889.

Green, William D. *A Peculiar Imbalance: The Rise and Fall of Racial Equality in Minnesota, 1837-1869.* St. Paul: University of Minnesota Press, 2015.

Grossman, Lt. Col. Dave. *On Killing.* Boston: Little, Brown and Company, 1996.

Hancock, Joseph Woods. *Goodhue County Minnesota: Past and Present.* Red Wing: Red Wing Printing, 1893.

Hand, Daniel. "Reminiscences of an Army Surgeon," *Glimpses of the Nation's Struggle*, Vol. 1. St. Paul: St. Paul Book and Stationery Company, 1887.

Haskell, Frank A. *The Battle of Gettysburg.* Madison: Wisconsin History Commission, 1908.

History of Goodhue County. Red Wing: Wood, Alley & Co., 1878.

History of the Hamline University of Minnesota When Located at Red Wing, Minnesota From 1854 to 1869. St. Paul: Hamline University Alumni Association, 1907.

Holmes, Oliver Wendell, Junior. *Speeches By Oliver Wendell Holmes, Junior*. Boston: Little, Brown, and Company, 1891.

Imholte, John Quinn. *The First Volunteers: History of the First Minnesota Volunteer Regiment, 1861-1865*. Minneapolis: Ross & Haines, 1963.

Jorgenson, Wayne D. *Every Man Did His Duty: Pictures and Stories of the Men of the First Minnesota*. Minneapolis: Tasora, 2012.

Junkin, D.H. and Frank H. Norton. *The Life of Winfield Scott Hancock*. New York: D. Appleton and Company, 1880.

Krom, Richard, ed. *The 1ˢᵗ Minnesota: Second To None*. Rochester: Richard Krom, 2010.

Lee, Arthur O. *Leftover Lutefisk: More Stories from the Lutefisk Ghetto*. Cambridge, MN: Adventure Publications, 1984.

Leehan, Brian. *Pale Horse at Plum Run: The First Minnesota at Gettysburg*. St. Paul: MHS Press, 2002.

Marquis, Albert Nelson, ed. *The Book of Minnesotans*. Chicago: A.N. Marquis and Company, 1907.

McPherson, James M. *Battle Cry of Freedom: The Civil War Era*. New York: Oxford University Press, 1988.

Milton, John. *Paradise Lost*, Book I. New York: Effingham Maynard & Co., 1889.

Moe, Richard. *The Last Full Measure: The Life and Death of the First Minnesota Volunteers*. St. Paul: MHS Press,1993.

Minnesota in the Civil and Indian Wars, Vol. II. St. Paul: Pioneer Press Company, 1893.

Stephen E. Osman. *Fort Snelling and the Civil War*. St. Paul: Ramsey County Historical Society, 2017.

Roberts, Thomas S. *Birds of Minnesota*, Vol. 1. Minneapolis: University of Minnesota Press, 1932.

Ronan, Margaret. *Girl From The Gulches: The Story Of Mary Ronan*. Helena: Montana Historical Society, 2003.

St. Paul, Minnesota, Directory for 1867. St. Paul: Bailey and Wolfe, Publishers, 1867.

Sanders, Helen Fitzgerald. *History of Montana*, Vol. I. Chicago: Lewis Publishing Company, 1913.

Searles, Jasper N. "The First Minnesota Volunteer Infantry," *Glimpses of the Nation's Struggle*, Vol. 2. St. Paul: St. Paul Book and Stationery Company, 1890.

Sears, Stephen W. *Gettysburg*. Boston: Houghton Mifflin Company, 2003.

Soldiers of the American Revolution: Who Were At One Time Residents Of, Or Whose Graves Are Located In Chautauqua County, New York. Chautauqua County, NY, 1925.

Shakespeare, William. *Shakespeare: The Complete Works*. New York: Harcourt, Brace & World, Inc., 1968.

Tanner, George Clinton. *Fifty Years of Church Work in the Diocese of Minnesota, 1857-1907*. St. Paul: Committee of Publication, 1909.

Tolstoy, Leo. *War and Peace*. New York: Barnes & Noble Classics, 2005.

Warner, George E. and Charles M. Foote. *History of Ramsey County and the City of St. Paul*. Minneapolis: North Star Publishing Co., 1881.

Webster, Noah. *An American Dictionary of the English Language*. New York: S. Converse, 1828.

Wert, Jeffrey D. *Gettysburg: Day Three*. New York: Simon & Schuster, 2001.

Williams, James Grant and John Fiske, eds. *Appleton's Cyclopedia of American Biography*, Vol. V. New York: D. Appleton and Company, 1888.

Wright, James A., and Steven J. Keillor, editor. *No More Gallant Deed: A Civil War Memoir of the First Minnesota Volunteers*. St. Paul: MHS Press, 2001.

U.S. Find A Grave Index, ancestry.com.

Young, Andrew W. *History of Chautauqua County, New York*. Buffalo: Matthews & Warren, 1875.

Journals

Albright, R.E. "The American Civil War as a Factor in Montana Territorial Politics." *Pacific Historical Review* 6, No. 1 (March 1937).

"A Partial Sketch of the Civil and Military Service of Major Martin Maginnis." *Contributions of the Historical Society of Montana* 8 (1917), Montana Historical and Miscellaneous Library.

Asher, Hellen Asher. "A Frontier College of the Middle West: Hamline University, 1854-69." *Minnesota History* 9, (December 1928).

Breckenridge, W.J. "A Century of Minnesota Wildlife." *Minnesota History* 30 (September 1949).

"Church of the Redeemer, Cannon Falls, Goodhue County." *Journal of the Forty-Eighth Annual Council of the Diocese of Minnesota*, 1905.

Hage, Anne A. "The Battle of Gettysburg As Seen By Minnesota Soldiers." *Minnesota History* 38 (June 1963).

Hanford, James Holly. "Milton and the Return to Humanism." *Studies in Philology* 16, No. 2 (April, 1919).

Hoffman, Larry. "The Mining History of Butte and Anaconda." Mining History Association, www.mininghistoryassociation.org/ButteHistory.htm.

Johnston, Daniel S.B. "Journalism in the Territorial Period." *Minnesota Historical Society Collections*, Vol. I. St. Paul: Minnesota Historical Society, 1905.

Malone, Michael P. "Midas of the West: The Incredible Career of William Andrews Clark." *Montana The Magazine of Western History*, 33, No. 4 (Autumn 1983).

Military Historical Society of Minnesota. "The First Minnesota and the Battle of Gettysburg." https://www.mnmilitarymuseum.org/files/7313/3799/8529/Rev._First_Minn_and_Battle_of_Gettysburg.pdf.

Upham, Warren. *Minnesota Geographic Names*. St. Paul: Minnesota Historical Society, 1920.

Wolf, Hazel. "Campaigning with the First Minnesota: A Civil War Diary." *Minnesota History* 25 (December 1944).

Zdon, Al. "Colvill of Minnesota." *Minnesota History* 61, No. 6 (Summer 2009).

Articles

Hendrickson, John. "Calvin Coolidge and the Joy of Fishing." Calvin Coolidge Presidential Foundation, coolidgefoundation.org.

"Summer White House on the Brule." Wisconsin Historical Society. wisconsinhistory.org/Records/Image/IM85171.

Swain, Col. Rick. "Grip Hands With Us Now." *Assembly Magazine of U.S. Military Academy Graduates*, July/August 2006.

"What We Believe: The Book of Common Prayer." www.episcopalchurch.org. "Vestry." www.episcopalchurch.org.

Newspapers

Due to digitization of historic newspapers, there are too many to list here, the reader will see these newspaper titles listed in the footnotes. The searching was done by means of Minnesota Newspaper Hub (Minnesota Historical Society); Newspapers.Com; Chronicling America (Library of Congress); and Community History Archives of Red Wing (MN) Public Library.

Government Documents

Biographical Directory of the U.S. Congress. bioguide.congress.gov.

Bureau of the Census. *1850 U.S. Census; 1860 U.S. Census; 1870 U.S. Census; 1880 U.S. Census; 1890 Veterans Schedules of the U.S. Federal Census; 1900 U.S. Census; 1910 U.S. Census.*

Goodhue County, MN. *Probate Court, Goodhue County, Minnesota.*

Colvill, William. *Annual Report of the Attorney General to the Legislature of Minnesota, Session of 1868.* St. Paul: Press Printing Company, 1868.

Davis, William C. National Park Service. "Civil War Series: The First Battle of Manassas," http://npshistory.com/publications/civil_war_series/17/sec7.htm.

Department of State. U.S. Passport Applications, For Native Citizens, 1795-1925, "Martin Maginnis," February 9, 1907.

Minnesota Department of Transportation. "Railroads in Minnesota, 1862-1956." MN Statewide Historic Railroads Study Final, www.dot.state.mn.us.

Minnesota Government Website. "Colvill Memorial Highway." https://www.revisor.mn.gov/laws/1933/0/Session+Law/Chapter/353.

Minnesota Legislative Reference Library. *Minnesota Legislative Manual, 1871.* State of Minnesota. "Minnesota Territorial and State Attorneys General, 1849-Present." www.lrl.mn.gov/mngov/attygen.

Montana State University. "Butte and the Richest Hill: History," and "William A. Clark." Montana State University Billings Library Guide, https://libguides.msubillings.edu.

National Park Service. "The Battle of Malvern Hill," https://www.nps.gov/rich/learn/historyculture/mhbull.htm.

National Park Service. Gettysburg video, 158th Anniversary, You Tube, accessed August 13, 2024.

State of Minnesota. *Minnesota Territorial Census 1857.*

Statutes At Large of the United States of America, Dec., 1891, to March, 1893; Fifty-Second Congress, Vol. XXVII. Washington, DC: GPO, 1893.

U.S., Minnesota Civil War Records, 1861-1865. Ancestry.com.

U.S. Senate. *Senate Election, Expulsion and Censure Cases From 1789 to 1960.* Washington, D.C.: GPO, 1962.

Other Unpublished Materials

Akers, Charles N. "Sketches: William Colvill, 1906-1910." Charles N. Akers and Family Papers, P2559, Minnesota Historical Society.

Bray, N.J. Bray. "Col. William Colvill, Jr., Cook County Pioneer Homesteader," March 16, 1933. William Colvill, 1830-1905, Biographical Sketches and Letters, P939, Minnesota Historical Society, St. Paul, MN.

Colvill, William. "Col. Colvill's Statement." Colvill, 1830-1905: Biographical Sketches and Letters, P939, Minnesota Historical Society.

Colvill, William. "Col. Colvill's Letter to Col. John B. Bachelder," August 30, 1866. Colvill: Biographical Sketches and Letters, P939, Minnesota Historical Society.

Colvill William, "The Old First Minnesota at Gettysburg," (as told to H.L. Gordon), typescript manuscript. "William Colvill Biography File," Goodhue County Historical Society, Red Wing, MN.

Hoyt, Mark Anthony. Hoyt Diary, "Colvill and Maginnis." John Franklin Hoyt & Family Papers, A/.H868j., Minnesota Historical Society.

Osman, Stephen E. "Speech at Cannon Falls, Colvill Memorial Rededication," Cannon Falls, MN, July 31, 1994.

Historian (retired) Steve Hoffbeck at his favorite fishing lake near Frazee, 2023.

ABOUT THE AUTHOR
Steve Hoffbeck

The author of *Colvill Smiled: The Legend of the 1ˢᵗ Minnesota Volunteer Regiment at Gettysburg* is Steven R. Hoffbeck, retired Professor of History at Minnesota State University Moorhead.

A native Minnesotan, Steve Hoffbeck grew up as a dairy-farmer's son on the family farm located five miles north of Morgan. His first book, entitled *The Haymakers: A Chronicle of Five Farm Families*, was a narrative of the blessings, toil, and woes of farming. The *Haymakers* won a Minnesota Book Award in 2001.

Hoffbeck's subsequent work, *Swinging for the Fences: Black Baseball in Minnesota*, explored the neglected history of almost-forgotten ballclubs and ballplayers in the North Star State. The book was awarded the *Sporting News*/SABR Baseball Research Award for 2005.

Both books were imprinted by Minnesota Historical Society Press, one the state's premiere publishers, and both are still available online.

His third book, *Hillcrest Lutheran Academy, Centennial Beacon: Hillcrest's Hundred Years of Stories, 1916-2016*, printed in 2017, told the history of the school located in Fergus Falls, Minnesota.

Dr. Hoffbeck has written many articles for *Minnesota History* magazine and in regional magazines, including *Minnesota Monthly, Farm & Ranch Living*, and *Lake Country Journal*. Since 2010, he has written over 300 short features for broadcast on *Dakota Datebook*, a program of North Dakota's Prairie Public Radio.

Hoffbeck and his wife, Dianne, live in Barnesville, Minnesota, and have four adult children, and six grandchildren.

The next writing project is tentatively called "Legends of Minnesota."

NOTES

NOTES TO INTRODUCTION

1. Sinclair Lewis, The Minnesota Stories of Sinclair Lewis (St. Paul: Borealis Books, 2005), p. 15.

NOTES TO CHAPTER 1

1. Based on "Col. Colvill's Funeral," Cannon Falls [MN] Beacon, August 30, 2001, p. 24.

2. "Big Figure in Montana Annals Dies," Helena [MT] Daily Independent, March 28, 1919, p. 3.

NOTES TO CHAPTER 2

1. "Blue and Grey Meet Again at Gettysburg; First Minnesota Made History," Minneapolis Star, June 29, 1938, p. 1.

2. Here and below, "Gettysburg," National Park Service brochure, nps.gov, accessed September 16, 2023; and the 1977 version of the N.P.S. "Gettysburg" brochure; and "Blue and Grey Meet Again at Gettysburg," Minneapolis Star, June 29, 1938, p. 1, 7.

3. James A. Wright, No More Gallant a Deed (St. Paul: MHS Press, 2001), p. 293.

4. Wright, No More Gallant a Deed, p. 295-296.

5. "Blue and Grey Meet Again," Minneapolis Star, June 29, 1938, p. 7.

6. "Blue and Grey Meet Again," Minneapolis Star, June 29, 1938, p. 7.

7. Wright, No More Gallant a Deed, p. 291.

8. "Reports of Capt. Henry C. Coates, First Minnesota Infantry," July 5, 1863, Minnesota in the Civil and Indian Wars, Vol. II (St. Paul: Pioneer Press Company, 1893), p. 372.

9. Here and below, "The First Minnesota and the Battle of Gettysburg," Military Historical Society of Minnesota, https://www.mnmilitarymuseum.org/files/7313/3799/8529/Rev._First_Minn_and_Battle_of_Gettysburg.pdf, accessed on September 19, 2023.

10. Wright, No More Gallant a Deed, p. 306.

11. "Statue to Colvill is Dedicated," Minneapolis Journal, May 30, 1909, p. 1.

NOTES TO CHAPTER 3

1. "His Long Active Career," Minneapolis Journal, June 13, 1905, p. 2.

2. Andrew W. Young, History of Chautauqua County, New York (Buffalo: Matthews & Warren, 1875), p. 418.

3. "His Long Active Career," Minneapolis Journal, June 13, 1905, p. 2.

4. Stephen E. Osman, "Speech at Cannon Falls, Colvill Memorial Rededication," July 31, 1994, unpublished manuscript, in possession of author.

5. "Big Figure in Montana Annals Dies," Helena [MT] Daily Independent, March 28, 1919, p. 3; "Life's Work of Pioneer is Finished," Anaconda [MT] Standard, March 28, 1919, p. 1; sworn as "native-born citizen" in U.S. Passport Applications, 1795-1925, "Martin Maginnis," Feb. 9, 1907; Belle Creek in "The Honorable Record of our Next Delegate," Daily Rocky Mountain Gazette [Helena, MT], Aug. 9, 1872, p. 2.

6. Hellen Asher, "A Frontier College of the Middle West: Hamline University, 1854-69," Minnesota History, Vol. 9, December, 1928: p. 363, 368, 369.

7. "Stories About Maginnis," Anaconda Standard, July 7, 1900, p. 9.

8. History of Goodhue County (Red Wing: Wood, Alley & Co., 1878), p. 408-409; Franklyn Curtiss-Wedge, History of Goodhue County, Minnesota (Chicago: H.C. Cooper, Jr., & Co., 1909), p. 650-651; "The Copartnership," Red Wing Sentinel, September 5, 1860, p. 2; History of the Hamline University of Minnesota When Located at Red Wing, Minnesota From 1854 to 1869 (St. Paul: Hamline University Alumni Association, 1907), p. 212, 251.

9. "Statue to Colvill is Dedicated," Minneapolis Journal, May 30, 1909, p. 2; "Wild Pigeons are About in Immense Numbers," Red Wing Sentinel, Aug. 29, 1857, p. 4; "Rare Sport," Emigrant Aid Journal of Minnesota [Nininger, MN], June 20, 1857, p. 5; "Wild Pigeons and Ducks Are Very Numerous," Red Wing Sentinel, April 23, 1859, p. 3; "Wild Ducks, Prairie Chickens and Pigeons," Red Wing Sentinel, Aug. 27, 1859, p. 3; "Sporting," St. Paul Weekly Minnesotian, October 1, 1859, p. 3; "Duck Shooting," Red Wing Sentinel, April 4, 1860, p. 3; "Prairie chickens and pigeons are plenty," in "Republican Men at Lake City," St. Paul Weekly Minnesotian, Sept. 3, 1859, p. 4; "Pigeons," Wabashaw County Herald, May 26, 1860, p. 3; Thomas S. Roberts, Birds of Minnesota, Vol. 1 (Minneapolis: University of Minnesota Press, 1932), p. 376, 385-386, 576-577, 585; W.J. Breckenridge, "A Century of Minnesota Wildlife," Minnesota History, Vol. 30, No. 3 (Sept. 1949): p. 223-227.

10. W.W. Sweeney in History of Goodhue County (Red Wing: Wood, Alley & Co., 1878), p. 223-224; "Statue to Colvill is Dedicated," Minneapolis Journal, May 30, 1909, p. 2.

11. William Colvill, "A Rare Trout," Red Wing Sentinel, Aug. 13, 1859, p. 2.

12. "Statue to Colvill is Dedicated," Minneapolis Journal, May 30, 1909, p. 2.

13. "Farewell," Red Wing Sentinel, Feb. 4, 1860, p. 2.

14. "Presidential Vote, 1860, 1864, 1868," Minnesota Legislative Manual, 1871, Minnesota Legislative Reference Library, www.leg.state. mn.us, accessed October 7, 2023.

15. James M. McPherson, Battle Cry of Freedom: The Civil War Era (New York: Oxford University Press, 1988), p. 274; "The War Begun; First Bloodshed," Red Wing Sentinel, April 17, 1861, p. 2.

16. "To Arms, To Arms," Red Wing Sentinel, April 17, 1861, p. 2.

17. "Red Wing, April 19," Weekly Pioneer & Democrat [St. Paul, MN], April 26, 1861, p. 4-5; Leo Tolstoy, War and Peace (NY: Barnes & Noble Classics, 2005), p. 563.

18. War-meeting legend written by Charles N. Akers in two sources: C.N. Akers, "Abraham Edwards Welch," in History of the Hamline University, p. 258; and Curtiss-Wedge, History of Goodhue County, Minnesota, p. 508.

19. C.N. Akers, "Abraham Edwards Welch," in History of the Hamline University, p. 508.

20. C.N. Akers, "Abraham Edwards Welch," in History of the Hamline University, p. 258.

21. C.N. Akers, "Abraham Edwards Welch," in History of the Hamline University, p. 258; and Curtiss-Wedge, History of Goodhue County, Minnesota, p. 508.

22. "Organization of the Goodhue Volunteers," Red Wing Sentinel, April 24, 1861, p. 2.

23. "Statue to Colvill is Dedicated," Minneapolis Journal, May 30, 1909, p. 2.

24. William Colvill, "Application for Membership, Minnesota Society of the Sons of the American Revolution, March, 1894, Ancestry.com; "Love, Robert," Soldiers of the American Revolution: Who Were At One Time Residents Of, Or Whose Graves Are Located In Chautauqua County, New York (Chautauqua County, NY, 1925), p. 47; "Celebration of the Fourth," Red Wing Sentinel, July 16, 1859, p. 4; "Concord's Battle," Minneapolis Tribune, April 2, 1894, p. 5.

25. "Celebration of the Fourth," Red Wing Sentinel, July 16, 1859, p. 4.

26. "Celebration of the Fourth," Red Wing Sentinel, July 16, 1859, p. 4.

27. "Col. Colvill's Narrative Told To A School Girl," Red Wing newspaper article, in "Colvill Biography File," Goodhue County Historical Society, Red Wing, MN.

28. "The Minnesota Regiment in Garrison," Weekly Pioneer & Democrat [St. Paul, MN], May 10, 1861, p. 8.

29. "Where Heroes Fell," St. Paul Globe, July 3, 1897, p. 7.

30. "Tale of the First," St. Paul Globe, Aug. 8, 1897, p. 10; "Dedication of the Monument to the First," St. Paul Globe, June 20, 1902, p. 4.

31. "Gallant Minnesota in the Field," Chicago Tribune, June 24, 1861, p. 4; "The Craft Represented," Chicago Tribune, June 24, 1861, p. 4, counted "two editors and sixteen printers" in the First Minnesota; Frank Mead, of the 1st Minnesota, wrote of the former occupations in

Frank J. Mead, "Minnesota's Glorious 'First,'" Minneapolis Times, June 13, 1897, p. 20.

32. "Statue to Colvill Dedicated," Minneapolis Journal, May 30, 1909, p. 2; Wright, No More Gallant a Deed, p. 22, 31.

33. Tolstoy, War and Peace, p. 911.

34. Wright, No More Gallant a Deed, p. 42-43.

35. "A Partial Sketch of the Civil and Military Service of Major Martin Maginnis," Contributions of the Historical Society of Montana, Vol. 8 (Helena: Montana Historical and Miscellaneous Library, 1917), p. 9; "Army of the Potomac," National Tribune [Washington, D.C.], May 24, 1883, p. 1.

36. "Died," Goodhue County Republican, February 12, 1864, p. 3.

37. Martin Maginnis, "The Battle of Bloody Run," Goodhue County Republican, Aug. 9, 1861, p. 1, (he wrote this letter on July 27, 1861 in Washington, D.C.); the same letter was reprinted in Joseph Woods Hancock, Goodhue County Minnesota: Past and Present (Red Wing: Red Wing Printing, 1893), p. 153.

38. McPherson, Battle Cry of Freedom, p. 335.

39. Maginnis, "The Battle of Bloody Run," Goodhue County Republican, Aug. 9, 1861, p. 1.

40. Maginnis, "The Battle of Bloody Run," Goodhue County Republican, Aug. 9, 1861, p. 1.

41. Here and below, Maginnis, "The Battle of Bloody Run," Goodhue County Republican, August 9, 1861, p. 1.

42. Maginnis, "The Battle of Bloody Run," Goodhue County Republican, Aug. 9, 1861, p. 1.

43. Henry R. Putnam (1832-1872), "Tribute to Great Hero," Helena [MT] Independent, June 3, 1910, p. 5; "Draft Riots Quelled," Minneapolis Tribune, July 10, 1910, p. 28; "Death of Major Putnam," Helena [MT] Weekly Herald, February 15, 1872, p. 7; "First Regiment Minnesota Volunteers," [St. Paul] Weekly Pioneer & Democrat, May 17, 1861, p. 9.

44. Here and below, Maginnis, "The Battle of Bloody Run," Goodhue County Republican, Aug. 9, 1861, p. 1.

45. William Colvill's account of Bull Run in William Lochren, "Narrative of the First Regiment," Minnesota in the Civil & Indian Wars, p. 11; Osman, "Cannon Falls: Colvill Memorial Rededication," speech, July 31, 1994.

46. Here and below, Colvill's story is combined from his own recollections found in Lochren, "Narrative of the First Regiment,"

Minnesota in the Civil & Indian Wars, p. 11; and William Colvill, "Bull Run: Address of Col. Wm. Colvill at the Re-Union of the Survivors of the First Minnesota, June 21, 1877," Red Wing Argus, July 5, 1877, p. 1.

47. "The First Minnesota," Minneapolis Journal, June 25, 1903, p. 4.

48. James A. Wright, "Our Army Correspondence; Aug. 4th, 1861," Goodhue County Republican, Aug. 16, 1861, p. 2.

NOTES TO CHAPTER 4

1. "1st Regiment Minnesota Volunteers," Chatfield [MN] Democrat, July 27, 1861, p. 3; Theodore C. Blegen, Minnesota: A History of the State (Minneapolis: University of Minnesota Press, 1975), p. 242; casualties in Wright, No More Gallant a Deed, p. 65 and in Al Zdon, "Colvill of Minnesota," Minnesota History, Vol. 61, No. 6 (Summer 2009), p. 264; the percentage who died in the 1st Minnesota regiment that day was therefore at about 5 percent. Union losses at Bull Run totaled 460 killed, 1,124 wounded, and 1,312 missing; those in the "missing" category, many had been killed and the rest were taken as prisoners of war, see William C. Davis, National Park Service, "Civil War Series: The First Battle of Manassas," http://npshistory.com/publications/civil_war_series/17/sec7.htm, accessed Oct. 18, 2023. The 42 Minnesotans killed were nearly 10 percent of the total Union dead of 460. Col. W.A. Gorman reported 44 dead at Bull Run, officially, in "Killed, Wounded & Missing of the First Regiment," Weekly Pioneer and Democrat, Aug. 2, 1861, p. 5.

2. Frank A. Haskell, The Battle of Gettysburg (Madison: Wisconsin History Commission, 1908), p. 143-144.

3. Lt. Col. Dave Grossman, On Killing (Boston: Little, Brown & Company, 1996), p. 10-11, 19-27; "everybody tears cartridges, loads, passes guns or shoots," in Rufus R. Dawes, Service with the Sixth Wisconsin Volunteers (Marietta, Ohio: E.E. Alderman & Sons, 1890), p. 90; Wright, No More Gallant a Deed, p. 306, 307.

4. "Soldiers Under Fire," Detroit Free Press, Nov. 28, 1880, p. 9; "Under Fire: A Soldier's Sensations," Minneapolis Tribune, Dec. 28, 1880, p. 2.

5. "The Battle at Springfield," Muscatine [IA] Evening Journal, Aug. 21, 1861, p. 2.

6. Here and below, Maginnis, "The Battle of Bloody Run," Goodhue County Republican, Aug. 9, 1861, p. 1.

7. Maginnis, "The Battle of Bloody Run," Goodhue County Republican, Aug. 9, 1861, p. 1.

NOTES TO CHAPTER 5

1. "The Richmond Enquirer," Goodhue County Republican, Aug. 1, 1862, p. 2.

2. "Veteran's Reunion," Minneapolis Evening Journal, May 17, 1883, p. 2; "Army of the Potomac," National Tribune [Washington, D.C.], May 24, 1883, p. 1.

3. "Where Heroes Fell," St. Paul Globe, July 3, 1897, p. 7; Jasper N. Searles, "The First Minnesota Volunteer Infantry," Glimpses of the Nation's Struggle, Vol. 2 (St. Paul: St. Paul Book and Stationery Company, 1890), p. 89; Wright, No More Gallant a Deed, p. 87, 96; "A Partial Sketch of the Civil and Military Service of Major Martin Maginnis," Contributions of the Historical Society of Montana, Vol. 8, p. 9.

4. "The First Minnesota in the Seven Days' Battles Before Richmond, St. Cloud Democrat, July 17, 1862, p. 1; Daniel Hand, "Reminiscences of an Army Surgeon," Glimpses of the Nation's Struggle, Vol. 1 (St. Paul: St. Paul Book & Stationery Company, 1887), p. 291-292.

5. "The First Regiment," St. Paul Weekly Pioneer & Democrat, July 26, 1862, p. 2. Hand, Glimpses of the Nation's Struggle, Vol. 1, p. 292.

6. "The First Regiment," St. Paul Weekly Pioneer & Democrat, Aug. 8, 1862, p. 8; promoted Aug. 28, 1862, see Curtiss-Wedge, History of Goodhue County, Minnesota, p. 511. Family in Young, History of Chautauqua County, New York, p. 418; "D.G. Colvill," Forestville, N.Y., 1870 U.S. Census; "William Colvill," Forestville, N.Y., 1860 U.S. Census and 1870 U.S. Census, Ancestry.com.

7. "The First Regiment," St. Paul Weekly Pioneer & Democrat, Aug. 8, 1862, p. 8; Wright, No More Gallant a Deed, p. 152, 158.

8. McPherson, Battle Cry of Freedom, p.469-470; National Park Service, "Battle of Malvern Hill," nps.gov/rich/learn/historyculture/mhbull.htm, accessed Oct. 31, 2023.

9. Report of General McClellan," St. Paul Weekly Pioneer & Democrat, Jan. 15, 1864, p. 5; "The Rebel Army Defeated," St. Paul Pioneer & Democrat, Sept. 26, 1862, p. 2.

10. Wright, No More Gallant a Deed, p. 182.

11. "Report of Col. Alfred Sully, Battle of Antietam," Minnesota in the Civil & Indian Wars, Vol. II, p. 125. Sully reported 1 officer killed and 3 officers wounded; and then "enlisted men killed, 15; wounded, 19; missing, 24. Total enlisted men killed, wounded, and missing 188;" Searles, Glimpses of the Nation's Struggle, Vol. 2, p. 98-99.

12. Curtiss-Wedge, History of Goodhue County, Minnesota, p. 511.

13. "A Partial Sketch . . . Major Martin Maginnis," Contributions of Historical Society of Montana, p. 10.

14. Searles, Glimpses of the Nation's Struggle, Vol. 2, p. 100.

NOTES TO CHAPTER 6

1. Theodore Ayrault Dodge, Great Captains, Vol. IV, Napoleon (Boston: Houghton, Mifflin and Co., 1907), p. 24; N.P.S., "Weapons, Accouterments and the Soldier," nps.gov/history/history/paal/thunder-cannon/chap4.htm, here and below.

2. Wright, No More Gallant a Deed, p. 78.

3. Wright, No More Gallant a Deed, p. 303.

4. Wright, No More Gallant a Deed, p. 49; 'Minnie Musket,' "Army Correspondence, First Regiment, June 23, 1862, Fair Oaks, Va.," Goodhue County Republican, July 11, 1862, p. 2.

5. "Tribute to Great Hero," Helena [MT] Independent, June 3, 1910, p. 5.

6. 'Minnie Musket,' "Army Correspondence," Goodhue County Republican, July 11, 1862, p. 2. The half tent helped to reduce weight in each man's knapsack/backpack.

7. Wright, No More Gallant a Deed, p. 153, here and 2 paragraphs below.

8. Mark Anthony Hoyt Diary, "Colvill and Maginnis," in John Franklin Hoyt & Family Papers, A/.H868j., Minnesota Historical Society, p. 32-33, here and 4 paragraphs below; "Death of Lieut. Hoyt," St. Paul Daily Press, July 14, 1864, p. 4.

9. "Major General Sumner Compliments the Minnesota First," St. Paul Weekly Pioneer & Democrat, Aug. 8, 1862, p. 8; and "Review of Sumner's Corps," Winona Republican, Aug. 6, 1862, p. 2; "Veteran's Reunion," Minneapolis Evening Journal, May 17, 1883, p. 2; "Army of the Potomac," National Tribune [Washington, D.C.], May 24, 1883, p. 1.

NOTES TO CHAPTER 7

1. Here and below, M. Quad, "Sixteen Years After: Why Lee Invaded the North," Detroit Free Press, April 2, 1882, p. 18; M. Quad was the newspaper name of Charles B. Lewis, Civil War veteran.

2. M. Quad [Charles B. Lewis], "Sixteen Years After," Detroit Free Press, April 2, 1882, p. 18.

3. M. Quad [Charles B. Lewis]," Detroit Free Press, April 2, 1882, p. 18.

4. "Great Battle Picture," Morris [MN] Sun, Feb. 3, 1887, p. 5.

5. Wright, No More Gallant a Deed, p. 218; Curtiss-Wedge, History of Goodhue County, p. 511.

6. Here and below, M. Quad [Charles B. Lewis], "Sixteen Years After," Detroit Free Press, Nov. 27, 1881, p. 18.

7. M. Quad [Charles B. Lewis], "Sixteen Years After," Detroit Free Press, April 2, 1882, p. 18.

8. Hazel Wolf, "Campaigning with the First Minnesota: A Civil War Diary," Minnesota History 25 (Dec. 1944), p. 360, diary of Isaac L. Taylor.

9. Martin Maginnis, "The First Minnesota," Washington [D.C.] Sunday Herald, May 28, 1882, p. 3; reprinted in "The First Minnesota: Graphic Description of the Charge by Hon. Martin Maginnis, Who Was one of the Participants," Helena [MT] Independent, June 21, 1882, p. 1; and reprinted in Ken Robison, "Major Martin Maginnis," [Fort Benton, MT] River Press, May 29, 2013, p. 6. In 1882, Maginnis wrote an "unpublished manuscript lecture," that got published in 1882, as listed above, in which he used information from a copy of a letter that had been written at a "camp near Warrenton, July 28, 1863," written by a member of the First Minnesota identified only as "SERGEANT," that had been published as Sergeant, "Battle of Gettysburg and the First Minnesota," St. Paul Weekly Pioneer & Democrat, Aug. 14, 1863, p. 3, and Maginnis copied some words directly from that article, changed some phrasings, and then added much information that he had learned since the time of the battle. Maginnis may have been the writer named "SERGEANT," but that is unclear.

10. Maginnis, "The First Minnesota," Washington [D.C.] Sunday Herald, May 28, 1882, p. 3; Wright, No More Gallant a Deed, p. 293 (Company F, as the reader will note, was the company from Red Wing, and Maginnis had

been promoted to be a lieutenant with Company H in 1862; while Colvill had been promoted by the time of Gettysburg to Colonel of the entire 1st Minnesota regiment).

11. "Our Returning Braves," St. Paul Weekly Pioneer & Democrat, February 19, 1864, p. 5, the "absent sick" total was 101 men, and the "Number on detached service" at that time was 63.

12. M. Quad, "Sixteen Years After: The Second Day at Gettysburg," Detroit Free Press, April 9, 1882, p. 17; M. Quad, "Sixteen Years After," Detroit Free Press, Nov. 27, 1881, p. 18.

13. William Colvill, "The Old First at Gettysburg," Minneapolis Tribune, July 28, 1884, p. 2.

14. Colvill, "The Old First at Gettysburg," Minneapolis Tribune, July 28, 1884, p. 2.

15. Anne A. Hage, "The Battle of Gettysburg As Seen By Minnesota Soldiers," Minnesota History, Vol. 38 (June 1963), p. 251, 252; "Carpenter's Letter," Minneapolis Tribune, June 30, 1963, p. 49; "Gallant First at Gettysburg," Minneapolis Tribune, June 27, 1897, p. 21.

16. Maginnis, "The First Minnesota," Washington [D.C.] Sunday Herald, May 28, 1882, p. 3.

17. Maginnis, "The First Minnesota," Washington [D.C.] Sunday Herald, May 28, 1882, p. 3.

18. Maginnis, "The First Minnesota," Washington [D.C.] Sunday Herald, May 28, 1882, p. 3; Wright, No More Gallant a Deed, p. 295.

19. Maginnis, "The First Minnesota," Washington [D.C.] Sunday Herald, May 28, 1882, p. 3.

20. Maginnis, "The First Minnesota," Washington [D.C.] Sunday Herald, May 28, 1882, p. 3.

21. "Col. Colvill's Statement," Colvill, 1830-1905: Biographical Sketches and Letters, P939, Minnesota Historical Society, p. 2.

22. Maginnis, "The First Minnesota," Washington [D.C.] Sunday Herald, May 28, 1882, p. 3.

23. "Col. Colvill's Statement," Biographical Sketches and Letters, P939, Minnesota Historical Society, p. 2; Maginnis, "The First Minnesota," Washington [D.C.] Sunday Herald, May 28, 1882, p. 3.

24. Colvill, "The Old First at Gettysburg," Minneapolis Tribune, July 28, 1884, p. 2.

25. Colvill, "The Old First at Gettysburg," Minneapolis Tribune, July 28, 1884, p. 2.

26. Colvill, "The Old First at Gettysburg," Minneapolis Tribune, July 28, 1884, p. 2; "One of Few Left After Terrible Charge Tells of Battling His Way Back Through Lane of Death," Minneapolis Journal, June 29, 1913, p. 6 of Gettysburg Section.

27. Colvill, "The Old First at Gettysburg," Minneapolis Tribune, July 28, 1884, p. 2.

28. Maginnis, "The First Minnesota," Washington [D.C.] Sunday Herald, May 28, 1882, p. 3.

29. Maginnis, "The First Minnesota," Washington [D.C.] Sunday Herald, May 28, 1882, p. 3; expectations in Colvill, "The Old First at Gettysburg," Minneapolis Tribune, July 28, 1884, p. 2; "First Minnesota," Mower County Transcript [Austin, MN], July 21, 1897, p. 1.

30. D.H. Junkin and Frank H. Norton, The Life of Winfield Scott Hancock (NY: D. Appleton and Company, 1880), p. 97; "Letters to the Old First," Minneapolis Tribune, July 24, 1884, p. 3.

31. Junkin and Norton, Life of Winfield Scott Hancock, p. 97; "Letters to the Old First," Minneapolis Tribune, July 24, 1884, p. 3.

32. Colvill, "The Old First at Gettysburg," Minneapolis Tribune, July 28, 1884, p. 2.

33. Maginnis, "The First Minnesota," Washington [D.C.] Sunday Herald, May 28, 1882, p. 3.

34. Maginnis, "The First Minnesota," Washington [D.C.] Sunday Herald, May 28, 1882, p. 3.

35. Junkin and Norton, Life of Winfield Scott Hancock, p. 97; Maginnis, "The First Minnesota," Washington [D.C.] Sunday Herald, May 28, 1882, p. 3.

36. "Col. Colvill's Letter to Col. John B. Bachelder," August 30, 1866, in Colvill: Biographical Sketches and Letters, P939, Minnesota Historical Society; Wayne D. Jorgenson, Every Man Did His Duty (Minneapolis: Tasora Books, 2012), p. 24, 27.

37. Colvill, "The Old First at Gettysburg," Minneapolis Tribune, July 28, 1884, p. 2.

38. Maginnis, "The First Minnesota," Washington [D.C.] Sunday Herald, May 28, 1882, p. 3.

39. Maginnis, "The First Minnesota," Washington Sunday Herald, May 28, 1882, p. 3.

40. Colvill, "The Old First at Gettysburg," Minneapolis Tribune, July 28, 1884, p. 2; "One of Few Left," Minneapolis Journal, June 29, 1913, p. 6 of Gettysburg Section.

41. "Heroic Charge of First Minnesota Recalled by Trempealeau Resident," Winona Republican Herald, July 25, 1931, p. 4; the account from John M. Rhorer (1840-1920), of Morristown, Minnesota (sometimes misspelled "Rohrer," or "Roher," sergeant, Company G, wounded on July 2, 1863, at Gettysburg).

42. Colvill, "The Old First at Gettysburg," Minneapolis Tribune, July 28, 1884, p. 2; "Col. Colvill's Statement," Biographical Sketches and Letters, P939, Minnesota Historical Society, p. 3.

43. Maginnis, "The First Minnesota," Washington Sunday Herald, May 28, 1882, p. 3; "Col. Colvill's Statement," Biographical Sketches and Letters, Minnesota Historical Society, p. 3.

44. "Heroic Charge of First Minnesota," Winona Republican Herald, July 25, 1931, p. 4.

45. "Heroic Charge of First Minnesota," Winona Republican Herald, July 25, 1931, p. 4.

46. Colvill, "The Old First at Gettysburg," Minneapolis Tribune, July 28, 1884, p. 2; "Col. Colvill's Statement," Colvill, Biographical Sketches and Letters, Minnesota Historical Society, p. 3.

47. Maginnis, "The First Minnesota," Washington Sunday Herald, May 28, 1882, p. 3.

48. William Colvill, "The Old First at Gettysburg," Minneapolis Tribune, July 28, 1884, p. 2: brush described by Edward H. Bassett in Richard Krom, ed., The 1st Minnesota: Second To None (Rochester: Richard Krom, 2010), p. 497. As explained by historian Wayne D. Jorgenson, Colvill was 30 paces (about 90 feet) behind the line of his soldiers during the charge and then he joined them all in the creek bed, in Wayne D. Jorgenson, Every Man Did His Duty (Minneapolis: Tasora, 2012), p. 26.

49. Colvill, "The Old First at Gettysburg," Minneapolis Tribune, July 28, 1884, p. 2; William Colvill, "The Old First Minnesota at Gettysburg," (as told to H.L. Gordon), p. 8, typescript manuscript, "William Colvill Biography File," Goodhue County Historical Society, Red Wing, MN.

50. Colvill, "The Old First at Gettysburg," Minneapolis Tribune, July 28, 1884, p. 2.

51. Colvill, "The Old First at Gettysburg," Minneapolis Tribune, July 28, 1884, p. 2.

52. Colvill, "The Old First at Gettysburg," Minneapolis Tribune, July 28, 1884, p. 2.

53. Colvill, "The Old First at Gettysburg," Minneapolis Tribune, July 28, 1884, p. 2; overlapping lines from Charles Muller, 1st Minnesota at Gettysburg, in "One of Few Left," Minneapolis Journal, June 29, 1913, p. 6 of Gettysburg Section.

54. Maginnis, "The First Minnesota," Washington Sunday Herald, May 28, 1882, p. 3.

55. Colvill, "The Old First at Gettysburg," Minneapolis Tribune, July 28, 1884, p. 2.

56. "Heroic Charge of First Minnesota Recalled," Winona Republican Herald, July 25, 1931, p. 4.

57. Colvill, "The Old First at Gettysburg," Minneapolis Tribune, July 28, 1884, p. 2.

58. Wright, No More Gallant a Deed, p. 301, 310; H.C. Coates, "Return of Killed, Wounded and Missing of the First Minnesota Volunteers at the Battles near Gettysburg, Pa., July 2d and 3d, 1863," in Minnesota in the Civil & Indian Wars, 1861-1865, Vol. II, p. 375-377.

59. H.C. Coates, "Return of Killed, Wounded and Missing of the First Minnesota Volunteers at the Battles near Gettysburg, Pa., July 2d and 3d, 1863," in Minnesota in the Civil & Indian Wars, 1861-1865, Vol. II, p. 375-377.

60. Deaths at Bull Run in Wright, No More Gallant a Deed, p. 65; and in Zdon, "Colvill of Minnesota," Minnesota History, 61, p. 264; deaths at Antietam in Richard Moe, The Last Full Measure (St. Paul: MHS Press, 1993), p. 189.

61. Wright, No More Gallant a Deed, p. 60.

62. Frank A. Haskell, The Battle of Gettysburg (Madison: Wisconsin History Commission, 1908), p. 56.

63. Colvill, "The Old First at Gettysburg," Minneapolis Tribune, July 28, 1884, p. 2.

64. Colvill, "The Old First at Gettysburg," Minneapolis Tribune, July 28, 1884, p. 2.

65. Frank Mead, "A World Famous Charge," Minneapolis Times, June 27, 1897, p. 9; Maginnis, "Army of the Potomac," National Tribune [Washington, D.C.], May 24, 1883, p. 1, a transcript of the speech that Maginnis delivered as the "annual oration" at the reunion of the Army of the Potomac in the national capital, again, Maginnis used phrases and information from a copy of a letter that had been written at a "camp near Warrenton, July 28, 1863," written by a member of the First Minnesota identified only as "SERGEANT," that had been published as Sergeant, "Battle of Gettysburg and the First Minnesota," St. Paul Weekly Pioneer & Democrat, Aug. 14, 1863, p. 3, and Maginnis copied some words directly from that article, paraphrasing most of it, and then added much information of his own. Maginnis may have been the writer named "SERGEANT," but that is uncertain.

66. Colvill, "The Old First at Gettysburg," Minneapolis Tribune, July 28, 1884, p. 2.

67. M. Quad, "Sixteen Years After: Last Day at Gettysburg," Detroit Free Press, April 16, 1882, p. 18.

68. Maginnis, "The First Minnesota," Washington Sunday Herald, May 28, 1882, p. 3.

69. Maginnis, "Army of the Potomac," National Tribune [Washington, D.C.], May 24, 1883, p. 1.

70. Haskell, The Battle of Gettysburg, p. 197; Maginnis, "Army of the Potomac," National Tribune [Washington, D.C.], May 24, 1883, p. 1.

71. M. Quad, "Sixteen Years After: Last Day at Gettysburg," Detroit Free Press, April 16, 1882, p. 18; Wright, No More Gallant a Deed, p. 305, 306.

72. Stephen Sears, Gettysburg (Boston: Houghton Mifflin Company, 2004), p. 415, 419.

73. M. Quad, "Sixteen Years After: Last Day at Gettysburg," Detroit Free Press, April 16, 1882, p. 18.

74. Maginnis, "Army of the Potomac," National Tribune [Washington, D.C.], May 24, 1883, p. 1.

75. Maginnis, "Army of the Potomac," National Tribune [Washington, D.C.], May 24, 1883, p. 1; Sears, Gettysburg, p. 415.

76. Maginnis, "Army of the Potomac," National Tribune [Washington, D.C.], May 24, 1883, p. 1; Wright, No More Gallant a Deed, p. 306, 307; "Our Returning Braves," Weekly Pioneer & Democrat, February 19, 1864, p. 6.

77. Maginnis, "Army of the Potomac," National Tribune [Washington, D.C.], May 24, 1883, p. 1.

78. Maginnis, "Army of the Potomac," National Tribune [Washington, D.C.], May 24, 1883, p. 1.

79. National Park Service, Gettysburg video, 158th Anniversary, You Tube, accessed August 13, 2024; Jeffrey D. Wert, Gettysburg: Day Three (N.Y.: Simon & Schuster, 2001), p. 201.

80. M. Quad, "Sixteen Years After: Last Day at Gettysburg," Detroit Free Press, April 16, 1882, p. 18.

81. Maginnis, "Army of the Potomac," National Tribune [Washington, D.C.], May 24, 1883, p. 1; "Our Returning Braves," St. Paul Weekly Pioneer & Democrat, Feb. 19, 1864, p. 6.

82. Haskell, The Battle of Gettysburg, p. 137.

NOTES TO CHAPTER 8

1. 'Sergeant,' "Battle of Gettysburg and the First Minnesota," St. Paul Weekly Pioneer & Democrat, August 14, 1863, p. 3; Tillie Pierce Alleman, At Gettysburg Or What A Girl Saw And Heard Of The Battle (New York: W. Lake Borland, 1889), p. 81; Haskell, The Battle of Gettysburg, p. 60.

2. 'Sergeant,' "Battle of Gettysburg," Weekly Pioneer & Democrat, August 14, 1863, p. 3.

3. H.C. Coates, "Return of Killed, Wounded and Missing of the First Minnesota Volunteers at the Battles near Gettysburg, Pa., July 2d and 3d, 1863," in Minnesota in the Civil and Indian Wars, 1861-1865, Vol. II, p. 375-377.

4. H.C. Coates, "Return of Killed, Wounded and Missing," in Minnesota in the Civil and Indian Wars, 1861-1865, Vol. II, p. 375-377.

5. "Our Returning Braves," St. Paul Weekly Pioneer & Democrat, Feb. 19, 1864, p. 6.

6. "Our Returning Braves," St. Paul Weekly Pioneer & Democrat, Feb. 19, 1864, p. 6; "History," St. Paul Press, July 18, 1865, p. 4.

7. Haskell, The Battle of Gettysburg, p. 125.

8. "Promotions in the First Regiment," Goodhue Volunteer, Sept. 23, 1863, p. 2; "Montana's First Citizen," Helena [MT] Independent, Dec. 1, 1912, p. 9.

9. Here and below, Colvill, "The Old First at Gettysburg," Minneapolis Tribune, July 28, 1884, p. 2.

10. "Col. Colvill Who Died Today," Montana Daily Record [Helena, MT], June 13, 1905, p. 1.

11. Here and below, Alleman, At Gettysburg Or What A Girl Saw, p. 73-74, 101-103.

12. "Col. Colvill's Statement," Biographical Sketches and Letters, Minnesota Historical Society, p. 4 (removal of bullet from shoulder); also Colvill, "The Old First Minnesota at Gettysburg, "William Colvill Biography File," Goodhue County Historical Society.

13. Colvill, "The Old First Minnesota at Gettysburg," p. 8, "William Colvill Biography File," Goodhue County Historical Society.

14. Young, History of Chautauqua County, New York, p. 418; "Forestville Loses Its Oldest Daughter (Mrs. Mary Colvill Sherman, 1828-1916), Dunkirk [NY] Evening Observer, May 5, 1916, p. 4.

15. Here and below, Tillie Pierce Alleman, At Gettysburg Or What A Girl Saw, p. 104-107.

16. "Col. Wm. Colvill," Goodhue County Republican, Jan. 29, 1864, p. 3; Young, History of Chautauqua County, New York, p. 418, lists Daniel G. Colvill (born 1800) as an uncle for Colonel Colvill, but census pages list him as "David"; N.J. Bray, "Col. William Colvill, Jr., Cook County Pioneer Homesteader," March 16, 1933, in Biographical Sketches and Letters, William Colvill, Minnesota Historical Society, p. 2; "Hospitals Closed," Reading [PA] Times, Dec. 14, 1863, p. 3; "For The Herald," Wayne County Herald [Honesdale, PA], Aug. 13, 1863, p. 3.

17. "Col. Colvill Who Died Today," Montana Daily Record [Helena, MT], June 13, 1905, p. 1, Charles M. Webster, who had lived in Red Wing, contended that Jane Morgan had been a nurse for Colvill.

NOTES TO CHAPTER 9

1. "Montana's First Citizen," Helena [MT] Independent, Dec. 1, 1912, p. 9; "Tribute to Great Hero," Helena Independent, June 3, 1910, p. 5.

2. "Montana's First Citizen," Helena [MT] Independent, Dec. 1, 1912, p. 9; "Tribute to Great Hero," Helena Independent, June 3, 1910, p. 5; "The First Minnesota," St. Paul Weekly Pioneer & Democrat, Dec. 11, 1863, p. 4.

3. "Entertainment to the First Minnesota," [Washington, D.C.] Evening Star, Feb. 8, 1864, p. 3; "Welcome to the First Regiment in Washington," St. Cloud Democrat, Feb. 18, 1864, p. 4.

4. Here and below, "Our Returning Braves," St. Paul Weekly Pioneer & Democrat, Feb. 19, 1864, p. 4.

5. "Our Returning Braves," St. Paul Weekly Pioneer & Democrat, Feb. 19, 1864, p. 4.

6. Charles N. Akers, "Sketches: William Colvill, 1906-1910," in Charles N. Akers and Family Papers, MHS, P2559.

7. "Our Chattanooga Letter," St. Cloud Democrat, June 8, 1865, p. 1.

8. "The State Capital," Goodhue Volunteer, July 20, 1864, p. 3; the friend was Edwin A. Littlefield, in "Personal," Goodhue Volunteer, May 25, 1864, p. 3.

9. "An Interesting Scene," St. Paul Press, March 1, 1865, p. 4; "Legislature of Minnesota," St. Paul Press, Jan. 4, 1865, p. 1; "Negro Suffrage," St. Paul Weekly Pioneer & Democrat, Feb. 10, 1865, p. 8; William D. Green, A Peculiar Imbalance: The Rise and Fall of Racial Equality in Minnesota, 1837-1869 (St. Paul: University of Minnesota Press, 2015), p. 142, 148.

10. "Heavy Artillery," Weekly Pioneer & Democrat, March 3, 1865, p. 2; "News of Our Own State," Weekly Pioneer& Democrat, June 16, 1865, p. 3; "Promotions in Heavy Artillery," Weekly Pioneer & Democrat, August 18, 1865, p. 2. Service with 1st Minnesota Heavy Artillery from April 18, 1865-July 26, 1865, "William Colvill" 1890 Schedules of the U.S. Federal Census, 2nd Ward, Duluth, MN, Ancestry.com.

11. "The Latest By Telegraph; Surrender of Gen. Lee," Pioneer & Democrat, April 14, 1865, p. 7.

12. "Thanks to Grant and his Army," Weekly Pioneer & Democrat, April 14, 1865, p. 7.

13. "The National Calamity," Pioneer & Democrat, April 21, 1865, p. 4.

NOTES TO CHAPTER 10

1. "Col. Colvill Who Died Today," Montana Daily Record, June 13, 1905, p. 1.

2. Charles N. Akers, "Biographical Sketches: William Colvill, 1906-1910," Charles N. Akers and Family Papers, MHS, p. 3.

3. "Col. Colvill Who Died Today," Montana Daily Record, June 13, 1905, p. 1.

4. George E. Warner and Charles M. Foote, History of Ramsey County & the City of St. Paul (Minneapolis: North Star Publishing Co., 1881), p. 249; "Minnesota Territorial and State Attorneys General, 1849-Present," www.lrl. mn.gov/mngov/attygen, accessed July 30, 2024; "Union State Ticket," St. Cloud Democrat, Nov. 2, 1865, p. 2; "Democratic Ticket," St. Paul Weekly Pioneer & Democrat, Oct. 6, 1865, p. 7; "Grand Rally To-Night," Winona Daily Republican, Nov. 6, 1865, p. 2.

5. "Hawkes Trial," Minneapolis Tribune, June 5, 1867, p. 3; "Hawkes Trial," Minneapolis Tribune, June 4, 1867, p. 3; "Help Wanted: J.H. Jones, 125 Dearborn-St," Chicago Tribune, Sept. 5, 1866, p. 4.

6. "Hawkes Trial," Minneapolis Tribune, June 4, 1867, p. 3; "Hawkes Trial," Minneapolis Tribune, May 30, 1867, p. 3.

7. "Hawkes Trial," Minneapolis Tribune, June 4, 1867, p. 3; "Hawkes Trial," Minneapolis Tribune, May 30, 1867, p. 3.

8. "Hawkes Trial," Minneapolis Tribune, June 4, 1867, p. 3: "Hawkes Trial," Minneapolis Tribune, May 31, 1867; "Hawkes Trial," Minneapolis Tribune, June 5, 1867, p. 3; "An Alleged Murder," Winona Daily Republican, Feb. 20, 1867, p. 1 (reprinted from Chicago Republican);

"The St. Paul Tragedy," Chicago Tribune, Aug. 25, 1866, p. 2 (reprinted from St. Paul Press).

9. "Hawkes Trial," Minneapolis Tribune, June 4, 1867, p. 3; "Hawkes Trial," Minneapolis Tribune, May 30, 1867, p. 3.

10. "Hawkes Trial," Minneapolis Tribune, May 30, 1867, p. 3; "An Alleged Murder," Winona Daily Republican, Feb. 20, 1867, p. 1; "T.T. Armstrong," St. Paul, Minnesota, Directory for 1867 (St. Paul: Bailey & Wolfe, Publishers, 1867), p. 28.

11. "Hawkes Trial," Minneapolis Tribune, June 4, 1867, p. 3

12. "Hawkes Trial," Minneapolis Tribune, May 30, 1867, p. 3.

13. "Hawkes Trial," Minneapolis Tribune, June 4, 1867, p. 3; "Minnesota Correspondence," Jackson [OH] Standard, June 27, 1867, p. 1.

14. "An Alleged Murder," Winona Daily Republican, Feb. 20, 1867, p. 1.

15. Here and below, Maggie White's testimony in "Hawkes Trial," Minneapolis Tribune, May 30, 1867, p. 3.

16. "An Alleged Murder," Winona Daily Republican, Feb. 20, 1867, p. 1.

17. Here and below, Maggie White's testimony in "Hawkes Trial," Minneapolis Tribune, May 30, 1867, p. 3.

18. Dr. A. Wharton, M.D., testimony in "Hawkes Trial," Minneapolis Tribune, June 4, 1867, p. 3.

19. "The St. Paul Tragedy," Chicago Tribune, Aug. 25, 1866, p. 2.

20. "The St. Paul Tragedy," Chicago Tribune, Aug. 25, 1866, p. 2.

21. Here and below, "An Alleged Murder," Winona Daily Republican, Feb. 20, 1867, p. 1.

22. "The St. Paul Tragedy," Chicago Tribune, Aug. 25, 1866, p. 2; Jacob Henry Stewart," in James Grant Williams and John Fiske, eds., Appleton's Cyclopedia of American Biography, Vol. V (N.Y.: D. Appleton & Company, 1888), p. 686; "J.H. Stewart, physician," St. Paul, MN, 1870 U.S. Census; "Brewer Mattocks, physician," St. Paul, MN, 1870 U.S. Census.

23. "An Alleged Murder," Winona Daily Republican, Feb. 20, 1867, p. 1.

24. Here and below, "Hawkes Trial," Minneapolis Tribune, June 4, 1867, p. 3.

25. "Hawkes Trial," Minneapolis Tribune, June 4, 1867, p. 3.

26. "Hawkes Trial," Minneapolis Tribune, June 7, 1867, p. 4; "Daniel Alexander Robertson," U.S. Find A Grave Index, ancestry.com, accessed July 20, 2024; "Daniel A. Robertson, Sheriff," St. Paul, Minnesota, Directory for 1867, p. 188.

27. "The Killing Of Mrs. Hawkes," Chicago Tribune, Feb. 17, 1867, p. 4; "The Killing of Mrs. Lizzie Hawkes," Chicago Tribune, Dec. 14, 1866, p. 2.

28. "Hawkes Trial," Minneapolis Tribune, June 4, 1867, p. 3; "Minnesota Correspondence," Jackson [OH] Standard, June 27, 1867, p. 1.

29. "Hawkes Trial," Minneapolis Tribune, June 4, 1867, p. 3; "Hawkes Trial," Minneapolis Tribune, May 30, 1867, p. 3; "Minnesota Correspondence," Jackson [OH] Standard, June 27, 1867, p. 1; "The Killing Of Mrs. Hawkes," Chicago Tribune, Feb. 17, 1867, p. 4.

30. "Detective Police Agency, William Turtle & Co., advertisement, Chicago Tribune, March 23, 1866, p. 1; "Capt. William Turtle: Obituary," Chicago Tribune, Feb. 15, 1887, p. 7; "Turtle's Detective Agency," A.N. Marquis & Company's Handy Business Directory of Chicago (Chicago: A.N. Marquis & Company, 1886), p. 454; "Hawkes Trial," Minneapolis Tribune, June 6, 1867, p. 3; "The Killing Of Mrs. Hawkes," Chicago Tribune, Feb. 17, 1867, p. 4. Detective D.J. Page's first name was usually spelled "Devillo," but was sometimes "Deville," see "D.J. Page Sinks to Rest," obit., Santa Cruz Evening News, March 28, 1914, p. 8.

31. "Hawkes Trial," Minneapolis Tribune, June 7, 1867, p. 3.

32. "The Killing Of Mrs. Hawkes," Chicago Tribune, Feb. 17, 1867, p. 4.

33. "M.A. Hawkes," Omaha [NE] Herald, April 17, 1867, p. 2; "M.A. Hawkes," Charleston [SC] Daily News, March 11, 1867, p. 2; "M.A. Hawkes," Memphis [TN] Daily Appeal, March 28, 1867, p. 2.

34. "The Hawkes Case," Rochester Post, March 2, 1867, p. 5. "Edward Lambert, city justice," St. Paul, Minnesota, Directory, 1867, p. 130; "Edward C. Lambert, lawyer," St. Paul, Ramsey County, U.S. Census 1860; Warner and Foote, History of Ramsey County & the City of St. Paul, p. 250; "Edward C. Lambert, 1816-1870," U.S. Find A Grave Index, ancestry.com, accessed July 26, 2024; "Judge Lambert, of St. Paul," St. Cloud Journal, June 16, 1870, p. 2.

35. "Committed," Freeborn County Standard [Albert Lea, MN], March 21, 1867, p. 3; "The Hawkes Case," Chicago Tribune, March 17, 1867, p. 3; "State News," Lake City [MN] Leader, March 23, 1867, p. 3.

36. Here and below, "The Hawkes Case," Chicago Tribune, March 17, 1867, p. 3.

37. "The Hawkes Case," Chicago Tribune, March 17, 1867, p. 3; "The Murderer Hawkes Held for Trial," Chicago Tribune, March 14, 1867, p. 1.

38. "Admitted to Bail," Rochester Republican, April 4, 1867, p. 1.

39. William Colvill, Annual Report of the Attorney General to the Legislature of Minnesota, Session of 1868 (St. Paul: Press Printing Company, 1868), p. 594-595.

40. W.T.L., "Minnesota Correspondence," Jackson [OH] Standard, June 27, 1867, p. 1.

41. Here and below, William Colvill, Annual Report of the Attorney General to the Legislature of Minnesota, Session of 1868 (St. Paul: Press Printing Company, 1868), p. 595.

42. W.T.L., "Minnesota Correspondence," Jackson [OH] Standard, June 27, 1867, p. 1.

43. "Hawkes Trial," Minneapolis Tribune, June 4, 1867, p. 3; "S.M. Flint, Lawyer," St. Paul, Ramsey County, Minnesota, U.S. Census 1860; "Judge Samuel M. Flint," obituary, St. Paul Globe, Oct. 7, 1881, p. 1; "Samuel Minot Flint," U.S Find A Grave Index, ancestry.com, accessed July 29, 2024.

44. "Hawkes Trial," Minneapolis Tribune, March 2, 1867, p. 5; "William Golcher, Gun Smith," St. Paul, Ramsey County, MN, Minnesota Territorial Census 1857; and U.S. Census 1860; William Golcher, 1834-1886, U.S. Find A Grave Index, ancestry.com, accessed July 30, 2024.

45. W.T.L., "Minnesota Correspondence," Jackson [OH] Standard, June 27, 1867, p. 1; "The Hawkes Case," Rochester Post, March 2, 1867, p. 5.

46. "The Hawkes Case," Rochester Post, March 2, 1867, p. 5.

47. "Hawkes Trial," Minneapolis Tribune, June 5, 1867, p. 3; "Hawkes Trial," Minneapolis Tribune, June 7, 1867, p. 3.

48. Here and below, "Hawkes Trial," Minneapolis Tribune, June 9, 1867, p. 3.

49. W.T.L., "Minnesota Correspondence," Jackson [OH] Standard, June 27, 1867, p. 1. Here and below, "The Hawkes Case; His Acquittal," Minneapolis Tribune, June 11, 1867, p. 3.

50. "The St. Paul Pioneer says one of the Hawkes insurance cases has been settled [with Aetna]," Chicago Tribune, Oct. 11, 1867, p. 3.

51. Here and below, Colvill, Annual Report of the Attorney General to the Legislature of Minnesota, Session of 1868, p. 594-595.

52. "Official Laws," St. Cloud Journal, April 9, 1868, p. 5; "Laws of Minnesota," Red Wing Argus, April 2, 1868, p. 3.

53. Here and below, "Police Court; Quite a Blunder," Minneapolis Tribune, June 12, 1867, p. 3.

54. Noah Webster, An American Dictionary of the English Language (N.Y.: S. Converse, 1828), Vol. II, "Puppy," meaning also a "whelp, the young progeny of a bitch or female of the canine species," [really an early version of 'S.O.B.'].

55. "City Council," Minneapolis Tribune, June 19, 1867, p. 3; "Council Proceedings," Minneapolis Tribune, July 17, 1867, p. 1.

NOTES TO CHAPTER 11

1. "The Local Democratic Ticket," Red Wing Argus, Nov. 1, 1877, p. 1; "Well Put," St. Cloud Journal, Oct. 25, 1866, p. 2; "Colonel Colvill," St. Paul Daily Press, Sept. 29, 1866, p. 1.

2. "Col. Colvill's Appointment," Morris [MN] Sun, June 2, 1887, p. 2; "Minnesota Legislature," Goodhue County Republican, Jan. 24, 1878, p. 2.

3. "Democratic State Convention," Brainerd Tribune, Sept. 27, 1879, p. 1.

4. "Col. Colvill Who Died Today," Montana Daily Record [Helena, MT], June 13, 1905, p. 1, Charles M. Webster, who had lived in Red Wing, stated that Jane Morgan had been a nurse for Colvill after Gettysburg. A letter, dated about the year 1908, as written by a relative of William Colvill, stated that Colvill had met "his wife-to-be, Miss Morgan," when Colvill was Attorney General (1866-1868), in Charles N. Akers and Family Papers, Minnesota Historical Society.

5. "Fires," Goodhue County Republican, Jan. 28, 1882, p. 5.

6. Sumner Ladd, "Colvill Had Green Thumb," Red Wing Daily Republican-Eagle, July 3, 1963, in "Colvill Biography File," Goodhue County Historical Society.

7. N.J. Bray, "Col. William Colvill, Jr., Cook County Pioneer Homesteader," March 16, 1933, in Biographical Sketches and Letters, William Colvill, 1830-1905, MHS, p. 4.

8. Sumner Ladd, "Colvill Had Green Thumb," Goodhue County Historical Society.

9. "The Annual Fair Last Week," Red Wing Argus, Oct. 14, 1869, p. 4; U.P. Hedrick, Cyclo-pedia of Hardy Fruits (New York: Macmillan Company, 1922), p. 29.

10. Sumner Ladd, "Colvill Had Green Thumb," Goodhue County Historical Society.

11. Sumner Ladd, "Colvill Had Green Thumb," Goodhue County Historical Society.

12. Gust E. Freeman, "Colvill Stirs Memories," Red Wing Republican-Eagle, July 1962, newspaper clipping in "Colvill Biography File," Goodhue County Historical Society.

13. "List of Premiums," Goodhue County Republican, Oct. 23, 1868, p. 2.

14. "Award of Premiums," Goodhue County Republican, Oct. 21, 1869, p. 4; "The Annual Fair Last Week," Red Wing Argus, Oct. 14, 1869, p. 4.

15. "The Fair," Goodhue County Republican [Red Wing], Oct. 20, 1870, p. 4.

16. Gust E. Freeman, "Colvill Stirs Memories," Red Wing Republican-Eagle, July 1962," newspaper clipping in "Colvill Biography File," Goodhue County Historical Society.

17. "Laying Of The Corner Stone Of Christ Church," Goodhue County Republican, July 1, 1869, p. 4; "What We Believe: The Book of Common Prayer," www.episcopalchurch.org, accessed August 7, 2024.

18. George Clinton Tanner, Fifty Years of Church Work in the Diocese of Minnesota, 1857-1907 (St. Paul: Committee of Publication, 1909), p. 375, 376; "Vestry," www.episcopalchurch.org, accessed Aug. 7, 2024; "Laying Of The Corner Stone Of Christ Church," Goodhue County Republican, July 1, 1869, p. 4.

19. Tanner, Fifty Years of Church Work in the Diocese of Minnesota, 1857-1907, p. 375; Email, Christ Church Pastor Aaron Twait, Red Wing, MN, to Author Steve Hoffbeck, Feb. 21, 2024; "Consecration of Christ Church," Goodhue County Republican, Dec. 21, 1871, p. 4.

20. "Hero of Gettysburg," Red Wing Republican, June 13, 1905, p. 1, in "Colvill Biography File," Goodhue County Historical Society.

21. "Mrs. Jane E. Colvill," Red Wing Advance Sun, Nov. 21, 1894, p. 5.

22. Here and below, "The Colvill Railroad War," Goodhue County Republican, June 22, 1871, p. 4; "War On The St. Paul And Chicago Railroad," Goodhue County Republican, April 20, 1871, p. 4; "The Railroad War," Red Wing Argus, June 22, 1871, p. 4.

23. "War On The St. Paul And Chicago Railroad," Goodhue County Republican, April 20, 1871, p. 4.

24. "Col. Colvill Who Died Today," Montana Daily Record, June 13, 1905, p. 1, story from Charles M. Webster.

25. "District Court," Goodhue County Republican, Dec. 28, 1871, p. 4; "Col. Wm. Colvill," Freeborn County Standard [Albert Lea, MN], Jan. 4, 1872, p. 2.

26. Minnesota Department of Transportation, "Railroads in Minnesota, 1862-1956," Minnesota Statewide Historic Railroads Study Final, Section E, p. 9, www.dot.state.mn.us, accessed on August 8, 2024.

27. "Col. Colvill's Appointment," Morris [MN] Sun, June 2, 1887, p. 2; "Col. Colvill A Winner," St. Paul Daily Globe, May 21, 1887, p. 1.

28. "Red Wing," St. Paul Globe, June 9, 1888, p. 10; "A Busy Week In Duluth," St. Paul Globe, June 3, 1888, p. 12.

29. "Red Wing," St. Paul Globe, July 1, 1886, p. 5.

30. "William Colvill," Hanover Township, Chautauqua County, NY, U.S. Census: Non-Population Schedules, 1860.

31. Here and below, Gust E. Freeman, "Colvill Stirs Memories,"Red Wing Republican-Eagle, July 1962," newspaper clipping in "Colvill Biography File," Goodhue County Historical Society; "Our Friend Col. Colvill," Red Wing Advance Sun, July 7, 1886, p. 2.

32. "Red Wing," St. Paul Globe, July 8, 1886, p. 5; "Red Wing," St. Paul Globe, July 1, 1886, p. 5; "Col. Colvill," New Ulm Weekly Review, July 7, 1886, p. 2.

33. "Red Wing," St. Paul Globe, June 9, 1888, p. 10; "A Busy Week In Duluth," St. Paul Globe, June 3, 1888, p. 12.

34. "Red Wing," St. Paul Globe, June 30, 1888, p. 12.

35. "Colvill Steps Out," St. Paul Daily Globe, Oct. 1, 1891, p. 1; "Col. Colvill Resigns," St. Paul Daily Globe, April 20, 1891, p. 1; "The Duluth Plums," St. Paul Globe, Jan. 9, 1890, p. 1; Judge Bert Fesler, "Reminiscences of Col. Colvill," August, 1936, Colvill, Biographical Sketches and Letters, MHS (copied from St. Louis County Historical Society), p. 2.

36. "Chap. 299; An Act Granting a Pension to William Colvill, of Minnesota," Statutes At Large of the United States of America, Dec., 1891, to March, 1893; Fifty-Second Congress, Vol. XXVII (Washington, DC: GPO, 1893), p. 790.

37. "Mrs. Jane E. Colvill," Red Wing Advance Sun, Nov. 21, 1894, p. 5.

38. "Mrs. Jane E. Colvill," Stillwater [MN] Daily Gazette, Nov. 16, 1894, p. 3.

39. "Red Wing," St. Paul Globe, Aug. 1, 1886, p.11; "Red Wing," St. Paul Globe, June 30, 1888, p. 12; "Katherine Tanner," Find A Grave Index, Ancestry.com; "William P. Tanner," Cannon Falls, Goodhue County, MN, 1880 U.S. Census, Ancestry.com; land in History of Goodhue County, p. 419.

40. "William P. Tanner," St. Paul Daily Globe, May 24, 1883, p. 2; "W.P. Tanner," St. Paul Globe, May 16, 1883, p. 2; "W.P. Tanner," Minneapolis Tribune, May 9, 1883, p. 7; "Correction," St. Paul Globe, May 21, 1883, p. 4.

41. "Mrs. Jane E. Colvill," Red Wing Advance Sun, Nov. 21, 1894, p. 5; "Mrs. Jane E. Colvill," Red Wing Advance Sun, Nov. 21, 1894, p. 7.

42. "Death of Mrs. Colvill," Duluth Evening Herald, Nov. 14, 1894, p. 5; "Mrs. Jane E. Colvill," Stillwater Daily Gazette, Nov. 16, 1894, p. 3; Visitors Throng Awaiting Arrival of President," Minneapolis Tribune, July 29, 1928, p. 5. Sisters are all listed in Find A Grave Index.

43. "Reminiscences of Col. Colvill," Aug., 1936, Colvill, Biographical Sketches and Letters, MHS (copied from St. Louis County Historical Society), p. 2.

44. Frank J. Mead, "The Old Soldier," Minneapolis Journal, Sept. 11, 1897, p. 16.

45. "Reminiscences of Col. Colvill," Aug., 1936, Colvill, Biographical Sketches and Letters, MHS (copied from St. Louis County Historical Society), p. 2; N.J. Bray, "Col. William Colvill, Jr., Cook County Pioneer Homesteader," March 16, 1933, in Colvill, Biographical Sketches and Letters, MHS, p. 3.

46. "William Colvill," and John Hussey family, Hovland Township, Cook County, Minnesota, 1900 U.S. Census, Ancestry.com; "Last Tuesday," Cook County Herald [Grand Marais, MN], July 4, 1896, p. 3; "Notice for Publication," Colvill homestead, "Section 10, Township 61 North, Range 2 East," Cook County Herald, June 1, 1901, p. 4; William Colvill, Homestead Certificate 3895, July 22, 1902, Cook County, MN, 167 and 30/100th acres, Township 81-N, Range 2-E, Section 10; "Col. Colvill Returned," Cook County Herald, June 29, 1895, p. 3; "Statue To Colvill," Minneapolis Journal, May 30, 1909, p. 1.

47. "George H. Durfee, Civil War Soldier, Dies at Age of 90," Minneapolis Journal, Jan. 1, 1929, p. 6; "Chester S. Durfee Funeral,"

Minneapolis Journal, Aug. 6, 1929, p. 3; Chester Durfee, George Durfee, 1890 Veterans Schedules of the U.S. Federal Census, Ancestry.com; "Col. Colvill Returned," Cook County Herald, June 29, 1895, p. 3.

48. "Colvill lived most of the time at Red Wing," in "Col. Colvill, Veteran of the Civil War, Dies Suddenly," Cook County Herald [Grand Marais, MN], June 17, 1905, p. 5.

49. N.J. Bray, "Col. William Colvill, Jr., Cook County Pioneer Homesteader," March 16, 1933, in Colvill, Biographical Sketches and Letters, P939, MHS, p. 4.

50. "Statue To Colvill," Minneapolis Journal, May 30, 1909, p. 1; "William Colvill," and John J. Hussey family, Minnesota State Census, 1905, Goodhue County, MN, Ancestry.com, accessed July 6, 2024; "Photograph of Colonel William Colvill standing on the porch of his house at 856 East 7th Street in Red Wing," Goodhue County Historical Society Collections, in MN Collections website, mncollections.org/Detail/objects/85542, accessed July 9, 2024; Fesler, "Recollections of Col. Colvill," Aug., 1936, in Colvill Biographical Sketches and Letters, MHS, p. 7.

51. Gust E. Freeman, "Colvill Stirs Memories,"Red Wing Republican-Eagle, July 1962," newspaper clipping in "Colvill Biography File," Goodhue County Historical Society, Red Wing, MN; Art Lee, Leftover Lutefisk: More Stories from the Lutefisk Ghetto (Cambridge, MN: Adventure Publications,1984), p. 5, 87-92.

52. Ruby Danenbaum, "Minnesota Woman Produces Striking Statue," Minneapolis Tribune, May 3, 1909, p. 24; "John J. Hussey," Grand Marais, Cook County, Minnesota, 1910 U.S. Census.

53. N.J. Bray, "Col. William Colvill, Jr., Cook County Pioneer Homesteader," March 16, 1933, p. 4.

54. N.J. Bray, "Col. William Colvill, Jr., Cook County Pioneer Homesteader," March 16, 1933, p. 4.

55. Fesler, "Recollections of Col. Colvill," August, 1936, in Colvill, Biographical Sketches and Letters, Minnesota Historical Society, p. 7.

56. S.M. Ladd, "Modesty Showed Through," Red Wing Republican-Eagle, July 3, 1963, "Colvill Biography File," Goodhue County Historical Society.

57. Fesler, "Recollections of Col. Colvill," p. 7.

58. "Hero of Gettysburg," Red Wing Republican, June 13, 1905, p. 1, in "Colvill Biography File," Goodhue County Historical Society.

59. Sumner Ladd, "Colvill Had Green Thumb," Red Wing Daily Republican-Eagle, July 3, 1963, in "Colvill Biography File," Goodhue County Historical Society.

60. "Carnegie-Lawther Library At Red Wing," Minneapolis Journal, Oct. 22, 1903, p. 13; "The Carnegie Library Building At Red Wing," Albert Lea Tribune, Oct. 23, 1903, p. 4; Fesler, "Recollections of Col. Colvill," p. 7.

61. Fesler, "Recollections of Col. Colvill," p. 7.

62. Fesler, "Recollections of Col. Colvill," p. 7.

63. Fesler, "Recollections of Col. Colvill," p. 7.

64. Gust E. Freeman, "Colvill Stirs Memories,"Red Wing Republican-Eagle, July 1962," newspaper clipping in "Colvill Biography File," Goodhue County Historical Society.

65. Fesler, "Recollections of Col. Colvill," p. 7.

66. Sumner Ladd, "Colvill Had Green Thumb."

67. Jim Freeman, "Biography of William Colvill," August 6, 2008, in "Colvill Biography File," Goodhue County Historical Society.

68. Jim Freeman, "Biography of William Colvill;" S.M. Ladd, "Modesty Showed Through," Red Wing Republican-Eagle, July 3, 1963; "Hero of Gettysburg," Red Wing Republican, June 13, 1905; and Gust E. Freeman, "Col. William Colvill," all in "Colvill Biography File," Goodhue County Historical Society.

69. "List of Books in Col. Colvill's Library, Aug. 4, 1906," Charles Akers & Family Papers, P2559, MHS.

70. "Goes Under The Hammer," St. Paul Pioneer Press, Oct. 2, 1905, in "Colvill Biography File," Goodhue County Historical Society, Red Wing, MN.

71. John Milton, Paradise Lost, Book I (N.Y.: Effingham Maynard & Co., 1889), p. 76.

72. John Milton, Paradise Lost, Book I, p. 55.

73. John Milton, Paradise Lost, Book I, p. 80.

74. John Milton, Paradise Lost, Book I, p. 54.

75. John Milton, Paradise Lost, Book I, p. 54.

76. John Milton, Paradise Lost, Book I, p. 82.

77. John Milton, Paradise Lost, Book I, p. 52.

78. "Hero of Gettysburg," Red Wing Republican, June 13, 1905, p. 1, in "Colvill Biography File," Goodhue County Historical Society.

79. James Holly Hanford, "Milton and the Return to Humanism," Studies in Philology, Vol. 16, No. 2 (April, 1919), p. 147.

80. "Hero of Gettysburg," Red Wing Republican, June 13, 1905, p. 1, in "Colvill Biography File," Goodhue County Historical Society.

81. Maginnis in "Major Maginnis Talks About Former Colonel," Montana Daily Record [Helena, MT], June 22, 1905, p. 3; "Battle Flags in New State House," Montana Independent [Helena, MT], June 27, 1905, p. 8.

82. "Colonel of the 'Old First' Dead," Minneapolis Journal, June 13, 1905, p. 1; "Hero of Gettysburg Answers Last Roll Call," Minneapolis Tribune, June 14, 1905, p. 6.

83. "Battle Flags in New State House," Montana Independent [Helena, MT], June 27, 1905, p. 8.

84. "Old First in Reunion," Minneapolis Tribune, June 14, 1905, p. 6.

85. Here and below, "Colvill Laid At Rest," Faribault Journal, June 21, 1905, p. 3; Tanner in "Church of the Redeemer, Cannon Falls, Goodhue County," Journal of the Forty-Eighth Annual Council of the Diocese of Minnesota (Red Wing: Red Wing Advertising Company, 1905), p. 117.

86. "Fighting Parson of Civil War Dies," Minneapolis Journal, May 26, 1918, p. 1; "Cannon Falls," St Paul Globe, Dec. 16, 1901, p. 3; Franklyn Curtiss-Wedge, History of Rice and Steele Counties, Minnesota, Vol. I (Chicago: H.C. Cooper, Jr., and Co., 1910), p. 209; "Rev. Thomas G. Crump, Minnesota Missionary," Find A Grave Index, Ancestry.com.; "Thomas G. Crump," Company B, Eighth Minnesota Volunteer Regiment, in Minnesota, U.S., Civil War Records, 1861-1865, Ancestry.com.

87. "Mrs. Jane E. Colvill," Stillwater Daily Gazette (from Red Wing Republican), Nov. 16, 1894, p. 3; "Jane E. [Morgan] Colvill," Find A Grave Index, Ancestry.com.

88. "William Colvill Estate," June 16, 1905, Probate Court, Goodhue County, Minnesota, Ancestry.com, accessed Dec. 6, 2023.

NOTES TO CHAPTER 12

1. "Appointment," Weekly Pioneer & Democrat, August 19, 1864, p. 4; "A Good Appointment," Goodhue Volunteer, Aug. 17, 1864, p. 3.

2. "Major of the Eleventh," Weekly Pioneer & Democrat, Sept. 16, 1864, p. 4; "Eleventh Regiment Roster," Weekly Pioneer & Democrat, Sept. 23, 1864, p. 4; Rufus Davenport, "Narrative of the Eleventh Regiment," in Minnesota in the Civil & Indian Wars, 1861-1865, Vol. I, p. 488-489.

3. "Narrative of the Eleventh Regiment," in Minnesota in the Civil & Indian Wars, 1861-1865, Vol. I, p. 488-491; "The Eleventh Regiment," St. Paul Press, July 6, 1865, p. 4; "Letter From The Eleventh Regiment," Weekly Pioneer & Democrat, Dec. 2, 1864, p. 4.

4. "Home From The War," Weekly Pioneer & Democrat, July 14, 1865, p. 3.

5. "Home From The War," Weekly Pioneer & Democrat, July 14, 1865, p. 3; "The Eleventh Regiment," St. Paul Press, July 6, 1865, p. 4.

6. "Montana's First Citizen," Helena [MT] Independent, Dec. 1, 1912, p. 9; "A Partial Sketch . . . Major Martin Maginnis," Contributions of the Historical Society of Montana, Vol. 8, p. 13, 14; "Claims Honor Of Naming City," Kalispell [MT] Bee, Jan. 16, 1906, p. 7.

7. "Organization of the Goodhue Volunteers," Red Wing Sentinel, April 24, 1861, p. 2.

8. Here and below, "Montana's First Citizen," Helena [MT] Independent, Dec. 1, 1912, p. 9; "A Partial Sketch . . . Major Martin Maginnis," Contributions of the Historical Society of Montana, Vol. 8, p. 13, 14, 15; "Claims Honor Of Naming City," Kalispell [MT] Bee, Jan. 16, 1906, p. 7.

9. "From Mitchell's Gulch," Rocky Mountain Gazette, Feb. 2, 1867, p. 1; "Helena Letter," Montana Post, March 31, 1866, p. 3; "A Cradle Worth Rocking," Rocky Mountain Post, Jan. 6, 1866, p. 3; "A New Auxiliary," Montana Post [Virginia City, MT], July 27, 1867, p. 8; "Items," Montana Post, July 10, 1868, p. 8; "Major Maginnis," Red Wing Argus, July 30, 1868, p. 4.

10. "Major Mart. Maginnis," Red Wing Argus, March 19, 1868, p. 4; Louise (sometimes recorded as Louisa) Elvira Mann (Maginnis), born 1838, in 1850 U.S. Census, Pontiac, Oakland County, Michigan; Louisa Maginnis, Find A Grave Index, Ancestry.com, tombstone (1838-1919), accessed May 2, 2024; "Mrs. Maginnis Dies At Advanced Age," Montana Record-Herald [Helena, MT], November 28, 1919, p. 2; Louise E. Mann was the sister of Sarah B. Mann (1832-1917), Sarah was the wife of William W. Phelps (1826-1873), and Martin Maginnis knew Phelps because of associations through the Red Wing newspaper in the 1850s and 1860s. Phelps was in charge of the U.S. Land Office in Red Wing from 1855-1859, and Phelps was in the U.S. House of Representatives, 1858-1859, so they met through Phelps. Maginnis worked with

Colvill and Phelps at the Red Wing newspaper. By 1861, the Red Wing Sentinel was under the ownership of Maginnis, with William Phelps as editor, see Daniel S.B. Johnston, "Journalism in the Territorial Period, Minnesota Historical Society Collections, Vol. I (St. Paul: Minnesota Historical Society, 1905), p. 280, 281, 323-325.

11. "An Incident Of The Fire," Helena Herald, Oct. 4, 1871, p. 3; "Another Disastrous Fire," Helena Herald, Oct. 2, 1871, p. 3; "Incident of the Burning of the Helena Herald," Red Wing Argus, Oct. 19, 1871, p. 1.

12. "The Great Fire In Helena," Helena Independent, Aug. 24, 1872, p. 2; "A Fire In Helena," Minneapolis Tribune, Aug. 25, 1872, p. 1.

13. "The New Senator From Montana," St. Louis Post-Dispatch, May 21, 1900, p. 8.

14. R.E. Albright, "The American Civil War as a Factor in Montana Territorial Politics," Pacific Historical Review, Vol. 6, No. 1 (March 1937), p. 36-46, many gold-miners had come from Missouri and from Confederate states, and they allied with Northern Democrats such as Maginnis.

15. Helen Fitzgerald Sanders, History of Montana, Vol. I (Chicago: Lewis Publishing Company, 1913), p. 397.

16. "The New Senator From Montana," St. Louis Post-Dispatch, May 21, 1900, p. 8.

17. "Major Martin Maginnis," Anaconda Standard, May 19, 1900, p. 1; Helen Fitzgerald Sanders, History of Montana, Vol. I, p. 397; "Martin Maginnis, 1841-1919," Biographical Directory of the U.S. Congress, bioguide.congress.gov, accessed March 19, 2024.

18. Helen Fitzgerald Sanders, History of Montana, Vol. I, p. 400, 402, 403.

19. "Butte and the Richest Hill: History," and "William A. Clark," Montana State University Billings Library Guide, https://libguides.msubillings.edu, accessed on February 20, 2024; Larry Hoffman, "The Mining History of Butte and Anaconda," Mining History Association, www.mininghistoryassociation.org/ButteHistory.htm, accessed February 20, 2024; "Senator W.A. Clark," Helena Weekly Herald, Dec. 14, 1899, p. 8.

20. Helen Fitzgerald Sanders, History of Montana, Vol. I, p. 409; "Senate," Chicago Tribune, April 17, 1900, p. 9; "Sanders and Power to Be Seated as Montana Senators," St. Paul Globe, Feb. 15, 1890, p. 1; U.S. Senate, Senate Election, Expulsion and Censure Cases From 1789 to 1960 (Washington, D.C.: GPO,

1962), p. 75-76; Michael P. Malone, "Midas of the West: The Incredible Career of William Andrews Clark," Montana The Magazine of Western History, Vol. 33, No. 4 (Autumn 1983), p. 9-10.

21. Helen Fitzgerald Sanders, History of Montana, Vol. I, p. 359; "Maginnis Met Gath," Anaconda Standard, April 3, 1892, p. 3.

22. Malone, "Midas of the West," p. 12-14; U.S. Senate, Senate Election, Expulsion and Censure Cases, p. 93-94; "Congress in Session," Chicago Inter Ocean, Dec. 5, 1899, p. 3.

23. U.S. Senate, Senate Election, Expulsion and Censure Cases, p. 93-94; U.S. Senate, "The Election Case of William A. Clark of Montana (1900)," https://www.senate.gov/about/origins-foundations/electing-appointing-senators/contested-senate-elections/089William_Clark.htm, accessed on February 20, 2024.

24. U.S Senate, Senate Election, Expulsion and Censure Cases, p. 934.

25. Paula Wilmot, "Clark Proved State's Seat in U.S. Senate was for Sale," Great Falls [MT] Tribune, Jan. 31, 1999, p. 36; Darrell Ehrlick, "The Absent Legacy of Montana's Most Successful Copper King," Daily Montanan, Oct. 4, 2023, dailymontanan.com.

26. "Robert Emmet," Butte Miner, March 4, 1886, p. 4; "Delegate Maginnis," Helena Independent-Record, Aug. 20, 1878, p. 3; "Tribute To Great Hero," Helena Independent, June 3, 1910, p. 5.

27. Here and below, "Congress," Philadelphia Times, June 1, 1879, p. 1; "Decoration Day," Helena Weekly Independent, June 19, 1879, p. 2; "Maj. Maginnis Oration," Helena Weekly Herald, June 1, 1879, p. 7; "More True Than Poetical," Pittsburgh Daily Post, June 2, 1879, p. 2.

28. "Army of the Potomac," National Tribune [Washington, D.C.], May 24, 1883, p. 1; "Veteran's Reunion," Minneapolis Evening Journal, May 17, 1883, p. 2; Martin Maginnis, "The Grand Army," Chicago Tribune, May 17, 1883, p. 1.

29. "Stories About Maginnis," Anaconda Standard, July 7, 1900, p. 9; "The New Senator From Montana," St. Louis Post-Dispatch, May 21, 1900, p. 8; "Portrait Of Martin Maginnis," Ravalli County Democrat [Hamilton, Montana], June 6, 1900, p. 4.

30. "Democrats In Session," Butte Miner, June 6, 1888, p. 1; "Stories About Maginnis," Anaconda Standard, July 7, 1900, p. 9; "Maginnis Of Montana," Butte Miner, Dec. 12, 1888, p. 1.

31. "Montana Dignitaries," Bismarck Tribune, June 29, 1888, p. 8; "Stories About Maginnis," Anaconda Standard, July 7, 1900, p. 9.

32. "Maginnis Of Montana," Butte Miner, Dec. 12, 1888, p. 1.

NOTES TO CHAPTER 13

1. "From Delegate Maginnis," Helena Independent, June 19, 1874, p. 4.

2. "Delegate Maginnis," Helena Independent, May 4, 1877, p. 3.

3. "The Following," Montana Daily Independent, Nov. 5, 1878, p. 2; "Hon. Martin Maginnis," Weekly Missoulian [Missoula, MT], Aug. 23, 1878, p. 2; "Personal," Helena Daily Independent, Nov. 1, 1878, p. 3; "Brevities," Helena Daily Herald, Oct. 10, 1878, p. 3.

4. "A Private Letter," Butte Weekly Miner, June 22, 1879, p. 4; "Personal," Washington, D.C., Evening Star, Oct. 28, 1879, p. 1.

5. "Social Intelligence," Washington Post, Dec. 12, 1880, p. 2; "The Washington Budget," Helena Independent, Jan. 8, 1887, p. 1.

6. "The Washington Budget," Helena Independent, Jan. 8, 1887, p. 1; "Gobbled Items," Butte Miner, Jan. 11, 1887, p. 3.

7. Here and below, Margaret Ronan, Girl From The Gulches: The Story Of Mary Ronan (Helena: Montana Historical Society, 2003), p. 67-68; "The Washington Budget," Helena Independent, Jan. 8, 1887, p. 1; "Faces and Fortunes," Helena Clock, May 18, 1895, p. 1.

8. "Major and Mrs. Maginnis," Helena Weekly Herald, April 26, 1894, p. 8; "Major Maginnis," San Francisco Chronicle, Jan. 19, 1894, p. 10.

9. "A Globe Trotter," Billings Gazette, Dec. 1, 1901, p. 4; "The Crook Sails," Baltimore Sun, Dec. 6, 1901, p. 8; "Major Martin Maginnis," Helena Independent, June 8, 1902, p. 1; "Fort Ethan Allen," Burlington [VT] Clipper, Jan. 25, 1902, p. 1; "6150 Miles From Home," Boston Globe, Jan. 28, 1902, p. 2.

10. "Has Girdled The World," Montana Daily Record [Helena, MT], June 21, 1902, p. 4; "What Martin Maginnis Saw Across The Sea," Anaconda Standard, Aug. 10, 1902, p. 23.

11. "Soldiers For Philippines," Philadelphia Times, Dec. 6, 1901, p. 2; "Obituary: Major General Alfred E. Bates," New York Tribune, Oct. 14, 1909, p. 7; "City of Peking Arrives," San Francisco Examiner, June 8, 1902, p. 21.

12. "A Globe Trotter," Billings Gazette, Dec. 1, 1901, p. 4; "People and Events," Montana Daily Record [Helena, MT], June 25, 1902, p. 8.

13. "Major Maginnis In Europe," Montana Lookout [Helena, MT], July 25, 1908, p. 6; "Major Maginnis Is In Europe," Butte Miner, Nov. 24, 1907, p. 9; "Major Maginnis Will Soon Depart For Home," Montana Daily Record [Helena, MT], May 9, 1908, p. 5.

14. "Major Maginnis Will Soon Depart," Montana Daily Record [Helena, MT], May 9, 1908, p. 5; "Major Maginnis In Europe," Montana Lookout [Helena, MT], July 25, 1908, p. 6.

15. Charles Akers, "In Memorium: Colonel William Colvill," Aug. 13, 1906, Charles N. Akers and Family Papers, MHS.

16. "Martin Maginnis," San Francisco Chronicle, Jan. 19, 1894, p. 10; "Firm On His Throne," and "Besides Bearing," in Anaconda [MT] Standard, Jan. 24, 1901, p. 6.

17. "People We Meet," Butte Daily Post, Aug. 1, 1902, p. 4; "Major Martin Maginnis," Butte Miner, March 28, 1919, p. 4.

18. "Major Maginnis Will Soon Depart," Montana Daily Record [Helena, MT], May 9, 1908, p. 5.

19. "Major Maginnis Back," Helena Independent, June 16, 1911, p. 5; "Personals," Montana Daily Record [Helena, MT], Dec. 5, 1912, p. 5.

20. "Life's Work Of Pioneer Is Finished," Anaconda Standard, March 28, 1919, p. 1; "Major Martin Maginnis," Montana Record-Herald [Helena, MT], March 27, 1919, p. 1.

21. Here and below, "Last Honors To Major Maginnis," Butte Miner, April 9, 1919, p. 3.

22. "Mrs. Maginnis Dies," Montana Record-Herald [Helena, MT], Nov. 28, 1919, p. 2; "Requiem Mass for Mrs. Maginnis," Montana Independent-Record, Dec. 1, 1919, p. 7; "Leaves $1,000,000 Estate; James Lawther, Wealthy Minnesotan," Albert Lea [MN] Evening Tribune, June 29, 1916, p. 1; "Mrs. Evalyn Lawther of Red Wing Is Dead," Winona Daily News, Feb. 19, 1932, p. 7; "Two Minneapolis Nieces Share in $400,000 Estate," Minneapolis Tribune, Feb. 25, 1932, p. 7.

NOTES TO CHAPTER 14

1. William Shakespeare, Shakespeare: The Complete Works (NY: Harcourt, Brace & World, Inc., 1968), p. 760-761.

2. Here and below, "Army Of The Potomac," National Tribune [Washington, DC], May 24, 1883, p. 1.

3. Martin Maginnis speech in Washington, D.C., "The Grand Army," Chicago Tribune, May 17, 1883, p. 1; "Gone Into History," Goodhue Volunteer, May 4, 1864, p. 2.

4. "Gone Into History," Goodhue Volunteer, May 4, 1864, p. 2.

5. "A Famous Russian Novel: War and Peace," New York Times, Jan. 31, 1886, p. 10.

6. Here and below, Leo Tolstoy, War and Peace, p. 358-359.

7. "The First Minnesota," Minneapolis Tribune, June 18, 1875, p. 4.

8. Stephen E. Osman, "Speech: Cannon Falls-Colvill Memorial Rededication, 31 July 1994," unpublished manuscript, p. 4, copy provided to author by Stephen E. Osman.

9. "Political Soldiers," Rochester [MN] Republican, July 5, 1865, p. 2.

10. "Colvill and Maginnis," St. Paul Globe, June 21, 1900, p. 9.

NOTES TO CHAPTER 15

1. "Lo, the Conquering Heroes Come," Winona Daily Republican, Feb. 13, 1864, p. 2.

2. Here and below, "Honor First Minnesota," Minneapolis Journal, Dec. 1, 1905, p. 7.

3. "Honor First Minnesota," Minneapolis Journal, Dec. 1, 1905, p. 7, "The First Minnesota," Minneapolis Tribune, June 18, 1875, p. 4.

4. "Col. Colvill Honored," Cook County Herald [Grand Marais, MN], July 10, 1897, p. 3; "Where Heroes Fell," St. Paul Globe, July 3, 1897, p. 7.

5. "A Charge of Peace," Minneapolis Tribune, July 3, 1897, p. 1.

6. "Col. Colvill Honored," Cook County Herald [Grand Marais, MN], July 10, 1897, p. 3.

NOTES TO CHAPTER 16

1. "Proposes Statue For Col. Colvill," Minneapolis Journal, June 14, 1905, p. 7; "Van Sant Suggests," Winona Republican-Herald, June 17, 1905, p. 2.

2. "Contest Over The Colvill Statue," Minneapolis Journal, April 23, 1908, p. 7.

3. "Catherine R. "Kate" Fallis, U.S. Find A Grave.com, Ancestry.com; "John R. Fallis," Toledo, Lucas County, Ohio, 1870 U.S. Census; "Work Of The Reaper: John R. Fallis," Minneapolis Tribune, Sept. 26, 1897, p. 8; John R. Fallis and Martha Fallis moved from Toledo, Ohio, to Minneapolis in 1887 and he worked in the "grain commission business."

4. "A Life Valentine . . . Geo. J. Backus and Catherine Fallis," Minneapolis Times, Feb. 15, 1894, p. 16; "Mrs. George J. Backus, 91, Dies," Stuart [Florida] News, Aug. 4, 1955, p. 1.

5. "Backus, Edward Wellington," and "Backus, George J.," in Albert Nelson Marquis, ed., The Book of Minnesotans (Chicago: A.N. Marquis and Company, 1907), p. 25; "E.W. Backus & Co.," Northwestern Lumberman, Feb. 10, 1894, p. 15; "Last Rites For George Backus," Stuart [Florida] News, Jan. 13, 1944, p. 1.

6. "Contest Over The Colvill Statue," Minneapolis Journal, April 23, 1908, p. 7.

7. "Contest Over The Colvill Statue," Minneapolis Journal, April 23, 1908, p. 7.

8. "What the Death Mask Shows," Sauk Centre Herald, April 17, 1902, p. 8; "Death Masks and Life Masks," Library Company of Philadelphia, www.librarycompany.org/artifacts/masks, accessed June 11, 2024 (Abraham Lincoln had two life masks made, in 1860 and in 1865, but not a death mask).

9. Ruby Danenbaum, "Minnesota Woman Produces Striking Statue of Brave Soldier and Hero, Colonel Colvill," Minneapolis Tribune, May 3, 1909, p. 24; "Contest Over The Colvill Statue," Minneapolis Journal, April 23, 1908, p. 7.

10. Danenbaum, "Minnesota Woman Produces Striking Statue," Minneapolis Tribune, May 3, 1909, p. 24.

11. Danenbaum, "Minnesota Woman Produces Striking Statue," Minneapolis Tribune, May 3, 1909, p. 24.

12. Danenbaum, "Minnesota Woman Produces Striking Statue," Minneapolis Tribune, May 3, 1909, p. 24.

13. "Statue of Col. William Colvill," Minneapolis Tribune, April 1, 1909, p. 9; "Statue In Honor of Hero Unveiled," Minneapolis Journal, March 31, 1909, p. 1; "Minnesota Soldiers in Western Hospitals," Weekly Pioneer and Democrat, Feb. 3, 1865, p. 1.

14. "Veterans Gather," Minneapolis Journal, May 29, 1909, p. 1; "Statue to Colvill," Minneapolis Journal, May 30, 1909, p. 1.

15. Here and below, "Statue to Colvill," Minneapolis Journal, May 30, 1909, p. 2.

16. "Coolidge Party Leaves Summer Lodge," St. Cloud Times, Sept. 11, 1928, p. 5; "Coolidges to Entrain," Minneapolis Star, Sept. 10, 1928, p. 15; "Summer White House on the Brule," Wisconsin Historical Society, wisconsinhistory.org/Records/Image/IM85171, accessed June 18, 2024; John Hendrickson, "Calvin Coolidge and the Joy of Fishing," Calvin Coolidge Presidential Foundation, coolidgefoundation.org, accessed on June 18, 2024.

17. Florence Lehmann, "Coolidge Praises First Minnesota," Minneapolis Journal, July 30, 1928, p. 1, 10; "Calvin Coolidge and the Joy of Fishing," Calvin Coolidge Presidential Foundation.

18. "President Coolidge," Green Bay Press-Gazette, July 17, 1928, p. 27; "Cannon Falls Ready," Winona Republican-Herald, July 26, 1928, p. 1, 8.

19. Lehmann, "Coolidge Praises First Minnesota," Minneapolis Journal, July 30, 1928, p. 1, 10.

20. Lehmann, "Coolidge Praises First Minnesota," Minneapolis Journal, July 30, 1928, p. 1, 10; "Unity of the Nation Hailed," New York Times, July 30, 1928, p. 1, 2; "Mrs. Coolidge Unveils," Minneapolis Tribune, July 30, 1928, p. 1.

21. Lehmann, "Coolidge Praises First Minnesota," Minneapolis Journal, July 30, 1928, p. 1, 10.

22. Lehmann, "Coolidge Praises First Minnesota," Minneapolis Journal, July 30, 1928, p. 1, 10.

23. Lehmann, "Coolidge Praises First Minnesota," Minneapolis Journal, July 30, 1928, p. 1, 10; "Unity of the Nation Hailed," New York Times, July 30, 1928, p. 1, 2.

24. Lehmann, "Coolidge Praises First Minnesota," Minneapolis Journal, July 30, 1928, p. 1, 10; "Unity of the Nation Hailed," New York Times, July 30, 1928, p. 1, 2.

25. Lehmann, "Coolidge Praises First Minnesota," Minneapolis Journal, July 30, 1928, p. 1, 10.

NOTES TO CHAPTER 17

1. "Further Honors For Col. Colvill," Cook County Herald [Grand Marais, MN], Sept. 21, 1907, p. 4.

2. "About Our Neighbors," Freeborn County Times-Enterprise [Albert Lea, MN], Oct. 16, 1907, p. 8; Franklyn Curtiss-Wedge, History of Goodhue County, Minnesota, p. 664-665.

3. "Four Persons Drown," Bricelyn [MN] Sentinel, July 17, 1908, p. 1; George B. Hauenstein," Red Wing, Goodhue County, MN, !900 U.S. Census.

4. "Red Wing Man Drowns," Minneapolis Journal, Sept. 1, 1905, p. 9; U.S. Find A Grave Index, Ancestry.com, George W. Hauenstein, 1856-1905, accessed July 5, 2024; "George Hauenstein," Red Wing, Goodhue County, MN, 1900 U.S. Census.

5. "Red Wing Has Picnic And Bathing Grounds," Minneapolis Tribune, Aug. 1, 1908, p. 15; "Work of Red Wing Women," Minneapolis Journal, Aug. 2, 1908, p. 50; "Mrs. Alice A. Neill," obituary, Fox Lake [WI] Representative, Sept. 8, 1939, p. 1; "Alice A. (Purdy) Neill," and "David Middleton Neill," U.S. Find A Grave Index, Ancestry.com, accessed July 5, 2024.

6. "Colvill Park," red-wing.org/facilities/facility/details/Colvill-Park-9; exploreminnesota.com/profile/red-wing-water-park/2897, exploreminnesota.com/profile/colvill-park/2969; accessed July 3, 2024.

7. Warren Upham, Minnesota Geographic Names (St. Paul: Minnesota Historical Society, 1920), p. 135-136, formerly Colville Township had been in Hovland Township in Cook County.

8. "Colvill Memorial Highway," https://www.revisor.mn.gov/laws/1933/0/Session+Law/Chapter/353, accessed July 3, 2024.

NOTES TO CHAPTER 18

1. "The Veterans," Minneapolis Tribune, June 15, 1870, p. 4.

2. Wayne D. Jorgenson, Every Man Did His Duty, p. 24, 26.

3. "Gallant Minnesota in the Field," Chicago Tribune, June 24, 1861, p. 4, "one of these soldiers is 6 feet 9 inches, and still growing," was actually William Colvill, 6' 5".

4. "Frank J. Mead," Minneapolis Times, July 3, 1895, p. 4.

5. "Regimental Meeting," Minneapolis Tribune, June 21, 1867, p. 4; "The 'Old First' Regiment," Minneapolis Tribune, June 23, 1867, p. 4; 2nd reunion, "The Reunion of the First Minnesota," Minneapolis Tribune, June 12, 1868, p. 1; 3rd annual reunion, "First Minnesota Infantry," Minneapolis Tribune, June 12, 1869, p. 4; fourth, "The Veterans," Minneapolis Tribune, June 15, 1870, p. 4; 64th, "3 Conduct Reunion of '61 Regiment," Minneapolis Journal, July 20, 1930, p. 9.

6. "Col. Colvill," Red Wing Republican, July 26, 1884, p. 1; "Reunion of the First Minnesota," St. Paul Globe, July 23, 1884, p. 5.

7. "Col. Colvill," Red Wing Republican, July 26, 1884, p. 1; "Reunion of the First Minnesota," St. Paul Globe, July 23, 1884, p. 5.

8. "Old Soldier," Red Wing Advance Sun, Nov. 2, 1887, p. 5; "Other People's Notions," Minneapolis Journal, Oct. 28, 1887, p. 2.

9. "Statue to Colvill is Dedicated," Minneapolis Journal, May 30, 1909, p. 2.

10. "Statue to Colvill is Dedicated," Minneapolis Journal, May 30, 1909, p. 2.

11. Here and below, Hubbs quoted in Paul Thompson, "Colvill Memorial Recalls History of Winona Volunteers," Winona Republican-Herald, July 26, 1928, p. 8; "Charles L. Hubbs," United States Biographical Dictionary, Kansas Volume (Chicago: S. Lewis & Co., 1879), p. 342-343.

12. Charles L. Hubbs," Minnesota Civil War Records, 1861-1865, ancestry.com, accessed August 13, 2024; "Charles L. Hubbs," Find A Grave Index, accessed August 13, 2024.

13. "Hubbs Isn't Worried By Losing Job," San Diego [CA] Sun, Jan. 29, 1914, p. 1; wrist wound in "Complete List of Casualties," Goodhue Volunteer, July 22, 1863, p. 3; "A Full List of the Casualties," Winona Republican, July 14, 1863, p. 2.

14. Paul Thompson, "Colvill Memorial Recalls History of Winona Volunteers," Winona Republican-Herald, July 26, 1928, p. 9; "A Full List of the Casualties," Winona Republican, July 14, 1863, p. 2.

15. Haskell, The Battle of Gettysburg, p. 107.

16. Martin Maginnis, "The Following Lines; Battle Field, Fair Oaks, Monday, June 2d, 1862," Goodhue Volunteer, June 18, 1862, p. 3.

17. Martin Maginnis, "The Following Lines; Battle Field, Fair Oaks, Monday, June 2d, 1862," Goodhue Volunteer, June 18, 1862, p. 3.

18. "Stephen Foster Lyrics: Was My Brother In The Battle," https://sites.pitt.edu/~amerimus/lyrics.htm, accessed Aug. 21, 2024; 'Songs of the Civil War, Ken Burns Civil War Soundtrack," Kate & Anna McGarrigle, You Tube, accessed August 21, 2024.

19. The soldier was from the 4th Michigan Infantry, initials C.H.B., "No Romance; Sixteen Years After the Gaines Mills Battle," letter to the editor, Detroit Free Press, April 8, 1882, p. 8, here and below.

20. McKune from a letter of Edward H. Bassett in Richard Krom, ed., The 1st Minnesota: Second To None (Rochester: Richard Krom, 2010), p. 42; Taylor in Patrick H. Taylor, "Diary of a Civil War Veteran," Cass County Democrat [Harrisonville, MO], May 31, 1934, p. 5; also in Richard Moe, The Last Full Measure: The Life & Death of the First Minnesota Volunteers (St. Paul: MHS Press, 1993), p. 50, 277. Detroit Free Press, April 8, 1882, p. 8, here and below.

21. Detroit Free Press, April 8, 1882, p. 8.

22. Detroit Free Press, April 8, 1882, p. 8.

23. Martin Maginnis, "The Grand Army," Chicago Tribune, May 17, 1883, p. 2.

24. Here and below, "What Shall We Do," Red Wing Sentinel, August 13, 1859, p. 2.

NOTES TO CHAPTER 19

1. "The Re-Union of the First Minnesota Regiment," Mankato Record, June 22, 1878, p. 3; "Famous Charge Recalled," [Washington, D.C.] Evening Star, July 5, 1897, p. 12.

2. Col. Rick Swain, "Grip Hands With Us Now," Assembly, Magazine of U.S. Military Academy Graduates, July/Aug. 2006, p. 35; Britannica.com, accessed Nov. 18, 2024.

3. "A Charge of Peace," Minneapolis Tribune, July 3, 1897, p. 1; "First Minnesota," Gettysburg Compiler, July 6, 1897, p. 3.

4. "The Most Gallant Charge of the War," Sunday Herald [Washington, D.C.] May 28, 1882, p. 3; "The Most Gallant and Desperate Charge," Helena Independent, June 21, 1882, p. 1.

5. Alleged to be from St. Paul Pioneer Press, in "The First Minnesota's Gettysburg Charge," Little Falls Transcript, May 15, 1885, p. 1; "First Minnesota's Charge," New Ulm Weekly Review, June 17, 1885, p. 4; "Hancock and the First Minnesota," Atlanta Journal, April 2, 1886, p. 3.

6. Aligning with soldiers described in Rufus R. Dawes, Service With the Sixth Wisconsin Volunteers (Marietta, OH: E. R. Alderman & Sons, 1890), p. 82.

7. "First Minnesota Men Gather at Monument," Minneapolis Tribune, July 4, 1913, p. 1.

8. "Minnesotans Leave Gettysburg Field," Minneapolis Journal, July 4, 1913, p. 15.

9. William F. Fox, Regimental Losses in the American Civil War, 1861-1865 (Albany: Albany Publishing Co., 1889), p. 26; "The First Minnesota," St. Paul Globe, Aug. 3, 1885, p. 4; "Gettysburg," National Tribune [Washington, D.C.], May 14, 1885, p. 8.

NOTES TO APPENDIX

1. Danenbaum, "Minnesota Woman Produces Striking Statue," Minneapolis Tribune, May 3, 1909, p. 24.

2. James Holly Hanford, "Milton and the Return to Humanism," Studies in Philology, Vol. 16, No. 2 (April, 1919), p. 147.

INDEX

238